THE PERILS OF PAULINE

PAULINE HICKS

A catalogue record for this book is available from the National Library of Australia

Linellen Press

265 Boomerang Road

Oldbury, Western Australia

www.linellenpress.com.au

Dedication

Home is not just a word or a name.
It's the connection to your roots.
It's where you feel safe.
It's a place where Love lives.
If I was able to keep that alive for you as you grew
then I achieved my goal.

Disclaimer

The names throughout this book have been changed to protect family members from public scrutiny, but this is basically a true story. This was my life until my divorce in 2003.

Contents

Introduction

I was born in Birkenhead, England, at 2 Gamlin Street in the North End on 28th August 1945. When I was a baby, we moved to Carnforth Street opposite the Birkenhead Library for eleven years and then back to Corporation Road in the North End where my grooming was completed for my adult life.

To understand my story, it's necessary for you to be aware of the social behavior and culture we kids were raised in right after the war. Rationing was accepted and threw a boundary around our wants and needs, hence we didn't ask or expect much to make us happy.

Birkenhead had been heavily bombed during the war. Cammell Lairds, the ship repair yard, was on our doorstep and those ships damaged during the war limped down the Mersey and into this yard for repair. Plus, munition factories and supply depots were built on any spare land here. Therefore, it was important for Hitler to attempt to destroy the shipyard and the surrounding land. Our parents (especially our mothers) had survived and had to deal with the aftermath of the loss of many people killed and buildings that had been damaged and destroyed, which created a different and special culture that we kids were raised in.

My mother's experience of the war will give you a snapshot of what these people in this area had lived through before we were born. To understand this unique and special culture we were raised in, it is necessary to understand what created it. And so, I begin with that story.

Chapter One

World War II

1941

Air raid sirens screamed and pierced the black starless night sky. Doris, fully dressed for escape, catapulted out of bed, frantic, her heart beating out of her chest. She plucked her twelve-month-old baby, Sarah, from her cot and wrapped her in yet another thick blanket. For the first time for days, Sarah seemed to be sleeping comfortably and Doris thought: *Why now? You bastard Hitler, why can't you give us one clear night so my baby can begin to recover?*

Her husband was somewhere out there fighting a war and she wasn't allowed to know where. *He's probably suffering more than me,* she thought. *The world and everyone in it needs strength right now.*

Racing out of her house at the bottom of Gamlin Street, she grabbed the pre-packed shoulder bag, threw the handles over her head and in terror ran toward Birkenhead North train station. Her friend Winnie's door was open in Buccleaugh Street as she bellowed into the hall:

"Winnie, do you need help?"

Winnie's husband was also away fighting in the war, and Doris admired how she managed her three children alone. Her middle child had polio and Doris knew she would be locking his leg splints onto him.

"I'm coming, Dot. Go on ... I'll be two minutes."

Doris's throat began to restrict her breath as she gripped her baby to her chest and ran, panicking, looking into the sky and vaguely seeing the lights of a fleet of approaching planes in the distance.

"Not now, God. Stop them. Not now. Let Winnie and her kids get to safety," she prayed as she ran into the Birkenhead North train tunnel which was now used as an air raid shelter. Glancing back, she saw Winnie and the kids running frantically, only a minute away. They would make it in time.

"Thank you, God."

The day's rain had created a twelve-inch-deep lake in the tunnel that she had to paddle through. Small train lamps flickered on the brick-arched roof through the middle of the tunnel and away from the entrance, giving enough light to identify faces. The shelter was already packed, people lining the walls as she threaded her way around knees, legs, and feet.

Yuk! Something slimy is wrapping itself around my leg. In alarm, she looked down but calmed on seeing it was only a piece of wet newspaper.

A gentle hum of voices filled the air. "Baby coming through. Baby coming through." It was a low chant that moved along with Doris as she walked between the crowd of tired faces, looking for a place to sit. Some had brought kitchen chairs but carrying Sarah meant that luxury wasn't an option. An elderly gentleman had been sitting on a square brick wall support. He stood saying, "'ere ye are luv. I can stand."

"Are you sure?" she asked as she peered into his frail face. If she took his seat, would he collapse if the bombs lasted most of the night? She couldn't have that on her conscience. She was about to gracefully refuse as she knew the guilt of her sitting and him standing would haunt her, but just then a younger man stood.

"'Ere, luv, take this kitchen chair."

"Thanks so much. This is really kind of you both." She smiled nervously. Sarah was awake in her arms and now struggling to breathe again. Doris needed to calm herself and concentrate on Sarah and how to keep her safe and breathing! The bombs had begun to explode above them as she wrapped the blanket around Sarah's head and ears to smother the sound as best she could. The ground vibrated then shook, and the explosions became deafening,

BOOM!! ... 10, 11, 12 ... BOOM! ... 10, 11, 12 ... BOOM! ... three close together, while the vicar of St James' Church prayed loudly, trying to be heard as he asked God for protection. Fear suffocated Doris as she silently, but over and over, prayed that they would survive the night. "Please, God, please!" (There are no atheists in air raid shelters.)

It was two weeks since Doris had visited the doctor with her 12-month-old child. Sarah had developed a cough which wasn't clearing. She had been given a small amount of penicillin by the doctor which, she'd been told, was the maximum allowance he could prescribe as the bulk of all medications were going straight out to the troops. Sarah's cough had grown worse and now rattled on her chest to the point Doris felt her child had pneumonia. She had planned to take her to the hospital the following day, hoping they could give Sarah something to help her breathe easier.

Sitting in this damp tunnel isn't helping my baby to breathe, she thought, even though she had no choice. But the thought stirred her guilt that she had brought her child into an environment that would harm her even more.

That feckin Churchill! That bloody idiot! In exasperation, her anger tried to replace her guilt as she vented with these thoughts. *Why did he decide to use Cammell Lairds to repair the damaged ships during the war? Birkenhead used to be a sleepy little town but it's all munition factories and supply depots now, a hive of industry day and night. How could he be so crazy as to think the damaged ships wouldn't be identified as ships of war, as they limped into the Mersey from the Irish Sea? How could he get it so wrong?*

Moving toward her out of the darkness, she saw Winnie and the kids. Her eldest boy caried a chair for his mum, and he set it beside Doris who rocked her baby automatically in her left arm as her right hand felt Sarah's little chest rattle with each breath she struggled to take.

"How's her breathing, Dot?" Winnie asked, concern in her eyes. Doris almost cried at this direct question because she was terrified her baby would not survive the night.

"I'm frightened, Winnie." She choked back the tears as she looked into Winnie's eyes.

Winnie grabbed Doris's shoulder firmly. "We'll all get through this, Dot. We won't let that bastard Hitler win."

Conversations circulated between the noise of the bombs. She heard Mrs Brown's voice.

"Our Mary lives in New Brighton on the top corner of the Mersey and the Wirral, looking out to the Irish Sea. She was telling me there's a rumour Lord Haw-Haw lives there watching for the ships entering the Mersey and coming here for repairs."

They discovered soon after the war had finished that Lord Haw-Haw turned out to be William Joyce, a Nazi spy living in Germany. Daily he sent out propaganda messages via radio throughout the war. He once lived with his relatives on the Wirral and it was thought they informed Joyce of the damaged ships sailing into the Mersey, but this couldn't be proved as the source of his information. He was arrested in Germany in May 1945 and accused of high treason. He was hanged on January 3rd 1946. William Joyce was born Irish.

"That toe rag has told Hitler all about this area," another joined in the conversation.

"Whoever he is has built a radio station in his attic and he's lettin' the Germans know about the damaged ships comin' into Cammell Lairds."

"Did you hear him on the radio this afternoon tellin' us all in his nasal voice 'Germany calling, Germany calling, Hitler will make the blood run down the seven roads of St James Church tonight and raze the buildings to the ground. Haw Haw Haw.' I wanted to pick up the radio and smash it to pieces on the kitchen floor!"

"He's thinkin' he's bein' humane," said another, "warning us so we can get into the air raid shelters early. But people are still being killed because of him, the bastard!"

"Yes, Hitler is trying to destroy those ships, but he even knows about the munition factories and supply depots that have been built here. That's why he's determined to wipe us off the face of the earth. Everything is neatly packaged in one place for him and marked by the Church. It's like Churchill wrapped us up in a bundle and handed us over to Hitler."

St James' Church sat on a central roundabout near the docks and had seven roads splaying out from it. From the air, this was a clear landmark for the planes as it looked like a wheel sitting on the docks. All the munition factories and supply depots had been built on any spare land on these roads. It was therefore important for Germany to wipe this part of England off the map. Unfortunately, all the locals also lived here.

Winnie and Doris began chatting, trying to hide the fear they both felt. They wanted the children to see and hear normal conversation to help them not feel too frightened through the night. Sarah's face was becoming ashen and losing its colour. Doris willed each breath as she looked into her child's face.

"Not long now, Dot, and you can take her straight to the hospital when we get out. I'll get me Dad to take ye in the lorry."

"Thanks, Winnie. That would really help (then whispering so the children didn't hear) I hope everyone managed to get into the tunnel tonight 'cos I don't think I can take another morning identifying those that died. I honestly do dread that scene as much as being here listening to the bombs."

Emerging from the air raid shelters was one of the nightmares everyone dreaded – not only because they weren't sure if their home was still standing, but the bodies of the dead were lined up along the streets with sacks covering their faces and a slate and chalk at their head. This task had been carried out by the Air Raid Wardens. Once they had laid the dead in the streets in this way, they then sounded the all-clear siren. Everyone's duty, out of respect for those who died, was to identify the dead. They had to lift the sack away from their face and if they recognised the person, they would write the name on the slate. They also had to read the names of everyone on the slates to discover who didn't make it through the night. Dread engulfed Doris each time and her body movements always felt automated and surreal as she lifted the sacks praying that it wasn't anyone she knew. This also became the recurring nightmare for most inhabitants. It was torture!

Rocking! Rocking! "Shh! Shh! Go to sleep, my baby," she quietly sang, looking into her baby's face, but Sarah's little chest still rattled in her struggle to breathe. Doris's hand lay on her baby's chest checking for each breath as she rocked and prayed and willed her to survive. And then … "Oh my God! My God!" she uttered when she didn't feel her little chest rising to breathe! She stood up with Sarah in her arms.

"A doctor!! A doctor!" she began screaming. Immediately all in the tunnel fell silent and looked in her direction. "A doctor! A doctor!" she screamed even louder. From some distance down the tunnel, a man began running toward her, vaulting over and around people as he shouted, "I'm a doctor, luv. I'm coming."

People moved out of his way as best they could, allowing him a clearer path through. She was now howling into the face of this man as he leaned in to hear Sarah's breathing. But there was no breathing. His eyes swiftly met Doris' and she understood what they were saying. She immediately went into a quiet shock. He firstly checked visually, then placed his ear on Sarah's chest and to be sure he then used his stethoscope as she stood holding her baby. Winnie repeated a mantra as she gripped Doris' shoulders.

"Please, God, no. Please, God no, please, God, no," but too late. The doctor looked mournfully into Doris' eyes and shook his head. Sarah had died in her mother's arms.

The all-clear siren was still sounding as Doris left the tunnel, clutching her deceased child and walking like a zombie. A rock sat in her chest, ice chilled her gut and her throat strained to hold back the tears that she couldn't or wouldn't release. People milled around her, all saying how sorry they were, but Doris didn't respond. They were merely voices talking over one another, a cacophony not making any sense. The doctor steered her toward his car, saying he'd take her to the hospital. Doris merely allowed him to move her. Once in the hospital, it took almost an hour for them to complete the official paperwork, and as they covered Sarah's beautiful little face and peeled her out of her mother's arms, only then did Doris release a tsunami of grief that had sat in her gut, dammed back by her throat. As it spewed forth, her body shook violently with every breath she took.

Her husband was informed and given compassionate leave of three days to attend Sarah's funeral. Doris's emotional support from then on were her friends and family. Nightly, fear filled her as she ran to the air raid shelters, and every morning she went through the torturous ritual of identifying the dead.

In this way, Doris learned how to be selfless throughout this war. She healed somehow by being strong, genuinely caring about those suffering around her and keeping busy helping her neighbours as best she could.

As she relived these stories to her children, she spoke about those worse off than herself. One night as she ran to the tunnel, she arrived and looked back to see her friend Winnie and her three children only then leaving their home and beginning to run frantically. Doris looked up to the sky when she heard the whistling of a bomb falling. Horrified she began shouting: "Faster, Winnie. Faster!" But she wasn't fast enough. Winnie and her kids perished right in front of Doris's eyes.

During that war, Doris suffered bombings, witnessed death, and had to identify body parts – but worst of all she had lost her only child at that time. She continued to live with the memories and endure the aftermath of the atrocities she had witnessed as she raised four more children, also supporting her husband and her neighbours in the community to simply survive another day, another week.

Her husband, and many of these men, returned from the war suffering shell shock, which was eventually called post-traumatic stress disorder, (PTSD), and counselling wasn't heard of then. Neighbours supported each other. The women in the community were strong, uncomplicated, selfless, and hardworking. Doris became the rock they offloaded to; her common sense, empathy and compassion helped them draw the strength to face another day.

Birkenhead was bombed relentlessly throughout the war with the death of over 4,000 residents and more than 2,000 seriously maimed and many buildings and homes destroyed.

Divorce was not an option and was never discussed by the women of my tribe. If by chance it did enter their heads after periods of physical violence at the hands of their men (who were deemed mentally disturbed), it was dismissed immediately – they thought of divorce as cowardly and weak. They never surrendered; never walked away; never gave up.

Young females born after the war and raised by these women in our village, learned quickly that stoicism was a must and women's lives should be sacrificial.

What these women in Birkenhead endured never reached a page in a history book but for me, Doris and those women that banded together to form our community, were the true heroes of the Second World War.

Doris was my mother. She was born the seventh daughter of the seventh daughter. This, in pagan terms, meant she had prophetic vision; she was a psychic and a clairvoyant. She was only nineteen years old when she lost her first child. That pain, plus the experience of surviving the war, was her baptism of fire. She became wise at an early age.

She had an aura and empathetic essence that drew people to her for emotional support. As her daughter, she opened my mind and taught me all she knew about the spirit world.

My mother and our female neighbours formed the 'village' I was raised in and its history formed the backdrop of my education for life.

Chapter Two

Pauline, the child

1949

The light of dawn began to creep around the edge of the curtains and into my bedroom. As I opened my eyes, I immediately thought, *It's t'morreh! Mum said we are going on holiday t'morreh, and that's now.* The excitement fluttered my tummy and I had to go to the toilet.

"Yer like a wee puppy," my father would often say; and it was true. Every time I got excited ,I nearly wet myself. I came out of the bathroom now bursting with my excitement and fighting to control it. Very slowly and quietly, I opened my parent's bedroom door. With my hand still on the doorknob, I peered at the back of Mum's head as it lay on her pillow, saying nothing and willing her to wake up. Mum slowly turned to look at me as I stood there in my nightie.

"It's t'morreh now, isn't it, Mum? Can I get ready t'go on holidays?" I half whispered, not wanting to be loud as Mum had told me so many times the rules of mornings – be quiet and slow! I was still trying hard to learn these rules.

"Oh, luv, it's not even six o'clock yet. We're not goin' till six o'clock t'night. Go back t'bed," she moaned.

I slowly closed the door, thinking, *How can she go back t'sleep when she knows she's goin' on holiday?*

I began skipping with my excitement, as I wasn't allowed to run, and I skipped back into my bedroom. *I'll put my best frock on now then I'll be ready before anyone else.* A squeal played in my chest that I wasn't allowed to let out. As I was always first to wake up, Mum had told me last night to quietly pack my bag as I waited for the others.

The small bag Mum had given me to pack my clothes in lay on the floor. I carefully went through all the clothes I owned and placed anything without a hole in it in the bag.

Most of my clothes were hand-me-downs from my sister, but that didn't matter to me. When she got new clothes, I would get as excited as she did, because I knew I'd get them eventually. My doll, which used to belong to my sister, but I wasn't supposed to know – and had appeared in my Christmas stocking with her face washed and wearing a new frock – sat looking at me from my bed. I loved my doll and I wasn't sure if she was allowed to come with me.

"It might be expensive to take dolls on holiday, Sally, but I'll ask if you can go?" I whispered to her. Back I went to my parent's bedroom door and slowly opened it again. Mum looked over at me.

I screwed up my face and eyes and crunched my head down into my shoulders as I asked sheepishly, "Can Sally come on holiday with us, Mum? Or is it too expensive for her?" I prepared myself for a no.

"Yes, luv, take 'er if ye want to, now don't come back again until I get up." She sighed.

Oh! My squeal nearly popped out of my mouth! I closed the door and excitedly hopped and skipped back into my bedroom and picked Sally up and hugged her as I danced around the room. "You can come with us on holiday, Sally. You can meet my Nana and Grandpa, and play with the wee pigs, and run in the fields, and we'll see the hens, and the beautiful swans on the lake, and *everythin'*!! *And* ... we're goin' on the big boat t'get there. Ooooh! It's goin' t'be lots of fun," I whispered as I wrapped her in my arms, trying hard not wake my brother and sister. Once my bag was packed, it seemed such a long time since I'd been awake that I felt if my brother and sister didn't wake soon they might be too late for our holiday. I peered right into my little brother Harry's face and pressed my nose against his as he started to wake. "Come on wee sleepy head," I whispered excitedly. "It's t'morreh!"

Our grandparents owned a pig farm in Moneyraegh, County Down in Northern Ireland. Cammell Lairds, where Dad worked building ships, closed every year for the last week in July and the first week in August. This was when we took our holidays. Mum would save all year round and, with Dad's holiday pay, we could usually afford to get the Irish Ferry across to Belfast and spend two weeks with our grandparents.

My world was measured in two halves. The two most precious moments in my life were Christmas and holidays. As soon as one was over, I counted the days until the other arrived.

We must be the luckiest people on earth to 'ave a Nanna and Grandpa in Ireland, I thought; pitying the rest of humanity.

"Don't ye go boastin' now, wee girl; that poor wee lass can 'ardly afferd a lace fer 'er shoe," my dad would say if he caught me bragging. So I was supposed to keep it to myself and say nothing; and I didn't know how anybody else did it! It was the hardest thing in the world for me to contain my excitement about anything I felt passionate about; and I felt passionate about a lot of things.

Sitting on the steps of our house with my bag packed, my best frock on, and Sally sitting beside me, I waited ... just waited ... for somebody to come along that I could boast to. I knew I would have to say it quietly in case my dad heard me, then the first person I could tell came around the corner.

Jumping off the steps, I ran to meet her and excitedly whispered in her ear, "We're goin' overseas, on holiday to Ireland!"

She stepped back and smiled while she looked at me, "Now?" she said.

"No, t'night at six o'clock, *and* we're goin' on the ferry boat, the big one that goes t' Ireland!" I squealed in excitement and jumped up and down. I wanted to go to the toilet again but not until I had finished boasting; so I put my hands between my legs and crossed them; then bounced on the spot.

"Yer lucky thing ye!" said my friend. "... wish I 'ad a Nan in Ireland." Then she looked sad; and I knew what my dad had meant, and I felt sorry for her.

"Not everybody's got a Nan in Ireland – we're just very, very, very lucky, that's all. I'll tell yer all about it when I get back, an' it'll be just like ye' went." I'd lost a bit of my spark now and I felt guilty for making my friend sad. "A'll 'ave t'go now 'cos a want a wee. A'll see ye when a get back." And I ran indoors to the toilet before I wet myself.

It's really hard being happy and not sharing it with someone in case you make them sad, I thought as I sat on the toilet; but I soon bounced back and sat on the steps again, waiting for my next 'victim.'

The Irish Ferry boat set sail for Belfast at midnight; but the six o'clock departure time my mother had given us for leaving the house seemed like it would never arrive.

"Come on," my mother shouted from inside the house. "It's time to go."

I jumped off the step squealing with pleasure and gave a little dance on the spot.

We began to walk down the street to Borough Road where

15

we would get the bus to the Birkenhead Ferry. We would then take the ferryboat across the Mersey to Liverpool where the Irish Ferry boat was docked.

My father was at the head of the procession, his small frame tipping to one side as he carried a large heavy suitcase that he tried hard not to drag on the ground. My mother followed, carrying my little brother Harry in one arm and a bag over the other. My sister Babs walked behind my mother and I brought up the end of the procession. Wanting to be like Mum, I carried my precious Sally in one arm and my bag of clothes on the other, but I had to skip along behind because I found it impossible to walk.

The entire neighbourhood seemed to spill out of their doors with everybody shouting goodbye to us. "Have a good 'oliday," they shouted. "See ye when yiz get back, we'll look after the 'ouse, don't worry. Hope the weather keeps fine fer yiz all."

And I waved to everybody and quietly squealed with pleasure.

At the bottom of our street on Borough Road, we boarded the double-decker bus and Dad placed the heavy suitcase under the stairs. The bus conductor rubbed the top of my head and said, "Goin' on 'oliday are ye, little un?"

"Yes!" I beamed. "To Ireland t'see me Nanna and Grandpa."

The seats on the bus were placed two abreast and my mother and father sat behind me and my sister, with Harry on Mum's knee. Babs had brought her book and began reading but sitting still in the seat was impossible for me. I fidgeted my bum, stood up and looked around, kneeled on the seat and leaned over toward Mum and Dad, gently pinching my little brother's cheek.

"We're on our way. We'll soon be there," I sang.

"Will you sit down, Pauline. Yer makin' me dizzy," my mother ordered. Oh I found it really hard to sit still when I was excited; I didn't know how to do it.

As I sighed and slumped down into the seat, I raised my legs in front of me. They reached the back of the next seat. I pushed my feet against it and the back of my seat snapped back. If I pushed my feet and straightened my legs, I could fit tightly into this space between the seats. Each time I did it, the back of my chair went back then immediately snapped forward, throwing me towards the back of the seat in front of me. So I did it again, and again, and again … until my mother said, "Get your feet off that chair and sit still, will you!"

Oh this really was the hardest part of goin' on holiday.

Eventually we reached the ferry and could see the water. The bus turned into the terminal and Mum told my sister and me to get off and stand on the kerb until Dad got the case off the bus.

We walked into the Birkenhead Ferry terminal where Dad bought the tickets, then we stepped onto the floating ramp and Babs and I skipped in excitement all the way down to the water's edge.

The Ferry Boat, *Woodchurch*, was a magical sight to me.

"Get hold of my frock you two 'till we're on the boat," Mum said. And I stood looking up at this beautiful old wooden ferry boat and thought, *my dad's probably built this!*

Dad led the way onto the gangplank. Mum followed with Harry in her arms, and my sister Babs and I brought up the rear, holding onto the hem of her skirt. As I bounced on the balls of my feet, holding Mum's frock at the end of the procession, I felt like a bridesmaid at a wedding.

"Now don't go near the rails without ye father," Mum said. "An' stay where I can see ye."

The ropes were thrown back onto the boat, the engines increased in power and the ferry boat left the dock side and chugged its way across the Mersey to Liverpool.

"Should we go an' see the sailors doin' their washin'?" said

Dad to Babs and me.

"Yes!!" we screamed and danced beside him, holding his hand as we moved toward the rear of the boat. I grabbed the rail tight and looked over at the foam and spray that came from the back of the boat as it cut its way through the water. Dad had told us that in the bowels of the boat, the sailors scrubbed their clothes, and the foam was the dirty soapy washing water that was draining away.

They must have an awful lot of washin', I thought.

Liverpool loomed in front of us. The large grey sandstone buildings with the eagle on top always made me feel as though I was entering a foreign land.

The Irish Ferry boat, *The Ulster Monarch,* sat further down the dock and was even more impressive than the boat we'd just got off. It ascended from the water, a monster dwarfing all around it, and the people looked like ants swarming all over it. The gang plank was wider than the last one, but longer and climbed much higher, and again we had to hold Mum's frock as we walked up to the top of this huge boat. Everybody seemed to know my dad, and shouts of "Hello there, Wally!" seemed to come from all around us as I walked, this time like a princess up the gang plank to the deck. I felt so important it was bursting out of me.

Everybody seemed to be Irish, and their beautiful singsong voices filled the air, shouting instructions and directions around the boat. We were taken to a cabin that had two sets of bunk beds either side of the small room. My father placed the case and bags under the bottom bunks.

"I want to sleep on that bottom bunk," Babs said.

"Ay, ye can do that and Harry can be at the bottom end," Dad said.

"And which bed will ye be wantin' t'sleep in t'night?" Dad asked me with a huge grin on his face.

"That top one," I said with excitement.

"Well now, put Sally t'bed in case ye lose 'er," said Mum, and I climbed the narrow little ladder to the top bunk and placed Sally between the sheets and pulled the covers around her chin.

"You stay there, Sally, cos I've got t'go with the grownups t'night t'have a beer," I told her importantly. We then all went up to the deck to inspect the ship.

"You two hold hands on the ship and don't go wandering off without being able t'see me and ye dad," Mum told me and Babs.

The atmosphere was magical. Everybody was happy and laughing. All these people were going on holiday just like us, so I couldn't make anyone unhappy by letting my enthusiasm out. Babs and I walked behind my mother, each holding onto our side of her skirt and holding each other's hand, looking up at the lovely Irish smiles that were all around us.

After inspecting the ship we went to the bar where Dad was surrounded by all his friends. The dark of the night drew in and all the different coloured lights went on and the music began.

This created a different atmosphere. Laughter and cigarette smoke, the smell of tar and the sea, singing and dancing, piano accordions, whistles and drums playing; and the night air swirled about my head and made me giddy with euphoria. Midnight arrived and we had been allowed to stay up to watch the boat leave the dock. I was surprised at how quiet the engines were, as they steadily began to thump … thump… thump… and move this monstrous vessel with all these happy people on board out to cross the Irish Sea.

As we stood waving from the ship to those standing on the dock, a great roar of delight swept around the ship throughout the passengers, and we all then went back inside to the bar where the music began again. Everybody sang. We knew all the songs because Dad had taught us them. So we sang along as we sailed through the dark on this magical, illuminated Christmas tree, all on our way to a fairyland.

THIS is holiday!

Forcing myself to stay awake as long as I could was hard, and I was woken by my dad, who picked me up from the floor where I sat against the wall.

"Come on, me beauty. It's bedtime fer you."

He carried me down to our cabin while I dozed on his shoulder, and lifted me into my bunk bed beside Sally. Harry and Babs were already fast asleep on the bottom bunk and Dad kissed me goodnight, the light was switched off and he left. The small porthole at the side of my bunk had moonlight streaming through it and it lit the cabin with its pale yellow, eerie glow. The water was swish, swish, swishing against the side of the boat as it rocked from side to side. The engines thump-thump-thumped to a heartbeat rhythm. The muffled singing and laughter and music all wrapped it's magic around me and transported me to another dimension.

I am the luckiest wee girl in the whole wide world, NUTHIN' could ever be better than this, ever … ever … ever … I thought as I drifted off into my fairytale dreams.

"Oh! I nearly forgot. Thanks very much, God, it's luvly. Eh! Men?"

And on my immediate return from my Ferry Boat and Ireland holiday I would begin counting down to Christmas.

I always woke on Christmas morning when it was still dark but lay perfectly still, hoping Father Christmas had already been yet knowing if I was awake and he found out he wouldn't stop at our house, so I squeezed my eyes, shutting them tight so he wouldn't know. I was aware of my heart beating as my excitement built. As soon as the light of day began to brighten our bedroom, I catapulted myself out of bed!

Yesterday was one of my nearly-the-very-best-days-of-my-life as we prepared for Father Christmas to come and visit our house and leave presents. Father Christmas is so very busy on Christmas eve as he zooms around the world on his sleigh with his magic, flying reindeers. Dad says he gets a bit tired now and again so he sometimes stops in a very special house and has a beer and a mince pie.

"Oh I hope he's picked our house!" I squealed as I skipped into the living room.

Last night we had taken three of Dad's biggest woollen working socks, ones without holes in them, and hung them on the mantle shelf over the fireplace for Father Christmas to fill for us – one for my big sister Babs, one for my little brother Harry, and one for me. I had insisted that my name was pinned to my sock because I knew my little brother had been naughty last week, and if he was going to get ashes in his stocking, I wanted to be sure there was no mix up between the socks. Mum kept saying that Father Christmas always knows which sock belongs to which child because he's magic, but I knew little Harry had been *very* naughty, so I almost cried while insisting that my name went on my sock.

Dad turned me by my shoulders and said sternly, "Now then, wee lass, yer'll be showin' ye Irish paddy here, an' I don't think Father Christmas will be impressed," as he lowered his chin and lifted his eyebrows in disapproval, but he still did it for me: my name was printed on the back of an envelope that had arrived with a Christmas card in it, and pinned it to the toe of one of the socks.

Mum put one of her home-made mince pies on one of our very best china plates and put it on the tray she used when special people visited. Dad placed a bottle of beer beside the pie and the tray was placed on the hearth for Father Christmas to see when he came down the chimney. He doesn't get burnt because Mrs Christmas makes him a special fireproof suit to wear each year that she sews with magic cotton to do the job.

There was a different quiet to this morning. The colour of the light in our bedroom was different as well. Instinctively, I ran to the window, parted the curtains, and the sight caught my breath in my throat as I became bewitched with the scene before me. The world was covered in a pure white blanket of snow. The whiteness lay on the ground and hung in the trees and covered the roof tops. The transformation was magical. The earth was covered in a white fur blanket.

A squeal of pleasure started in my stomach and, as it began its journey up through my body to my throat, it engulfed my whole being with a feeling of total joy that burst out through my mouth as I squeezed my eyes and smiled as I hugged this feeling all around me. I ran to the living room and gasped again in awe!

The first thing I noticed was the tray with an empty bottle of beer and plate. Leaning against the bottle was an envelope with writing on it that looked a bit like my Dad's writing and later Dad read it for us. It said "Thank you, from Father Christmas."

The socks were filled and now lay on the hearth, each one on top of a present. One for each of us.

'Oh!! He's been and he picked our house to rest in. OH!!" I squealed out loud as I clapped my hands and did a little dance on the spot. Then I desperately needed a wee before I opened my presents and ran to the bathroom where I tried to wee quickly. Then I ran into our bedroom to wake Harry and Babs. I peered into my brother's little face as I loudly whispered, "Father Christmas has been, Harry. Come and see what he's brought you."

Placing my arms around Harry's little chubby body, I carried him into the living room. My brother was one and a half years old now and great fun to share things with. He was still sleepy as I sat him on the floor in front of his present and sock. "Look!"

I said excitedly. "It's from Father Christmas for you."

His eyes lit up and a big smile began to cover his sleepy face as he sat looking at a wooden train and then at me. "Go on, look in your sock. It's yours," I squealed and smiled, enjoying his reaction.

I fell to my knees beside him and moved the sock with my name on it from the top of a big brown teddy bear – he had one shiny brown eye and one brown button eye, and a paper blue and gold dicky bow around his neck. "Oh! You're beautiful!" I exclaimed as I picked up this magical present and hugged him to me. I looked over at Babs' sock sitting on top of two books. "Babs, he's been!" I shouted and began to empty my sock on the floor. "Empty your sock out, Harry, like I did," and we discovered we both had an apple, an orange, a tube of smarties and a bag of jelly beans. I did feel relief when I didn't have any ashes in my sock after losing my paddy last night. I looked at my brothers sock and he didn't have ashes either so I guessed that Father Christmas must have been too busy to have noticed us both being naughty. Whew! That was a relief.

Mum and Dad and my big sister Babs appeared in the doorway. They were all smiling, and Dad put his arms around Mum and gave her a big smakaroo kiss. I loved seeing Mum and Dad do that. It always made me smile and feel happy inside. Then they all sat on the floor with us and gave us all smakaroo kisses as well.

Babs opened her books and, smiling, she looked at me saying, "I'll read you a bedtime story from this book tonight." I was so happy I just sat for a while in the middle of all this love and grinned and squealed with some happy tears coming out from my eyes.

"G'way wid ye," said Dad with a big smile as he tweaked my cheek and wiped a tear from it. "Tell me ye teddy bear's name t'be?"

"I don't know yet," I replied. "I want a wee first," and I jumped up, grabbed my new teddy bear and ran to the bathroom. I place him on the floor and sat looking at him as I sat on the toilet. *Freddie*, I thought. *His name is Freddie.*

Hearing a knock at the front door, I hurriedly finished on the toilet and ran back to the living room to meet our first visitors of the day. My Auntie Winnie was there in her real fur coat. She was my Mum's sister and she always gave us presents. My dad said she lived in the posh part of town but didn't wear any knickers. "Here's your Winnie," he would say to Mum when he saw her walking toward our house from the road. "Fur coat and no drawers." Mum told me it would be rude to repeat that to her, so I never told her I knew she didn't have any knickers.

By the end of the afternoon, all my aunts, uncles and cousins were congregated in our house. After our Christmas dinner we gathered around the piano where Dad played and led us into singing all the Christmas carols. In between renditions of carols, he would sometimes do silly noises on the piano, playing out of tune songs and singing alone until he found the right note.

"Oi've never had one lesson," he'd shout as he played this out of tune racket. "Oi discovered I had dis wonderful talent and taught meself to play by ear, though I did 'ave to learn to do it wid me fingers as me 'ead started to hurt when I played with me ears! Oi dedicate this next song to me luvly wife," he'd announce. Then he'd start to play an out of tune racket and singing, "She was! She was!" over and over, nothing else! They were the only words. But somehow it meant something different with every version of 'She was'. Everybody fell about laughing and Mum used the corner of her apron to wipe away her happy tears.

At 7 o'clock that night I sat in the corner listening to all this happiness. I was really tired, and my head kept falling on to Freddie because it was trying to go to sleep without the rest of me. Mum picked me up and hugged me to her cushions and whispered in my ear, "My wee girl's had a big day. Come on, sleepy head, it's time for bed."

She carried me to bed and put Sally on one side of me and Freddie on the other and kissed me good night. I loved the smell of Mum – it was face powder and lipstick and lifebuoy soap, and I thought she was the prettiest person I'd ever seen. I was so lucky to have her as my mum.

From my comfy bed I could still faintly hear the singing and laughter, and though I wished I could stay awake and be with them all, I knew my mum was right. I was too tired even to say my prayers out loud, but I remembered to say thank you in my head before I went to sleep. Mum and Dad had told us that God and Father Christmas could hear the silent thank yous in your head so I always did that before I went to sleep. And I added, *this was the best Christmas ever so thank you for that too.*

In the build up to Christmas and over the Christmas period we sang songs over and over around the house. Babs would sing to Harry and me in our bedroom as we were going to sleep and Mum had told her many times she wasn't to sing various songs because it made me cry so much. After wonderful happy days I could be found crying into my pillow as she sang:

> *He's the little boy that Santa Claus forgot,*
> *And goodness knows he didn't want a lot.*
> *He wrote a note to Santa for some soldiers and a drum;*
> *It broke his little heart when he found Santa hadn't come*
>
> *In the street he envied all those lucky boys,*
> *Then wandered home to last year's broken toys,*
> *I feel sorry for that laddie,*
> *He hasn't got a Mum or Daddy,*
> *He's the little boy that Santa Claus forgot.*

Chapter Three

Childhood happenings

1950-1954

It was sure to be a Saturday night. The time would be around midnight, and I was five or six years old. My father woke me from my sleep and lifted me out of bed.

"Come on me beauty. I want ye t'watch ye father beat the shit outa 'this feller."

With my tightly curled Irish red hair all tousled, and the sleep still gritty in my green eyes, I was carried into the living room wearing only my night-dress.

The neighbours and most of the drinkers from the local pub, *The Happy Valley*, which was on the corner of our street, were gathered around the perimeter of our living room where they had been called to witness my father 'beat the shit' out of this man. Dad had been insulted by something this man had said in the pub and so had 'offered him outside' to sort it out. The police had moved them on and so Dad had brought him home to fight him there.

My father normally stood five feet two inches in his stocking feet, but tonight he believed he had grown another foot in stature, as he did most Saturday nights after 'a belly full of ale', as my mother would often state when he'd been drinking.

A wing-back chair was pulled to the front of the audience and

I was placed on this to give me a ringside seat. My father took up his boxing pose, legs bent at the knees and straddled wide, back straight and arms held with fists lined up in front of his nose. He had removed his shirt and his 'Persil white vest' had a hole beneath one arm. My mother was tutting to the other females in the audience about him letting her down, "taking off his shirt when he's got an old vest on!" It was probably one of two that he owned.

His thick leather belt with a large brass buckle was tight around his waist holding up his trousers and his shoulder braces were hanging either side of his legs.

My father and the man shadow-boxed while they bounced around the floor, aiming pretend blows at each other but not hitting their mark. There were Oooh's and Aaah's from the audience when a fist shot out from either man, and Dad pranced around enjoying the performance he was putting on for them, his Irish grin never leaving his face.

The man jumped too far forward and caught my father with a left to his chin. Then! ... I became frightened for the man, because I knew my father – he wouldn't let him get away with that. The smile on my father's face twitched in the corners and his eyes took on a steely glare. He lunged at the man with a swift right to the chest followed by a left uppercut to his chin, putting the man on his backside in shock.

"I knew it! He shouldn't have done that to my dad."

The audience went crazy and accolades from everyone flowed to my father as they held his right hand in the air. He walked forward with a different smile now, and stood before the man with his legs astride, his head on one side, and he held out his hand to the man on the carpet and hauled him up.

"Fair fight, fair fight," he said. They shook hands, put their arms around each other's shoulders, and everyone had a party. Dad had made another friend out of an enemy.

Dad helped in a local boxing club with the youth of the area and so his performance was merely an opportunity for him to show off his boxing skills. Plus being Irish, a good scrap was a necessity in his life. Nobody was ever seriously hurt and a sing song and a knees-up always followed.

We grew up never knowing what Saturday night would bring.

Love and fear created happy and frightening memories of our childhood, and the two extremes were entirely dependent upon my father – whether he was drunk or sober.

As children we never thought we were any different from any other family, but as an adult, I realised that our upbringing was different from most.

The house we lived in was a prefabricated rectangle block sitting in its own piece of ground. It had been hastily built, along with the rest of the street, after the war to re-house the returning soldiers and their families. It was on a hill, the street carved down the centre of it. The houses on the left side were placed two abreast rising two overlooking two as the hill rose up from the main road. Our house was number two and the first on the left. On the right side of Carnforth Street, the houses faced the street. Each house had two bedrooms, one bathroom, one living room and a kitchen.

Because it housed the men that had fought in the war, I was raised hearing stories of war from all the neighbours and the pain it inflicted and the damage it had left on the souls of men that had fought. The bombs that had dropped on their wives and families and the people they had killed were spoken of regularly, never forgotten. Many men in our neighbourhood had been shell shocked and their nerves destroyed. Allowances were made for all our neighbours because they had suffered in one way or another because of the war. Our street was one large family unit. Neighbours cared and helped each other in any way they could.

My mother had six older sisters and was the recipient of their hand-me-downs of stockings, make-up and shoes. Our house was the place other female neighbours called on to be dressed when they were going somewhere special. It didn't matter if they weren't the same shoe size, they would jam their feet into Mum's shoes for the evening, If Mum didn't have any stockings to lend them she would stand them on a kitchen chair and carefully draw a line down the back of their legs to give the impression they were wearing seamed stockings.

If a neighbour was ill or found themselves in financial hardship, the rest of the street fed the family until they were on their feet again. Summer evenings found everyone out in the street sitting on their front garden walls and chatting. On weekends, when it became dark, Mum and Dad would sometimes invite them all in around our living room while Dad played the piano and everyone sang. Because we had a piano, we were classed as the 'posh' ones in the street.

Within the 'family unit', they would criticise a neighbour for one thing or another but when the chips were down for that person they still rallied around and helped.

Mrs Murphy was such a soul. She had no idea how to organise her family. She could not budget her money to make it last through the week and her house looked poor and bare. There were no curtains on Mrs Murphy's windows and she had one small easy chair without cushions in her living room, and only mattresses on the bedroom floors. As the housing corporation owned the houses, someone had reported this state of affairs to them and Mrs Murphy was told if she didn't furnish her home and take care of it she would be put out and a family that would appreciate it would be placed there. She was given four weeks to create a home.

The neighbours immediately rallied around; they dyed sheets and placed them as curtains on her windows. They scrubbed and cleaned and gave her pieces of furniture they didn't need anymore. The rag and bone man that called each week with his horse and cart was asked to find some half decent furniture and some beds for them, which he did. When the housing authorities came four weeks later, they saw a neat tidy home and she was told they would inspect every three months after that, but for now her family was allowed to stay. Every three months, the neighbours cleaned Mrs Murphy's home for the housing inspection.

Mrs Murphy was a 'simple soul', my mother used to say. At the end of each day when the siren would blast out from the local ship building yard to announce the end of the working day, the housewives would powder their face, put a clean apron on and stand on the front steps with their children awaiting their man returning home from work. All the men worked in Cammell Lairds and would begin to walk home along Borough Road, all climbing the streets and disappearing inside their homes. They would file past the women on the steps of their homes and touch the tip of their caps and nod their heads in their direction.

Mrs Murphy was a very large round lady. She would stand on her steps along with the rest of the women in the street to welcome her man home. On this day, her youngest was crying and she lifted her up on to her hip. As the men looked up to tip their cap, they began to click their tongues and smile, saying "Hello there, luv!" one after the other. Mrs Murphy acted coy, smiled and said words such as "Ooh go on with ye! My fella will 'ave yer life if ee 'eard ye."

My father tipped his cap to Mrs Murphy and walked on to my mother and whispered in her ear. My mother immediately ran to Mrs Murphy, saying, "Ye frock, look at ye frock!" Mrs Murphy had lifted her child onto her hip but the child's foot had caught the hem of her dress and hitched it up and Mrs Murphy was showing the world – she had no knickers on!

Opposite *The Happy Valley* pub at the bottom of the street and across Borough Road was a magnificent white stone library with a bust of King George in bronze in its grounds. I mention this building because reaching our seventh birthday was burned into our memories – it was the day all the Hicks kids joined the library. We would be playing in the street and, on our birthday, we would eagerly watch for Dad to turn the corner of the street from Borough Road on his way home from work. As he came into sight, we'd run squealing with excitement back into the house shouting,

"Dad's nearly home, Mum!"

She would grab the damp flannel from the side of the kitchen sink and run it over our face, our hair would be brushed and off we'd go holding Dad's hand as he took each of us in turn on our seventh birthday, over Borough Road to join the Birkenhead Library. Dad would have the copy of our birth certificate to prove we were seven years old that day. This was our birthday present.

Proudly, he would say to the librarian, "My wee girl 'ere is seven today an' it's 'er birthday and she'd like t'join the library please."

I can remember nearly wetting myself with excitement! With both Mum and Dad being avid readers and all their children then members of the library, our house was always full of books, and each of us would read the books that all of us had borrowed before they were returned.

Our parents always knew where to look for us: if not lying on the floor reading, we'd be either playing in the street or in our local Birkenhead Park.

We had a small, enclosed back garden and, as a child, I would perform a concert all on my own and charge the kids in the street a halfpenny to come in and sit on the grass to watch me. They never did have a halfpenny so I would say they could have it on tick (drip payment!). I had heard the women in the neighbourhood using this expression often when they wanted to buy something and didn't have the money. They'd say, 'I'll have to get it on tick.'

So I thought that meant for free. 'Mister Umberella' (Flanagan and Allen) was my favourite song as I could dance to that with Mum's umbrella.

Most Saturday nights, Dad would bring those in the pub back to our house as he played the piano and we'd have a sing along. I classed my childhood in this street as magical.

Chapter Four

Dads influence over our lives

1954

The area where we lived was called Merseyside, and Birkenhead was a town on the other side of the Mersey River from Liverpool. This part of England became known as the second capital of Ireland. The Irish Ferry boat docked in the port twice a week bringing Irish immigrants that were escaping the IRA and looking for a better life. Most of them created their new life where they docked, on the banks of the Mersey, choosing Liverpool or Birkenhead.

Drinking alcohol was the main pastime of the majority of the men in this area and so my father didn't stand out as being any different.

Dad was sober more than he was drunk, and he took an interest in all his children and spent time with us when he could. He had a passionate pride in his family, and his home, and all his possessions, which included us, were better than anybody else had and he made a point of telling people this often, especially when he was drunk.

The stories of his past were exaggerated more each time he told us them, and his children sat and listened spellbound. He boomed them out to the ceiling or the walls while he talked as though he was speaking to a huge audience.

Dad played the piano often throughout the week as we, his kids, sang along with him. And he often amused us by singing and playing out of rhythm and tune, and we would roll around the floor in fits of laughter.

(As an adult I came to realise, if you know how to play the piano properly, then to purposely play it badly was quite a clever thing to do).

We would be convulsed with laughter at the noise he made, but he, sombre-faced with a twinkle in his eye, would play on, then ask us what we were laughing at.

A boring job or situation could be turned into a fun filled adventure. He taught us how to tend the garden and grow from seed. With one tuppenny packet of flower seeds he would carefully count them into our hands. We had to give each seed a name then he would show us how to prepare the ground and plant them. We were told to water our seeds and talk to them every day. If they weren't watered and talked to they wouldn't grow, he said. After school, instead of playing with the other kids in the neighbourhood, we could often be found lying on our stomachs, talking to a patch of earth.

Redecorating the house was great fun when we were each given a door to varnish and then shown how to draw a grain in it with a piece of cardboard cut like a comb. As the years went on, we must have improved in this art form but in the early days, those doors must have looked a mess but our dad showed our handy work to everyone who entered the house, boasting that any one of us could paint as good as that "Vangoof fella". I was in my early twenties before I realised who he was referring to.

He encouraged us to daydream. On a cold and rainy day when we couldn't play outside, he would lean on the windowsill with us as we stared waiting for the rain to stop, and say,

"Now let's make dem black clouds go away,. Keep staring at dem and dey jus' disappears. Can ye see de sunshine? I can see it shinin' on de water. I can sees a field wid wee lambs in it, playing in de sunshine. What kin youse sees?"

Today it would be called visualisation, but as children it was our rainy day game.

On some occasions it would get us into trouble. In Christchurch school on Borough Road, we sat on the floor in the hall and listened to Mrs Maddocks, our music teacher, play the piano. Oh! she was my idol. I would sit and listen to the gentle, tinkly way she played the piano which was different from the heavy fingers of my dad. I dreamed of playing the piano like that myself one day in front of a large audience like the one I was sitting in. Approximately one hundred children. My day dreaming took over and although I had never had piano lessons at this stage in my life, I sat in my dream world staring at Mrs Maddocks knowing she would soon be asking for someone to help her to play something beautiful on the piano. As soon as she did, I would raise my hand and she would announce me in front of all these people and I would be famous.

Mrs Maddocks stood up from the piano and walked to the front of the stage and said 'something', which in my daydream was asking for this wonderful piano playing person she had heard of. My hand shot up and she said my name. Excitement engulfed me as I uncurled my legs from my squatting position on the floor, I climbed over all the other children and walked with my back straight and my curls bouncing on my head, down the aisle left between the children and on to the stage. With a smile that stretched from ear to ear, I stood beside Mrs Maddocks looking down on all the children and I felt ten feet tall.

"Yes, Pauline?" said Mrs Maddocks with half a smile.

I looked up at her. *What does she mean 'Yes'? I've come to play the piano with her.*

"Well, do you know the answer to my question?" she asked.

"What question?" I asked.

"You've been daydreaming again, Pauline, haven't you?" she said crossly. "Now go and sit down and pay attention."

This was one of my most embarrassing moments. My face burned and I wanted to cry as I had to walk off the stage, back down the stairs and pick my way through the crossed legs of all the audience as they giggled and laughed at me. But in the morning break from lessons when we all went into the play yard, Peter stood before me struggling to say something. He was one of the boys in my class and said nothing about my embarrassment but leaned into me and gave me my first kiss. My embarrassment was over! I was in love!

Dad worked as a 'spider man', which was a name they gave to steel erectors on Birkenhead Docks. He boasted that he could walk across a four-inch beam suspended seventy feet in the air, without a nerve in his body. We believed him. Cammell Laird's, the company he worked for on the docks, built a lot of famous ships, and on their launching, he would take us to witness the ships that 'he' had built, and as kids we believed he had done it single-handed. He wanted us to be proud of him, and for a lot of things we were.

The times we didn't boast about were his drunken bouts of rage; the violent arguments with my mother after his drinking. On occasions she ran into our bedroom to get away from him but he burst through the door, roaring abuse at her. We huddled together in fear in the corner of the double bed that we children shared. He never ever hurt us but this scene would make us terrified. We would want to cry but we were too frightened to make a noise in case he noticed us, and all the while our little hearts hammered away in our chests as we held onto each other for comfort. Our mother would be dragged from our room and the door slammed and we could hear her being physically knocked around the living room.

After an evening of my father's drinking and a violent argument, my mother waited until he was asleep in the chair. It was late and the rest of the world was fast asleep safe in their beds. Mum dressed us all and placed Harry in a large pram with Babs and I holding on to the handle, we walked some miles through Birkenhead Park in the black of night to my aunt's house in Leinster Street in the North End of Birkenhead. This memory haunted all three of us for years, firstly because of what we had endured in the house followed by the fear of the dark outside. To this day, it is a nightmare I can still remember.

As children we had been born with the Irish passion for life but it was occasionally suffocated in our young bodies, never knowing if now was the time to show our enthusiasm or to shut up.

We were never short of home comforts, my mother saw to that; she was an excellent manager with money and supplemented the household income by doing cleaning jobs. She was a good mother and sat in with us kids every night. She wasn't one to go to the pub as she only drank alcohol for an occasion. I can only remember when we were older that she began to have a movie night out with her sister from time to time. She never spoke to anyone about the abuse she suffered, she had her pride, and we all knew not to talk to anyone about Dad's drunken rages. She could only hold her head up high if she thought no one knew. Consequently, only a rare few people were aware of the life she led. There were those who were critical of her, not knowing the life she led behind closed doors with my father. People would see this funny little Irish man and loved his company but couldn't understand why his wife had such a poker-face at times.

Dad mellowed as he got older and stopped being argumentative in drink, but he never stopped drinking. The two extremes of emotion we children endured because of Dad's personality, made it difficult, because we really loved someone we also feared. He would turn in his grave if he thought he had harmed us in any way because he loved us all passionately.

In 1952, we had a new baby born into our family, a beautiful baby boy. His name was Sam. Personally, I felt this baby boy was mine. Harry was four now and didn't always want me to baby him. At the age of seven, I felt quite grown up as I shared Sam's care. I learned how to change his nappies, bathe him, feed him, dress him. I would place him in his pram and walk around the neighbourhood with him, stopping and talking to all the neighbours while showing him off. I was so proud of our new baby; he was the most beautiful child in the world. I would sit for hours teaching him to walk and talk. At the end of my school day, I would run home to spend some time with him, singing him songs as he clapped his hands, letting me know he loved my singing. Nobody else was allowed to put Sam to bed. I made it my sole responsibility to dress him in his night clothes, feed him his last bottle, then quietly sing and rock him until he was asleep. Oh I did love that time with him.

While he was a newborn, he slept in his cot in Mum and Dad's room but as he grew he was moved into my room to sleep with me and the other kids. My life was complete again now that I had another baby to care for. Mum and Dad told everybody I was a born mother.

Chapter Five

Birkenhead North

Teenage years - 1956-1966

When I was twelve years old, my parents decided to move house. Sam was our fourth child and so the detached two-bedroom prefabricated house was now too small for us all. Before we had left Carnforth Street, all four of us children had slept in a double bed in one room. To begin the night, the two girls were at one end of the bed and the two boys at the other. As soon as the light was switched off, Babs would take her position on one third of the bed and me and the boys nested together at the other end. This was how we liked to sleep, arms and legs entangled. The girls and the boys now had to be separated and so a three-bedroom house was found. The two boys slept in one room and the two girls in another. Not having my little brothers to cuddle each night was something that took some time to come to terms with, but the bonus was Babs and I had our very first single beds all to ourselves.

At this point in our lives, Babs found another song that made me cry and she would sing it every night for weeks when we first moved in. Mum and Dad would tell her not to but she would whisper-sing it so they couldn't hear:

Rocking alone in an old rocking chair
I saw an old mother with silvery hair
She seemed so neglected by those who should care
Rocking alone in an old rocking chair

Her hands were all callused and wrinkled and old
A life of hard work was the story they told
And I thought of angels as I saw her there
Rocking alone in an old rocking chair

Bless her old heart, do you think she'd complain
Though life has been bitter she'd live it again
And carry that cross that is more than her share
Rocking alone in an old rocking chair

It wouldn't take much just to gladden her heart
Just some small remembrance on somebody's part
A letter would brighten her empty life there
Rocking alone in an old rocking chair

I know some youngsters in an orphans' home
Who'd think they owned heaven if she was their own
They'd never be willing to let her sit there
Rocking alone in an old rocking chair

I look at her and I think "What a shame"
The ones who forgot her she loves just the same
And I think of angels as I see her there
Rocking alone in an old rocking chair

I loved my sister, she helped me with my schoolwork and would read me bedtime stories and gave me all her clothes when she had outgrown them, but it made her laugh that she could easily make me cry. (As adults we often sang this song as a reminder of our childhood. We loved it!)

Though the house had an extra bedroom, the living areas were smaller than our prefab. The world we had become familiar with was about to change drastically. More than anything else we didn't want to leave our library behind but Mum assured us that there would be one near to where we were going to live.

It was a brick terraced house with a handkerchief-sized front garden and a small fence separating it from the pavement. The back garden wasn't much bigger and was surrounded by a high wooden fence. It was in the North End of Birkenhead. Corporation Road was one of the seven roads circling St. James' Church.

When I decided to write my life story, I found a small book written by Bill Houldin called *Up Our Lobby* and the following historical information was gleaned from that book.

> This area had become famous in the late 1800s for a set of buildings called the Dock Cottages. They had been situated at the nearest end of Ilchester Road to the church.
>
> The Birkenhead Dock Company, finding they needed accommodation for their numerous workers, decided in their wisdom to build the first block of flats in England. This was a new concept then and the whole country looked on with interest to see if this idea would work and how it would affect the lives of the average working-class family. The name 'Dock Cottages', conjures up the wrong picture of what were huge concrete blocks of one room flats standing four high surrounding a concrete central community recreation area. These addresses were even Block One, Block Two, etc. It resembled one of the old English Asylums.
>
> The Dock Cottages housed over one thousand people

and after ninety years they eventually were demolished in 1940 and Ilchester Square, again another block of flats but more rooms to each flat and modern facilities, was erected.

Once again, more than one thousand people were herded together to share family life. It created closeness unheard of anywhere else. If children fell over or hurt themselves they would run to any Mum to be cleaned up and kissed better. The centre of the blocks of flats, the concrete area, always had sports of some description being played there.

It was known as a tough area, but these people wouldn't see one of their own kind 'down and out'. Everybody supported each other and behind their tough exterior was a big fat heart.

Though the way of life in the flats did not create comfortable living, it did create two generations of excellent sports people, some of them famous and placing their names in the archives of English history.

Their names were bandied around these parts because they were neighbours and were classed as part of our extended family.

Dixie Dean, the famous footballer, he played for Everton and England.

Wally Thom, British and Empire welterweight boxing champion.

The Sutton brothers, Bill and Norman, golfers at the West Cheshire Artisans, Norman becoming World Champion in 1958.

The area also produced many successful caddies to the rich and famous golfers and stories of lives we could only imagine, were spread throughout the community from the *many pubs in the area where the men gathered regularly.*

We learned soon after moving into this house that those living in the roads surrounding Ilchester Square were also part of this community.

Opposite our house in Corporation Road was a high brick wall surrounding a huge building called *The Prince Albert Memorial Industrial School*. The building was designed to accommodate one hundred boys. Those admitted were deemed to be in need of care or they had been committed for some misdemeanour. The school had been closed since 1924 and now sat idle and empty. It still didn't stop Mum from threatening us with it.

"If you don't behave yourself I'll put you in the naughty boys home!" It was always just a huge brick wall to us.

Dad had been used to having a garden to potter in and this little piece of land that came with the house was a challenge to him. The front garden was transformed within weeks. It hadn't had any care for many years, Dad said, and he immediately went to work with horse manure, digging it in and aerating the soil. He then planted a privet hedge and a small rose garden under the front window. As his hedge grew, he trimmed it back into a tidy shape. Every week he went out there with his hedge clippers and meticulously cut any quarter inch of branch that dared to grow and spoil his tidy shape. As the neighbours began to take an interest in his little patch of land, Dad offered them privet cuttings to grow a hedge of their own. Neighbours either side took advantage of his generosity and so Dad planted cuttings in their garden and began to grow a hedge like ours. Dad liked things to be tidy so, as their hedge grew, he offered to trim their hedges to match the shape he had in ours.

Over the next few years 'The Privet Hedge' in Corporation Road got longer and longer as Dad planted cuttings in front gardens whether they wanted them or not. Dad spent any spare time he had going up and down the road trimming the hedges.

"The Hedge" stretched right down the road in front of at least twenty properties. Within two years of moving into an untidy row of houses, Dad had transformed the entire road with his 'Privet Hedge'. It now looked a treat as you approached the block of houses with front gardens maintained by the local Irish man.

Dad smoked Embassy cigarettes and they started to put coupons in the packet. When you had saved enough coupons you could choose to exchange them for gifts out of a catalogue. Dad puffed away at his cigarettes saving the coupons for a motorised hedge trimmer.

On the day his hedge trimmer arrived, there was great excitement in the house. Dad immediately went out to trim his hedge in a box shape but with the top in the shape of a wall resembling a fort. High at one side of the gate in a block about two feet square then dropping two feet for another two feet, then rising again into another block, two feet square and so on. All meticulously measured as he went. Our whole family looked on with pride and pleasure.

As Dad got to the boundary line between our house and the house next door he didn't stop. Along the neighbour's privet hedge he went meticulously shaping his fort wall.

"Ye can't do that, Wally, it's not your hedge," Mum reminded him in consternation.

"*Ahck*! It is my hedge; I gave it to dem, didn't I? Anyway, thaze will luv dis shape."

And he continued to go on his merry way, thoroughly enjoying himself, grinning from ear to ear and singing his Irish songs all the time – the neighbours didn't have the heart to object and spoil his fun. Once he'd finished moving to the right, he went off to the left. In the space of one weekend, Dad and his motorised hedge trimmer had transformed the entire road. Every week from then on until he died, Dad trimmed the hedges in Corporation Road. He was most definitely a frustrated horticulturist.

The house had also been sadly neglected before we moved in. Dad said there were at least seven sheets of wallpaper on every interior wall and the house would be bigger once it was all removed. We immediately began ripping it all off and redecorating the entire house. It was great fun. From that day on, Mum had a standard phrase: "Don't stand still too long there or ye father will paint ye." He always seemed to have his paintbrush in his hand inside, and his much-loved motorised hedge trimmer outside.

Respect for our elders was built into us and they were always called Mr or Mrs. I look back now and fail to understand why our parents used the same titles for each other. Always referring to each other as Mr or Mrs, when their peers were the same age as themselves.

Mr McGuiness was our next door neighbour. He was the same age as my Dad and about the same height. Mr McGuiness was southern Irish Catholic; my Dad was Northern Irish Protestant. They were very good friends. They called for each other to go for a pint and supported each other home from the *Shamrock Pub*, which was now Dad's local. As they walked home from the pub on Laird Street, we could hear them singing and they'd appear around the corner with their arms around each other's shoulders. On arriving at their respective gates; now both painted green by Dad, they would close the gates behind them and continue to sing their Irish songs in their front gardens. Mr McGuiness would harmonise with the high notes as they sang. Head held back and chest puffed up, they would direct their singing toward each other with gestures from their opened arms. This would continue until either Mrs McGuiness or my mother would go out and drag them in.

They also went to the local football matches together and

were inseparable … until the 17th March, which was St Patrick's Day. Then Dad would shout over the fence to him, "Yer a heathen, that's what ye are, McGuiness, a bloody heathen."

Mr McGuiness would come out of his house rolling up his shirtsleeves. "Ye call me a bloody heathen agin', 'icksie, an' al be puttin' ye on ye arse."

"Yer a bloody heathen, McGuiness, a bloody heathen. Come out an' fight like a man instead o' hidin' behind the skirts o' ye Mrs," my father would shout again while he too would start to roll up his sleeves.

At this point 'the wives' would come out of the house and start to drag them both indoors while they would both attempt to protest with "Let go of me, woman, while a wipes 'im off de face o' de erf."

Somehow at this point in the arguments the women were stronger than the men and were able to get them both inside.

Mr McGuiness and Dad would then ignore each other all day. If they happened to be in their gardens at the same time, they would shake their fists at each other and growl something that resembled "Geeerrrrawee-witcha."

The following day they would be off to the pub as usual as if it hadn't happened.

The only other day in the year they would fall out would be 12th July – Independence Day for Ireland or Orange Lodge Day, as Dad would call it. Dad would take his piano accordion outside and prance up and down in front of Mr McGuiness's house playing the orange marches with a huge smile on his face, knowing he was irritating his friend. On hearing the piano accordion, the neighbours would all begin standing in their front gardens knowing what was about to happen and waiting to be entertained. Mr McGuiness would come out and shout at Dad, in the same fashion as he was abused on St Patrick's Day.

"If ye don't git away from me 'ouse, 'icksy, yer'll be feckin sorry, am warnin' ye"

The following day they would be off to the pub as usual.

They had a strange relationship.

Chapter Six

My Dad – Wee Wally

1960

My dad was the wisest and funniest little Irish man that ever walked this planet. He was the size and build of a leprechaun and his face was carved with a permanent smile. His name was Walter, shortened to Wally and referred to as Wee Wally. Negativity wasn't in his psyche. His words were "Problems and challenges are the school of life. You must learn from them and work them through until ye find the silver lining, 'cos there'll always be one." Wee Wally's Words. He was a human magnet, always surrounded by people and laughter. He told the most outrageous stories that were obviously untrue but would be boasting or roasting himself – that the Irish could make fun of themselves epitomised Dad's life.

He had served in the Second World War as a dispatch rider and told us many stories of how he crept over the enemy lines, swinging his motor bike from this way to that as he dodged the bullets but delivered his dispatches every time. But he wouldn't talk of the bombs and trenches.

"We'll not give that life again wid the gift of words," he would say. But he did return with ' the night demons' in his head – as he called them – but counted himself lucky he had returned at all as many didn't.

Cammell Lairds was a shipyard on the banks of the Mersey River south of Liverpool that offered to employ the returning soldiers that lived in the vicinity. Dad was a steel erector and went straight into work as he felt keeping busy was the only way to keep the demons in his head at bay. The shipyard was full of damaged men – and Dad had an innate empathetic gift – he could reach into the skin of those in mental pain, soothe their souls, lift their spirits and make them laugh. Watching him was watching a master at work.

Cammell Laird's management quickly acknowledged his gift and they made him a supervisor, giving him time in the mornings to counsel those who arrived at work depressed or with the demons still in their heads from their night's sleep. The shipyard employed more than a thousand men, most of them returning soldiers and every one of them knew my dad. Helping people was his purpose in life, plus his skill as a steel erector was something he was proud of. Dad boasted to everyone that "he had the best job in Cammell Lairds."

Some years later, Dad employed an apprentice, a fifteen-year-old boy straight from school. After a couple of months of working in the shed learning the rudiments, Dad decided it was time to take him up on the steel. He placed the harness on the young boy and grabbed the end of the rope. He told him to watch how he climbed – this was called crabbing. He identified a beam about thirty feet in the air. Climbing to this beam, he threw the rope over it and came back down and fed the rope into the winch and pulled the right tension on it.

"Off ye go!" He smiled at him as he climbed in exactly the right way and then straddled the 30ft high beam, smiling down at Dad, so proud of himself.

Ships are built in dry docks, and cranes run on tracks along the edges, lifting the beams for the steel erectors and holding them in place until they are secured. On that day, a crane slipped off its track and the huge arm came hurtling down crushing and killing the young boy before Dad's eyes.

Over the next months we mentally lost Dad. He was at the bottom of a black pit of pain, consumed with self-blame and guilt. He spent his days sitting staring into the fire and quietly crying. The weeks turned into months. Depression continued to hover over the yard and the town. So many people called to say they were thinking of Dad but he didn't want to speak to them – he couldn't talk about the tragedy of that young boy, or of himself, to anyone.

Management was now dealing with absenteeism and the entire shipyard had a depressing cloud over it. They intuitively knew Dad's return would be the answer – they needed him back and called periodically.

"Your job's there for you, Wall, when you're ready," until one day he answered, "No, I'll not be going up on the steel again. I couldn't do it without seeing the face of that wee lad."

The shipyard was like a ghost town. Cammell Lairds were becoming desperate, the morale of their workforce wasn't lifting.

Then, some weeks later, a representative from the yard called to offer Dad a job, that of a toilet cleaner for a new block of toilets just completed. We, his family, stood listening at the living room door, horrified. This we felt added insult to injury. We stared at Dad waiting for his response, tears beginning to fall from my mother's eyes. Dad sat listening quietly and said he would think about it. The very next day he dressed for the first time in months and went down to the shipyard to see the toilet block. That evening as we sat at the dining table he described to us the long brick building built in the centre of the yard which had a huge storage room at the end of it that was surrounded by windows. He could see from there all that was going on. He had told them he would take the job providing he could fit the storage room out for himself with somewhere comfy to chat to the men who needed help in the mornings.

"We've thought of that," management said. "We're renewing the office reception furniture – would you like a leather settee and two chairs? They are almost new and in perfect condition."

"Thank you – that's kind of you," Dad said. "I would be very grateful."

He then smiled for the first time in ages and, leaning into the table as he caught our eyes, he boasted that 'he would be the only toilet cleaner ever on this earth to have his own office with a three-piece suite t'boot! Plus he was offered the same salary as before. Dad began to come back to us.

The buzz around the yard and town was 'Wee Wally was going back to work next week'. People in the streets and the yard were all saying, 'did you hear? Wee Wally's going back to work Monday'. The entire area could feel the depression lifting.

As Dad walked through the gates on Monday morning the entire work force had turned out to welcome him back. To get to his office, he had to push his way through the throngs of cheering people who were slapping his back. His three-piece suite was in situ, plus the old boardroom table and chairs, a cupboard with dishes and an urn. That day the black cloud lifted from the entire yard and absenteeism became a thing of the past.

Daily, he chatted to everyone that visited his office, and it was packed to capacity with standing room only every lunch break. As his work routine settled in, throughout the day those that needed counselling went in with shoulders drooped and came out smiling. And by Friday of that week Dad again announced "he had the best job in Cammell Lairds."

He had found the silver lining.

How many times have you said, 'I can't deal with this and put the problem into the too-hard basket, waiting for it to disappear, and it does in time. My Dad would say, you have robbed yourself of a valuable lesson in life that would build your character and add to your wisdom … plus … you have missed out on the sheer joy of a silver lining.

'cos there'll always be one! 'Wee Wally's Words'

Chapter Seven

Rock and Roll

1960s

During my first year in Corporation Road, I took the bus to the junior school I attended: Christ Church School on Borough Road. The schooling system at that time was a junior school from age five to eleven or twelve. The eleven plus examination was sat by everyone and, if you passed, you would go on to a high school in the area; if you failed, you went to a secondary modern school. I sat the eleven plus examination and passed to go to Park High School for Girls.

My parents were so proud of me. Mum and Dad went about telling everyone "our Pauline is going to High School". I was the talk of the neighbourhood for a while. Mum got in touch with the school I was about to attend to ask if they had a second-hand school uniform department. She couldn't afford to buy me new school clothes and the amount of sports equipment that was needed for me was a problem Mum needed to work on.

The second-hand uniform room in the school I was about to attend had old sports equipment also and Mum was excited for me. "We can get everything you need here, Pauline. Isn't that just grand."

Mum picked out a school uniform that had belonged to a sixteen-year-old who had just left school. "This'll do yer fine,"

Mum said as she held up this huge maroon pinafore dress. "I'll take it in and put a hem on it and if ye look after it it'll last ye till ye finish school." We then picked out a lacrosse stick, a tennis racket, a hockey stick, a school satchel and two pairs of shoes, one for wearing every day and one for sports, a maroon mackintosh, a beret for my head in winter and a boater hat for summer. I was as thrilled as Mum. We carried them home and set about putting tucks in this and hems on that. Dad sanded, stained and polished the sports equipment and Mum made me a cotton draw string bag to put them all in.

As I stood before Mum and Dad wearing all my 'new' clothes, they looked on me with pride. Mum escorted me to the bus and waved me off to my first morning at this school saying, "Yer'll make many new friends. It'll be lots of fun and remember to be respectful to the teachers."

I walked into the hall for my first day at this school and felt everybody was whispering and laughing at me in groups. I'd arrived looking like a pack horse in comparison. Their clothes all fitted them 'now', and I saw no sign of any of them with second-hand anything. The twelve-inch hem on my dress and mackintosh were rather obvious and seemed to cause titters of laughter as I dragged my drawstring floral cotton bag across the hall. The other girls all had neat leather cases for their sports equipment. My shoes were a size too big for me but Mum had bought them knowing I would grow into them so they were packed with newspaper in the toes. My heel would hit the floor a split second before the splat of the sole arrived. I must have looked like the school clown. I also seemed to be the smallest and skinniest person there. I did as Dad had told me and walked up to various groups of girls to meet them, but they all turned away from me laughing.

Lunch time arrived and we lined up outside the dining hall to pay for our weeks lunches. The cost was six pence per day, being two and six for the whole week, which was a half crown. My family received welfare support for school dinners and so I handed over my welfare dinner token. The teacher looked up at me and asked, "What is this, dear?"

My face began to burn. "It's my dinner token' miss."

"Just one moment I need to ask another teacher about these," she said and left her chair. All the girls giggled and whispered behind their hands again and I was engulfed with humiliation. I wanted to grab my things and leave this school there and then.

My time at this school was not a happy one. I was encouraged by Dad to "show 'em what yer made of" ... "yer as good as any one of 'em and better than most."

We had only recently moved into this area and when I was seen in my school uniform the children in this area decided I must have thought I was better than them and wouldn't befriend me. The children in the high school I was attending looked down on me because I came from the poor area and I didn't have the clothes and equipment they had. Consequently, I concentrated on my school and homework because I had no distractions. I studied hard so I wouldn't let my parents down and received high marks when I eventually sat my school 'O' levels at the age of sixteen but leaving this school to start work was the best day of my life. I had been out of my 'class'.

Miss Rice was my maths teacher and asked me if I was considering going to university.

I told her, "No. Mum wants me to start work to help with the housekeeping, Miss Rice." She handed me a letter at the end of the day asking me to give this to my mum and dad.

Mum read it and exclaimed, "What a lovely letter, Pauline. It could be used as a reference for a job. She says you should think of going on to university as you're clever enough. If ye would rather do that, luv, I'll see if I can make it happen."

"No, Mum, I've had enough of school. I really want to start

working now."

My auburn hair and green eyes made me an attractive teenager and I loved to dance. It was the 1960s and I was lucky enough to live around Merseyside when the world had Beatlemania. Every Friday and Saturday night my friend and I would get the ferry across the Mersey to Liverpool. We could then be found in any one of Liverpool's many clubs, rock and rolling through every dance. If a 'fella' didn't ask us up to dance, my friend and I would dance together until two of them came to 'split us up'.

Winkle picker shoes with 6-inch stiletto heels were something I quickly adapted to and jammed my feet into them every day, tottering around appreciating the extra height these shoes gave my small slight frame.

Having naturally curly hair was too 'square' in these times and I put large fat foam rubber rollers in it every night, trying to straighten it to produce the sleek bouffant style that Dusty Springfield made popular in our time. Unfortunately, one puff of wind or downpour of rain would make it frizz up again and so I used hair lacquer. This was part of my essential wardrobe and was as necessary to me as lipstick. I sprayed my hair until it was as stiff as a board and looked set in concrete before I went through the door of the house, then proceeded to spray every wisp of hair that escaped the bouffant shape I had so painstakingly worked on.

Skin-tight miniskirts and clothes with stiff net petticoats that we starched to hold out a felt skirt under a waspy belt were two of the main fashion choices. The petticoats were my favourite because they didn't prevent me from rock and rolling and they swirled out beautifully when I twirled around. In my mind, this made a lovely picture but on reflection I can see that my pink net petticoats, skinny legs and six-inch stiletto heels must have had me resembling a pink flamingo in a frenzy when I was dancing. At the time though I felt like 'the bees knees' and stepped out every weekend in full war paint resembling a fairy on a Christmas tree.

The boys we fancied wore what we called 'Teddy Boy' clothes – suits with long single-breasted jackets that had sleeves that ended halfway down their hands. The collars of these jackets were velvet. The pants were 'drainpipes' and their shoes were winkle pickers – that meant pointed toes. They brylcreamed their long straight hair back on their head and it met in the middle at the back which was called a D.A. This meant a 'duck's arse'. The front was pulled forward over their eyes. We used to call this style a Tony Curtis or an Elvis hair-do.

The *Mardi Gras* club on the left at the top of Matthew Street in Liverpool was a jazz club and our favourite venue. *The Cavern* was too small for our liking but sometimes we would finish at the *Mardi Gras* at about 10pm and walk down the hill to sit on the top step of the Cavern club listening to whichever band was on at the time. We visited in the early days to listen to the Beatles but the cigarette smoke was thick and you couldn't see your hand in front of your face so we'd sit outside just listening. John Lennon came out one time to have a cigarette and we chatted. My friend Jesse told him it was my birthday soon and he said the next song was for me. We heard him announce this when he went back in, and many years later when the Beatles were famous Jesse and I rummaged through our brains trying to remember which song he sang for me. We couldn't remember it.

Life was exciting and fun. Boy friends were never a shortage to me and I would have dates through the week with the latest 'feller' that I'd met on Saturday night. Heartaches were a plenty as most teenagers of any generation experience, but the plus we had was the newfound freedom our generation had with its 'flower power' and hippies, 'Hari Krishnas' and 'love not war'

57

values, pushed upon the unsuspecting world. Drinking alcohol was something I wasn't good at: 'one Babycham and I'm anybody's' was my favourite expression. I didn't smoke, never took drugs and didn't tell anyone that I still went to church on Sunday.

The peer pressure was more than I wanted to cope with and I knew I would have my leg pulled if they found out that I was a Sunday school teacher, so I began to lead a double life. I attended Bidston Parish Church – St Oswald's – because it was like having a sing song every Sunday morning. The Reverend Singleton had been an army chaplain and he would play the guitar and beef up the rhythm of the hymns. I'm sure he must have been the first to do this in his time. He would give me a bible story every Sunday and ask me to read it throughout the week and teach it to the kids at my next Sunday class. I would read it a couple of times through the week and then deliver it without notes the next Sunday. On this day, he stood at the door of the room I was in, listening to my interaction with the children. I started off OK teaching them about Lott and his wife leaving Sodom, and then I began to improvise:

"And Lott said t' God – ar eh, God, look what yerve gone and dun! Yerve turned me wife inta a pile of salt! Oo's gunna cook me tea now?" And I looked up to see his head lowering into his wide open hand, his fingers covering his face as he shook his head. I guess I should have stuck to the correct script but I'd guarantee those kids would remember my version more than the bible story!

My younger brothers had grown out of wanting to listen to the stories I used to read to them, and being a Sunday school teacher gave me the opportunity to read to children and watch their faces. They would listen in awe to the magical happenings that I would read to them from the bible with my own modern-day twist to them. I had inherited my father's ability to tell a story, set the scene and involve my listeners in all I told them. In looking back, I can see some of the distorted messages I was giving these young impressionable minds. I had an audience and more often than not made the stories up as I went along, just like my father did. There were times when I'd finished the story but it didn't really resemble the bible at all.

God was mentioned around our house as an invisible member of the family, along with the spirit world, fairies and leprechauns. If any personal possession had been moved overnight the leprechauns had been up to their mischief again. The fairies were kind; they used to leave sweets under your pillow if you were unhappy or leave a penny in exchange for a tooth that had come out. They paid for these because they needed them for gravestones. If we asked for anything extravagant or posed a question that Mum decided we should give some thought to, she would say:

"'ave a word with God t'night an' see what 'ee says."

By the following morning of course we'd forgotten what it was we needed answers to.

Dancing and singing in my teenage years gave me the outlet I needed to express my 'love of life'. I was exuberant, bubbly and had an infectious sense of humour and gathered people because I surrounded myself with amusement.

At the age of eighteen, after working for over two years, I now had my own money and could have a holiday of my own choice. Of course, I chose to go to Ireland.

My experiences of Ireland, in the telling of them, had impressed my friend Jesse so much that I was able to convince her it was the place for us to go.

My aunt and uncle were informed of our visit because they had transport and they arranged to meet us at the ferry and transport us to the farm where we would spend two whole weeks with my grandparents.

I felt the same giddy pleasure on the boat, which was spoiled by Jesse's obvious lack of enthusiasm for all the 'unseen' attributes of the journey.

"What the 'ell are thee sayin', a carn understand any of em!" she moaned, and "God al be glad when a get there, this boat's makin' me seasick."

My aunt and uncle met us. They had brought the horse and trap for our journey to the farm.

"Am not getting' in tha' thing," Jesse whispered indignantly as my Uncle dropped the step. "War'if someone sees us! It's a bloody rag an' bone man's cart."

"No one knows ye over 'ear," I reminded her. "Jus' ger'in."

We arrived at the pig farm and beautiful childhood memories came flooding back with the smells that surrounded it.

"War'a pong!" shouted Jesse. "'ow can thee live wit'dat!"

My aunt informed us that there would be a dance on Saturday night at the village hall.

"We'll send ye cousins along t'fetch ye both. It'll be great fun," she announced and she and my uncle left.

Jesse looked around the farm and her face said the words before they left her mouth. "Are we stuck 'ere till Saterday? There's nuthin t'do!" she exclaimed.

Tentatively I said, "We can go fer walks, an' see the countryside ... an' just wait 'till after tea, me Nan tells great stories, yer'll luv it." But her negativity worried me along with the guilt I felt for talking her into something she couldn't see the beauty of.

She pouted and sulked and dragged her feet around the farm, holding her nose and constantly complaining. "Dis is unbelievable. A don't know 'ow ye talked me inter'it."

The evening arrived and Nan's stories began.

Nan had a large wooden rocking chair beside a pot belly stove in the corner of the kitchen. She always sat here rocking as she looked into the air to tell her stories in a manner that made the observer feel they were eaves-dropping on a private conversation she was having with herself. Her audience sat on a rug at her feet.

To make a point reach its mark in our minds, she would stop rocking and slowly bring her gaze down to our eyes. Leaning over, peering into our very souls to utter a line that would bring shivers or shock; until our eyes reflected the effect she was trying to create. She was magic! Her stories were all about the spirit world and the goulies and ghosties and fairies and leprechauns and anything that went bump in the night. While this performance went on, she would drink a bottle of stout and sniff her 'snuff'.

Nan had a friend that had died many years ago, but who met her from the bus on the main road where it dropped Nan once a month after a visit to town. It would be dark when the bus arrived at this spot, and Nan wouldn't walk home until 'Mary' arrived to escort her. She talked of her conversations on these walks with Mary as though she was alive and Jesse's eyes were like saucers and obviously shocked at what she was hearing. Nan looked straight at Jesse on witnessing this and said;

"ne're be afeared o' the dead wee one. It's the livin' ye need be afeared o'," and Jesse's face was a picture.

That's done it, I thought. *She'll love bein' here now.*

At 8.30p.m. Nan announced it was time for bed. Being farmers, they were up before dawn. Jesse sat on the edge of her bed in shock.

"'ave never been t'bed at arf eight in me life!" she screamed, "an' ave gorra do it on me 'olidays!"

"We'll be up early in the mornin', ye see, 'elpin' t'muck out the pigs so we 'ave t'go t'bed now," I pathetically explained.

Her face went bright red and her voice went up another couple of octaves. "*Muck out!*" she screamed. "Muck out the friggin' pigs! Am not bleedin' well muckin' out nuthin'. This is like a friggin' nightmare. She's daft, your Nan, talkin' about ghosts an' tha'. She gives me the willies!" and no amount of talking could make Jesse appreciate where she was.

The week dragged on with Jesse spoiling all my pleasure at being there and wishing the days away until Saturday when we could go to the dance.

Jesse started putting her 'war paint' on not long after she got out of bed on Saturday morning. We both went through the clothes we had brought and chose our outfits for the dance.

Nan stared in shock at us when we appeared in the kitchen in our rock and roll gear. My choice had been my swirly petticoats and Jesse had chosen a little black leather number that was skin tight and barely covered the essentials.

The journey cart arrived with my cousins, who were both boys near our age. Their short hair was brylcreamed down flat with parts in the middle. Their brightly coloured, woollen, check shirts topped their wide denim jeans, ironed with creases down the front, and their outfits were completed with black, round-toed, highly polished, lace up shoes.

"Oh Jesus!" remarked Jesse as she saw them alight from the cart – she had to turn her head away to hide the laughter. They stood in the doorway staring at us with interest, while Nan poured compliments all over them about how smart they looked.

They politely stood at the back of the cart waiting to help Jesse and myself onto it. We tripped out over the cobbles, nearly breaking our ankles as our six-inch stilettos got stuck between the stones. My lift onto the cart was graceful compared with Jesse's in her tight mini-skirt as she tried to keep her knees together while she spanned the distance between the ground and the high step.

The ride was only a short one through the dark country lanes, which used to hold magical memories for me, and now I was rushing the procedure in my mind worrying about Jesse's feelings.

We alighted from the cart in the most ladylike fashion that we could, under the circumstances, and again tottered over the cobbles to the door of the village hall. Jesse hung onto me tightly whispering: "I 'ope these two aren't a sample of the fellers around 'ere!"

They were!!

The door opened onto a hall full of them, with girls our own age in dainty pretty floral dresses, white socks, patent leather, flat, round-toed shoes and ribbons in their hair.

The activities seemed to come to a stop as we stood in the doorway, peering at them with as much shock on our faces as they had on theirs. We looked like the entertainment for the night, and we were!

The stage was lifted only two feet off the floor at one end of the room, and had two fiddle players, a piano and a set of drums. Around the edge of the hall were benches, and a door on the left led to a kitchen, which was the passageway to the back door. One had to pass through this area to go to the loo, which was a wooden hut outside with a 'long drop' in it. The lighting in the room must have been a drain on the main grid that night and was quite a contrast to the dim club lighting we were used to.

The vicar was on stage with a beautiful Irish beaming smile, encouraging the young men to choose a partner for the next dance, while the girls sat on the benches giggling behind their handkerchiefs. Nobody was allowed to be left out of the dancing, and if they didn't have a partner, a parent would step in, and there were plenty of them in the kitchen preparing supper.

I thought Jesse was going to cry. She was dragged around in her stiletto heels, hating every minute of it, but not allowed to sit on a bench and sulk. I kicked off my shoes and joined in with the crowd and thoroughly enjoyed myself. I had decided that I couldn't allow Jesse to spoil another moment that should be fun.

The musicians played all the country dances I had learned in school. We held hands in circles and danced like children again. Then suddenly the musicians gave a loud "Dah Dah!!!" and the vicar announced that supper would be served as soon as we were ready. All the boys turned and grabbed part of a bench and set them in rows down the middle of the hall. We all sat down on the benches while the tea urn was pushed up and down the rows on a trolley. The procession began with a parent carrying a large tray and handing each of us an empty white mug, which was duly filled by the next parent who pushed the trolley. The tea in the urn already had milk and sugar added. A succession of parents then followed the urn. The first one with a tray of plates followed by someone's mum, each with a tray of their home-made cakes and biscuits, and they encouraged us to take as much as we could eat.

The supper now over, the benches were replaced around the room. The girls sat on them, the music began again, and the evening continued as before. Jesse couldn't wait to get out, but I didn't want the evening to end.

The second week went much like the first, with Jesse wishing the days away until she got back to Birkenhead.

Before I left, Nan took me to one side and said, "Don't be dragged inter the pleasures o'the flesh, me girl. Ye have the gift an' it's too precious t'waste. Be careful ye look at yer signposts afore ye take ye path. An' don't deny what ye can see as plain as the nose on ye face."

She died at the grand old age of ninety-six, with her family weeping and wailing around her, crying: "We warned 'er the stout would take 'er one day!"

I knew what Nan was talking about. I had many 'strange'

experiences which could only be explained by acknowledging the spirit world. I didn't want to be different and so never talked about these happenings to anyone. But Nan knew I was 'fey' like her, I just wasn't ready to acknowledge it yet.

Chapter Eight

Inheriting Mum's spirituality

1960s

The first time I experienced any spiritual strangeness, that I can remember, was when Uncle Frank died. He had been in hospital for what seemed a long time and I can't remember what it was exactly that he died of. Mum told me I had to go and visit Uncle Frank with her. I was twelve years old at the time and remember Mum taking me with her on the bus. As I walked into the hospital ward I felt as though I had bumped into a huge inflatable rubber balloon. It took my breath away and I gasped as I entered the ward.

"What's the problem with ye, Pauline?" asked Mum.

"I felt as though I bumped into a big balloon," I said, which was the only way I could explain it.

Uncle Frank lay still in the bed and as we approached him I could see that his bed had more light around it than the others did. We sat quietly at the side of the bed until he opened his eyes.

"She's here, Frank," Mum said, and I looked at her in astonishment. I didn't know Uncle Frank had asked to see me especially.

Uncle Frank held out his hand to me and smiled weakly. I gently held his hand and a strong surge ran through me. I felt as though my spirit had completely engulfed him. Uncle Frank acknowledged it by giving me a small nod of the head, then he sighed and closed his eyes again, and I felt his hand go limp in mine.

"Come on now, Pauline, and let Uncle Frank get some rest," Mum said.

I left the hospital with a strange feeling, 'knowing' that something had transpired between us.

Uncle Frank died that night. His was an Irish wake and we gathered in his home with my aunt and all the relatives, while Uncle Frank was placed in his open coffin in the front parlour. The day before his funeral people came and paid their last respects to him while he lay in his coffin. We supplied everybody with tea and biscuits right through until the evening when the men had finished work and gathered in the house and the alcohol began to be consumed. People walked around the house singing and talking to Uncle Frank as though he was still alive.

"Here's ye favourite, Frank. Are ye ready, boys!! Alt'gether!

Oh Patrick McGinty an Irish man of note,

Came into a fortune, and bought 'imself a goat."

Anything they wanted to say to Uncle Frank in private was said behind the closed door of the parlour. When they had finished their private conversation with him, the door was opened again and everybody was allowed to wander in and out.

An Irish wake goes on throughout the night and nobody goes to bed. As a twelve-year-old, I found it hard to stay awake and, in the early hours of the mornin,g I wandered into the hall and sat on the bottom stair with my chin in my hands. As I stared ahead of me, Uncle Frank came out of the front parlour. I wasn't afraid or shocked, I remember just smiling at him.

He came and sat beside me and asked how I was feeling. "I'm fine," I said. "How are you feeling, Uncle Frank?"

"Couldn't be happier, lass. Couldn't be happier. No more

pain." He smiled "Ave always loved ye Aunty Lil an' a knows she'll be upset fer a while. But a want ye t'tell 'er that al be lookin' after 'er still. Me brother will be waitin' fer them in Ireland an' a wants them t'go an' visit 'im fer a while. It'll do them a power o'good. T'ings will be well taken care of while they're away, an' ave left them well provided fer. Me brother will explain. Will ye tell dem dat?"

"A will, Uncle Frank," I said. He stood up and gave me a big smile and walked back into the parlour.

Just then Mum walked into the hall.

"What are ye doin' sittin' there, luv?" she asked.

"Ave just been talkin' to Uncle Frank," I replied.

"Oh, 'av ye!" she remarked. "An' what did 'ee ave t'say?"

I repeated our conversation word for word. She wasn't shocked and said she'd tell Aunty Lil. Because it was the middle of the night, my child-reasoning kept me thinking I may have dreamt it all. When Aunty Lil felt stronger, she went to Ireland to visit Uncle Frank's brother. The family farm had been sold and Aunty Lil was presented with half the proceeds. When Mum repeated this fact before our family she just looked at me and with a wink gave me a half smile, so I just smiled back.

A few years later, my Uncle Freddie was ill in hospital. Again Mum said I was to go and visit him. I was probably around fourteen years old. This strange feeling of bumping into a rubber balloon was with me again as I entered the ward. His bed was also surrounded by light. Uncle Freddie opened his eyes and smiled at me. He didn't say anything and Mum told me to give him a kiss. As I did, the same feeling of energy that I felt with Uncle Frank ran through my body. With this energy came a strong feeling of empathy for him. I found it hard not to let him see me crying and I wanted to hug him but was afraid of hurting him. That night, Uncle Freddie died. During that night I had a vivid dream. I was talking to Uncle Freddie and he gave me a message for my aunt. In telling Mum I realised that this was something more than a dream. But Mum never explained it properly to me, she simply passed on the messages I had been given.

This strange 'gift' I was becoming aware of then started to frighten me. As there was always talk about 'the next world', 'the spirit world' and an acceptance of a God around our house, I had heard about 'The Angel of Death''. I was convinced that this was what I was. If I visited anyone that was ill, they would die. I couldn't talk to anyone about it, as I didn't want to frighten people away from me. I made a strong promise to myself that I would avoid anyone that was ill for fear I made them die. Anytime Mum asked me to go and visit a sick friend or relative in hospital I began to invent all sorts of reasons why I couldn't go. If Mum tried to insist, I would throw a tantrum and raise my Irish paddy until she gave up. There was no way I was going to be responsible for anyone else dying.

When we lived in Carnforth Street, my best friend Bernadette was a Catholic and attended a Catholic school throughout the week and a Catholic church on Sundays. I attended a Protestant school and a Protestant church on Sunday. Somehow we knew we could do nothing about going to different schools but I asked Dad if Bernadette and I could go to her church one Sunday and my church the next Sunday.

"Ey, a don't see no harm in ye both doing that," said Dad.

This we did for some time and we loved it as we could spend more weekend time together. We also learned the difference in the teachings between the two religions and often discussed this with our parents. As we explored our new neighbourhood around the north end of Birkenhead we noticed there was a Baptist Church not far away.

I asked Dad, "What happens in the Baptist Church, Dad?

How is that different?"

He thought for a while and said: "Oi've never been inter a Baptist Church meself so why don't ye both go along der 'dis Sunday and come back and tell us all about it."

So excitedly we visited the next Sunday. We walked back to our house and Dad was working in the front garden. He saw us and a smile appeared on his face and his eyes began to laugh as he asked, "Why is de back of ye hair wet?"

"They dunked us in the water, Dad!" I said with concern. "They said it has to be if we want to go to that church!" And Dad burst out laughing.

"Well there ye go!" he chuckled. "Yer'll both be a Protestant, a Catholic and now a Baptist as well."

In the times we lived, you attended the schools of the faith you followed. Mum and Dad weren't religious, though we casually talked about God in the house. Dad would always say:

"Never put a label on yerself saying ye this or that religion."

I believe he felt like this because of his experience in Belfast and the IRA. Dad was Protestant and his best friend was a Catholic and they were threatened by the IRA to discontinue their friendship. For this reason, they left Belfast and raised their families in England. Therefore, Bernadette and I visited any church we wanted to and often compared one with another. It even became something we researched without consciously recognising we were doing this. Sunday was our day to visit churches of any faith and then discussing them with our parents. But we ended up acknowledging the spirit world but not being religious at all.

When I left school, I went to work in the office of an engineering company. I was so proud that I could earn money to help Mum with the household expenses. My sister Babs was already working and helping Mum so she led the way for us all to follow.

During these times when everyone knew everyone in our community, the milk man Ted, who called early each morning delivering our milk, was thrilled when I'd found a job nearby. He saw me through the front window.

"Pauline, luv," he shouted, indicating for me to go outside as he had something to tell me. I stepped out.

"I finish my round at St James Church at 8 o'clock each mornin'. I'm then goin' back to the depot in Old Bidston Road with an empty cart, so I can give ye a lift to work as I'm passin' your door each day and the engineering company yer'll be working at is right next door to my depot." He grinned from ear to ear as he said this because he was able to help me.

"Oh, thanks so much, Ted. That would be really helpful," I answered.

So, each morning I stood at our gate waiting for Ted. The electric milk carts had a compact, domed cab big enough for the driver only and the small truck had a roof over a deck that held the milk crates. Ted would pull up in front of me each morning, jump out of his driver's cab and move the crates to one side so I had room to sit with my legs dangling over the back of the deck. Mum gave me a piece of plastic tablecloth to place on the deck for me to sit on so my clothes wouldn't get spoiled. Off I went every morning, my bag on my lap and the electric truck quietly purring along the road on my way to work. If it was raining, I sat there with my umbrella open over me, no doubt looking a little like Mary Poppins.

The neighbours became used to seeing me.

"Mornin', Pauline. Lovely day, eh!"

"Mornin', Mrs Foster," I'd call back. "Mum said she'll call and see ye near midday."

"Thanks, luv. 'ave a lovely day."

"Allo, Pauline, luv."

"Allo, Mr Wentworth."

I'd be shouting to each and every person I passed by. They might only wave and I'd wave back like the queen as I sailed along seated on my milk float. People talked of telling the time by me when they saw me pass on my trip to work! It was a great start to my day. I always arrived at work smiling.

Mum was able to buy a few luxuries for the house now Babs and I were working and we hired a bigger television from Radio Rental. My family had gone up in the world and was now being classed as one of the posh ones in the street because we had a piano *and* a television.

If something special was being televised, the neighbours would sit around our living room watching the TV while the kids sat on the floor. The interest in my singers began with Flanagan and Allan, Gracie Fields, Vera Lyn and The Andrew Sisters on the television and I could sing every one of their songs. As a teenager, of course, my singers changed to Cliff Richard, The Beatles, Elvis, Tom Jones, Dusty Springfield and all the 60's songs, and music filled our house constantly. Most Saturday nights, Dad would bring those in the pub back to our house as he played the piano and we'd have a sing-song, singing some of the war songs.

It was common knowledge that Mum had a strong intuitive/spiritual ability, and spoke to the recently dead on many occasions. Mum's eyes would flicker from yours to your guide that stands behind you at difficult times throughout your life. They would speak to her. From my childhood, I watched her do this as she read the tea leaves in cups for neighbours, friends and family members. She would also read tarot cards. When I asked her how she did that, her answer was,

"Interpreting the shapes of the tea leaves keeps me focused on a small, enclosed space, and as I do I check in to the person's guide and their aura. With the cards, it is a visual for both me and the person I'm reading. I can tap into their being and, as we both look at the face of the card with its meaning, the right words about their concerns and events that are about to happen pop into my head. But it's a responsibility and must never be abused as some people aren't ready to hear that a loved one is about to die, or a tragic event is about to happen. You therefore must be selective in what you pass on. I'll teach you how to do this when you're older because you have the gift."

Mum had what we, her family, called 'the evil eye' which, translated, meant she could see and feel an evil spirit. She could walk into a room full of strangers and be immediately drawn to a black aura. Standing stock still, she would bore her eyes into the back of their skull, so much so that they could feel it and would turn to make eye contact with her. She would scowl until the person couldn't take this powerful gaze anymore and would usually leave the room, if they could. If they didn't, Mum would turn and leave the room, saying words such as:

"I can't be in the same room or breathe the same air as evil; I feel sick."

She would talk of speaking to a spirit of someone who was deceased and that person had given her some message or was sending support to their loved ones through her. She could also sense when her kids were trying to lie about something, and she would stare and take on a scowl that was saying, 'Don't try lying to me; I can see your soul.'

I was very close to my siblings and another time something strange happened to me was when Harry was on holiday in Spain. I'd been helping Mum with the washing in the kitchen and my nervous debility began to vibrate in me. Mum would keep an eye on me at these times and help me to settle down.

"Everybody's out," she said. "Make the most of it and go and sit in the front room and do that meditating yer've just learned."

I began sitting in the front parlour, staring.

John Lennon had brought the Maharishi to a concert in the Empire Theatre in Liverpool and asked us all to line up to learn how to meditate. I was almost first in the queue.

Emptying my mind as the Maharishi had taught me, I learned to stare at blank spaces to settle me before a meditation and so I was staring at the blank wall above the piano when I saw Harry's face. He was behind bars and he was crying for me. He seemed to be saying, "Get me out, Pauline. Get me out!!"

Just at that point Mum walked into the room and it shocked me back to the here and now. I looked at her, wide-eyed.

"What's troublin' ye, Pauline?" Mum asked.

"Ave just seen our Harry, Mum. He was behind bars and was crying for me t'get 'im out," I replied.

A troubled expression crossed her face and she stared at me for a while, then said, "A knew 'eed get 'imself inter trouble over there!" And went back to the kitchen and her work.

The next day we received a telegram from the British Consulate to say Harry was in prison for smoking dope and they needed Mum and Dad's permission to bring him home. He was being deported and Mum and Dad had to meet the costs.

This was a different type of 'knowing' and didn't bother me. Being an Angel of Death was too scary, but I didn't mind this sort of thing. So I began to visit the parlour regularly to merely sit and stare if I didn't have time to meditate. I didn't always get 'messages' but I found the experience very relaxing. It became a necessary part of my life and wherever I moved to I always had to create my own private space. I would announce to everyone that I was going to my room for a 'think'. But I didn't 'think'; I tried hard not to think about anything; I just sat and stared into nothing for as long as I could and if I wasn't disturbed I would follow this with meditation.

Transcendental Meditation became my saviour in my future life. In my early 30s, I joined the School of Philosophy that used this method of meditation as I studied the various Eastern schools of thought and religions. I have a fascination with how the human mind creates these channels of thought and beliefs and I still read and study writers that have new ideas on explaining the workings of our brain and mind. All of this information that I gathered over the years led to me researching spirit and my personal experiences confirmed what I'd read.

Another personal trait I had was the amount of energy that fuelled my being. Why walk when you can run? And why stop because the dark has set in? It appeared I had more energy than almost any other person I knew. If I was determined to complete something, anything, no matter what, the time of day or night wasn't an issue. I never ran out of energy and sometimes I would feel that having to sleep was a waste of my time.

At times, this energy coursed through my body for no particular reason. My nerves would be vibrating and, as I aged, I would sometimes get out in the fresh air and walk the dog until my nervousness settled. For me, being alive was action! I was not a person to be found lying on the couch or in my bed if I wasn't ill. My only health problem was that I suffered from migraines as a teenager and then I had to take to my bed, sometimes for two or three days. Migraines were the only blight on my health through to my mid-fifties.

My childhood, before marriage, was idyllic. Six of us in the house, plus the dog, family friends and neighbours calling day and night was the life I was used to and loved. Constant chatter, laughter, Dad playing the piano, singing and even bickering with my brothers and sister, but that crazy, funny, out there love of living, didn't prepare me for my lonely life with Dave.

Chapter Nine

My wedding & early marriage

1967 - 1970

We met when I was eighteen. He lived in the same working-class area that I did and my father and brothers approved of him. He was well liked by the lads in the local pub and was handsome. He played football and enjoyed life. But my mother disapproved of my choice.

"Yer'll rue the day yer ever met 'im. 'Ee's got a dirty aura that tells me ee's a liar and can't be trusted and ee's a drinker like ye father." She went on:"Never once has he looked me in the eye so ask yeself, what does that mean? What's 'ee hidin'?"

She made her feelings known to me about Dave but never tried to stop me from making my own choices. I even remember being surprised at my mother's assessment. He didn't drink any more than other men in the area and, if he was like my dad; then I loved my dad, so why shouldn't I love Dave?

He didn't work for a company but for himself, doing cash jobs for motor body repairs from a friend's one-car garage. He had no boss and no restrictions on his life and talked about owning his own business one day. I saw this as someone who wanted more out of life than what this working-class area offered. I fell in love with the perfect dream: a man that loved me and wanted to be with me, and us both raising the perfect family. His outbursts of anger and jealousy when I was being admired by another male confirmed to me that he really loved me and would protect me. Mum could be intimidating and I felt that, in time, he'd be comfortable talking to her and then be able to look her in the eye. My thoughts were that Mum was being too judgmental as she felt no one would be good enough for her kids. We set the wedding date.

I had been saving money since I started work. My aim was always to buy a house before I married as I was not going to start my marriage living with my parents as a lot of newlyweds did in this area. Dave and I discussed all of this, and he confirmed he wanted to get married as soon as possible and so I informed him of my savings, and asked him to aim at matching it so we'd have the deposit for our home quickly. As my salary went straight into my bank account, my plan was to now leave all my money that I earned in the bank and have it paid into my savings account to gain more interest. I only had to pay Mum and she offered to take a pound less each week to help me save. At the end of each month when I was paid, I'd tell him how much money I had in my savings, and he would tell me he had about the same amount. Unfortunately, this was the start of the lies he told me as I discovered he never had any savings.

Mum's face flinched when I told her I was marrying Dave "Pauline luv, I'm disappointed with your decision. Heartaches are all I see for you with this man."

But I wouldn't listen. I told myself I knew more about Dave than Mum did and really believed he'd get used to Mum and make eye contact when he felt more comfortable with her.

During the period of time we were supposed to be saving, each time I asked him how much he had saved he would lie and state an amount. Then, near to the date of our wedding, he eventually told me he had no savings after purchasing a shot gun to go shooting with his pals. I voiced my objection to this purchase and was angrily told to never tell him again what he can and can't do with his own money. Here was lesson number one, and I failed. My savings became the deposit on a new house and, as he worked for himself and couldn't prove a salary to the bank to obtain a loan, the mortgage was also in my name only. I threw my geographical net wider when I learned we only had my money for the deposit and found a house a little cheaper than I'd been aiming at. Eastham was a quiet suburb outside of Birkenhead on the Wirral.

25th March 1967 was the day we married and I planned every detail of what was going to be a wonderful day. I had my wedding dress made and was married by Reverend Singleton in St Oswald's Church in Bidston, the church where I had been a Sunday School teacher. All of this I paid for.

My cousin Alfie and I were the same age. He had the physique of a rugby player, but unfortunately, he had the mental capacity of a child. He loved me!! I visited him regularly and would play his games, and he would place his head on my shoulder, hugging and kissing me, always saying, "I love you, Pauline."

When I walked into the Church on my father's arm, over the sound of the organ playing the wedding march I could hear Alfie screaming, "Pauline, Pauline!!"

Uncle Bill was trying to hold him back but Alfie wanted to be with me and he was becoming stressed. "Pauline, Pauline!" He was not prepared to be stopped and I knew he would keep this up throughout the ceremony, so as I was passing their pew, I stopped and said to Uncle Bill. "Let him come here."

Alfie shot out of his dad's arms and placed his head on my chest as he grabbed me around my shoulders, shouting, "I love you, Pauline."

I peeled his head away from my chest. "You must be very quiet and say nothing now, Alfie, because the vicar has some very important words to say. Will you be very quiet for me,

Alfie?"

"Yes, Pauline. I'll be very quiet for you."

"Will you wait here with your mum and dad until the vicar has said his very important words and then you can walk out of the church with me. Will you be good and do that for me?"

"Yes, Pauline. I'll be very good," and he *was* good in the church.

We reached our wedding reception, which was at the Bidston Hotel on Hoylake Road. Once again Alfie began shouting and screaming; he wanted to sit by me. The tables were in the traditional U shape with Dave and I sitting in the centre so I instructed the waitress to place a chair and setting opposite me for Alfie.

Our wedding breakfast began with the speeches and the various standard wedding photographs of the two families and of us cutting the cake etc., as the photographer had another wedding he had to attend soon after ours and had to leave early. As it turned out, it was a blessing that we'd done all the official photographs because Alfie had been quiet throughout the speeches as I'd asked him to. Now happy he could speak again, he picked up the wine glass in front of him and announced he could crush this glass in his hand.

"No, Alfie!!" I shouted. Frantic, I stood and leant over the table to grab his hand to stop him but … too late; he crushed the glass and cut the artery in his wrist. As I was leaning over him, the blood pumped up into my face and down the front of my wedding dress. Alfie saw his blood everywhere and became so frightened, he screamed with full force. His mother, my Aunt Tess, stood up when she heard him scream and saw the blood and fainted. Uncle Bill was torn between saving his wife or his son.

"I've got Alfie, Uncle Bill. It's okay," I shouted, as I instructed Dave to go and get the car out because we'd have to take him to the hospital. I pulled off Alfie's jacket and tied the white cotton napkins that were near to me into a tourniquet around his arm. I knew Alfie wouldn't go to the hospital with anyone else but me, so Dave and I left our own wedding reception. Not only that, I was always the best person to be with in a crisis – I would jump into action immediately.

Knowing how to manage a difficult situation was another of my innate automatic responses.

"Please go ahead with the reception. The food is about to be served. We'll be back soon," I shouted as I ripped the veil from my head and left it on the table. I left the room with Alfie screaming into my bosom. Blood had spurted everywhere and was splattered all over my dress and, as I turned to leave, I saw my mother's eyes staring at me in shock. I could almost see the colour drain from her face and I knew what she was thinking: this was a really bad omen for a wedding.

We walked into the reception area at Birkenhead General Hospital on Park Road North with Alfie screaming and me in my traditional long white wedding dress covered in blood. There was quite a gathering of people at this time on a Saturday afternoon after the footie matches etc., but, on seeing the blood on my wedding dress, a nurse came running toward me and tried to peel Alfie away from my arm.

"He won't leave me, I'm sorry. I'll have to come with him, and he'll need to be sedated for you to stitch him." Alfie heard the word 'stitches' and, as he'd been stitched before and it frightened him, the screaming now reached fever pitch. I sat him on the bed behind the screen and pulled his head into my bosom and nodded to the nurse as I held his arm for her to administer the sedation. Almost instantly he was unconscious. Together, we rolled him over and tied him onto the bed then she and another young nurse began to attend to his cut wrist.

The nurse gave me a wet disinfectant paper cloth to wipe the blood from my face and hands and the skin around my neck. This powerful smell well outdid my *Estee Lauder Youth Dew*. It was just as well I loved the smell of disinfectant. But the blood had almost dried on my dress and there was so much, it had simply destroyed it. I walked back into the reception area where Dave had sprawled in a chair, his outstretched legs crossed at the ankles. His arms were crossed, and his head had slumped forward so his chin rested on his chest. I could see and feel his mood – he was trying to contain his agitation and anger. I sat beside him, and he turned his head to look at me.

After a few seconds he said, "You smell like a bleedin' lavatory and look a bloody mess!"

I knew I did, but there was nothing I could do about it now so rather than get upset I could actually see the funny side of this whole situation. So, with a straight face and being very blasé I said: "I told you last week that I'd planned a day we would never forget. I was right, eh?"

Looking around the emergency room, I realised everyone was staring at us, and probably bursting to ask if we had survived a death threat or some such thing on our wedding day.

The nurses attended to Alfie as a priority after I'd told them we needed to get back to our wedding reception. Probably only thirty minutes later he was brought out to us, stitched but thankfully still recovering from the sedation and therefore calm and in a dream state. We climbed back into the car with Dave driving and Alfie and I in the back seat. He was still hanging onto my arm with a vice grip. We began our journey back up to The Bidston Hotel where the reception would hopefully still be going on, but as we were about to drive past a fish and chip shop in Laird Street, Dave shouted, "I'm bloody starvin'. Does anyone else fancy fish and chips?"

"Yes!" we both shouted back, so on the afternoon of my wedding day I was sitting in the back of a mini car, covered in blood, smelling of disinfectant and eating fish and chips out of newspaper! And boy did they hit the spot for each of us!

A guy Dave played football with saw us sitting in the car on the side of the road eating our food. He stood for some seconds looking at us with a confused stare and then leaned down and said, "I thought you were getting married today, Dave?"

Dave just looked back and said without smiling, "We did".

Chapter Ten

Relief from a lonely marriage

1967-1970

The house I was able to buy was a two-storey, semi-detached brick house on a new housing estate in Eastham. It was a box shape with a glass porch. The front door was off the porch and the stairs were directly ahead, finishing in this long room that was a combined lounge and dining room, with a kitchen on the far right of it. Upstairs. there were three small bedrooms and a bathroom. The driveway ran down the left side of the house and there was a garden in front of the lounge window, ending on the pavement of the street. The back garden was long and was grassed with a fence separating it from the neighbours.

Dave was happy enough with the house but constantly complained about the distance he had to travel for work and to be with his drinking pals. Around Merseyside, and at this time in the 60s, the culture we lived in was the women were dominant, hardworking, nurturing types that made all the decisions for their family. This allowed the men to be the providers and nothing more. The men, of course, were happy to fill this role. They worked to provide the money for their families and were waited on hand and foot by their wives. The men would hand their pay packets over to 'the wife' at the end of the week and receive their beer money in return. They would gather in the pub to discuss the latest football results, who was having it off behind his wife's back, and how many pints they could 'down' and still walk home.

The macho image was very strong in these parts and the macho men had to compete to be part of the pack. If he didn't compete, he was ostracised – nobody in the pub would be too friendly toward him. The men would go home and tell their wives about these mean buggers and the women would agree with them and reassure their man that 'they' were real men and they were glad to have them that way. These men didn't know how to wash a dish, cook a meal, or use a vacuum cleaner or an iron. If the baby cried, they would shout for 'the wife' to shut 'em up.

Weekends were for the men. They lay in bed all Saturday morning because they had 'worked hard all week'. Saturday afternoon was the football match, either playing or watching, and Saturday night they took 'the wife' to the local pub for a drink. The men stood at the bar while the women sat around in a circle and talked about their kids, the increasing price of food, and how their men were good workers. The token of affection from the men to their wives, was how many drinks they sent over to their wife during the evening. The drunker the wife, the more her husband must love her. The singing would begin, and the husband and wife would direct their singing towards each other in one of the latest love songs.

"Put your sweet lips, a little closer to the phoooooooooone!"

"Let's pretend, that we're together, all aloooooooooone!"

At the end of the evening, they would put their arms around each other for support and walk home singing all the way. At home, they would have a bottle of beer or a nip or two of their favourite tipple, go to bed and have a quick 'nookie' that neither of them would remember the next morning because they were too drunk.

For the men, Sunday morning wouldn't start until at least eleven o'clock when their cooked breakfast would be placed before them once they were up and dressed. This was followed by a read of the *News of The World* newspaper then off to the pub until three o'clock. As they came in the door, their roast dinner would be placed on the table, which they would eat and then go off to bed for an afternoon's 'kip'. Awake again at seven o'clock, a quick wash to freshen up, then off to the pub until eleven o'clock.

This ritual went on week in and week out and the women never thought they were getting a raw deal. Everyone else lived like this, so this must be 'Life'.

From the moment I married, I started to kick 'the system'. I wasn't going to have a marriage like this. We were in love and Dave wanted to be with me – I thought I knew this. But the rows had started over his constant drinking and not producing any housekeeping money.

Twelve months earlier, I had found a job as a receptionist in an opticians in Bold Street, Liverpool and, though I missed my job in the engineering company, I was earning almost twice as much money at the opticians. Dave benefitted from this as I paid for our living expenses and mortgage. If we went out for a drink or threw a party, Dave would pay for that but kept saying he hadn't earned enough to give me a regular amount for household expenses each week. So, he was living for free off me. I didn't see it like that at the time.

The first three months of my pregnancy were a nightmare. Dave would pick me up from the train station after work and we would drive home together. The moment I stepped out of the car I would propel myself through the door and up to the bathroom to be sick.

Dave would sit down with the newspaper and announce that he wasn't in any hurry for his dinner; he could wait until I felt well enough to cook it. He thought he was being considerate. After a few evenings of the same procedure, my Irish flared up. In my state of pregnancy and with my emotions running high, I started screaming at him about how selfish he was. Dave was shocked! Absolutely nobody had ever heard me behave this way. I even shocked myself! Out of my mouth came all the abuse and insults I could think of and then I promptly burst into tears and ran upstairs where I threw myself onto the bed howling like a banshee, hoping Dave would feel sorry for me and come up to apologise and comfort me.

After lying there for almost thirty minutes, forcing as many wails as I could muster so that he could hear it clearly downstairs, Dave shouted, "Fer God's sake, will ye stop that bloody noise an' get down 'ere an' cook my meal. I've been workin' all bloody day an' a need feedin'!"

Up came my Irish anger again and I stormed into the bathroom and picked up a glass bottle of foul-smelling body lotion that had been a gift. During my pregnancy smells were a problem, even on television if I saw a product that was particularly strong smelling, I would be reminded of its smell and would feel sick. This bottle of body lotion had the same effect each time I saw it sitting beside the bath. So, it was no sacrifice to grab it and run half way down the stairs where I could see Dave sitting and hurl it at him. It hit the wall above the fireplace and shattered, spraying the entire room with this awful smell that made me feel sick. Dave announced that he'd had enough and changed his clothes and went off to the pub.

While he was gone, I felt lonely, it was better to have him there doing nothing than to be alone and upset like this. So, after cleaning up this foul-smelling mess that was making me nauseous, I decided to cook his dinner and placed it on a pan of boiling water with a plate over it for his return from the pub. He arrived home the worse for drinking on an empty stomach and I apologised for my outburst. He accepted my apology and forgave me, as long as it never happened again.

I loved Dave dearly, but I couldn't get him to hear my

frustration with this life. He simply didn't understand what I had to be frustrated about. We had a new house and we lived well enough. He thought I was asking for too much out of life. We both worked but it was only my money that paid for everything including the mortgage, and only sometimes Dave would give me money toward food if he earned any. I didn't question this division of wealth.

"You expect life t'be a bed of roses!" he once accused me. "Other women haven't got as much as you – ye should be bloody grateful."

This used to stop me in my tracks. I was paying the bills for my lifestyle, but I would still mentally look around and see the hardship that other women endured and count my blessings. BUT! I wasn't happy with my life. This lonely marriage was something I hadn't bargained for. I was from an Irish family: I was used to lots of talking and bickering and discussions around the house. The singing, the laughter, the banter … but the silences I endured were crushing me. I couldn't get Dave to discuss anything with me. If I as much as hinted that I was upset about anything he would lose his temper and go off to the pub earlier. If I talked about anything he knew nothing about he would tell me to shut up – I was talking a load of rubbish. When I asked him not to drink so much because it made me afraid of him at times, he told me I was exaggerating. I was "known as an exaggerator", he said. I knew never to argue with him when he was drunk, I always kept my criticism of the night before until the next morning when he was sober (in the early days). He would fiercely deny ever doing anything that I had said he'd done and told me I blew everything out of proportion. Then he would stop talking to me which lasted for a day or two at the beginning but over the years it grew to silences that could last up to eight or nine months. This destroyed me. I would do anything to stop the silences.

It seemed a constant battle for me right from the start to make sure my life would never be boring. What I wouldn't accept was that, in my efforts to alter that situation for myself, it didn't alter it for Dave. I could fill my life with meaningful happenings, get pleasure from some of the things I organised. Join a drama group, a book club, have holidays that were a bit different. Have parties; invite people around for dinner to keep them in the house all evening – all this to make sure my life did not end up with sitting in the pub talking about the price of food as the only highlight of my week.

When my twenty-second birthday was due, I was five months pregnant. I decided to throw a party in our new home and invited all our friends from Birkenhead, plus the neighbours to get to know them. Jack and Jesse, Margy and Steve, were the friends we mainly went out with for the evening – Dave and I very rarely had a night out on our own. They were good fun, and every gathering was a heavy drinking session which invariably ended with something that marked the occasion one way or another. In the early days, it was usually something mad that created lots of laughter, which one or all of us would do.

I worked all day preparing food for my birthday party and Dave made sure there was plenty of beer and short drinks – he could always find the money for that. Everybody loved our parties because they knew that, no matter what time it finished, the beer would never run out. Dave was proud of his reputation and spent a small fortune on ensuring it was upheld.

Our friends from Birkenhead arrived couple by couple and the neighbours then appeared and sat in a row on the settee quietly sipping sherry or a soft drink as our friends began hitting the alcohol with their usual vigour. Music played and the dancing began in the middle of the lounge. Around eleven o'clock when the noise and laughter was deafening, someone in our usual group had a wild idea of going to the local outdoor swimming pool. This suggestion was met with a hearty agreement from all our rowdy friends, and they took off to the nearby swimming baths in the transport that was available. The neighbours sat on the settee and didn't join the exodus from the room. I would have loved to have gone but, being the hostess, I felt I should stay and entertain our new neighbours.

The Oval in Eastham had the local outdoor swimming pools that were surrounded by a five-foot hedge that proved a little difficult for most of the 'ladies' to scale. The men were true gentlemen and helped them all over the hedge. They all began to race toward the pool, shedding their clothes as they ran. They had dived into the water in the dark and others were climbing the steps to the diving boards and creating havoc by jumping from this height onto the unsuspecting in the pool. There was a great deal of frivolity and laughter and suddenly the lights surrounding the pool were turned on. A voice boomed out over the loudspeaker, warning that they were trespassing and that the police had been informed and would be there in five minutes.

There was a mad scramble out of the water and they grabbed their clothes and ran toward the hedge to get back to the cars. The women that needed help over this hedge in the first place were, in the main, the first ones back over it without help.

I heard the cars arriving back to the house only forty-five minutes after they had left. I had been the perfect hostess to our new neighbours and had been talking politely to them in the absence of our friends and was generally trying to give a good impression.

The door opened and Dave came bursting in with the story of the event. He was dressed only in his wet underpants and was carrying his clothes. The rest of our friends followed; the men were in the same state of undress as Dave, and the women had on wet bras and knickers. The shock on the faces of our new neighbours was quite apparent and they all quickly finished their drinks and left. We all sat around until early hours of the morning drinking and laughing and telling stories of similar events that had happened to us on previous occasions. We were a wild crowd, and each gathering was fun, chaotic and exciting.

Most of them would sleep anywhere they found a cosy corner in the house and wouldn't leave until perhaps the following afternoon. I loved these evenings. These were my pressure valve releases. Perhaps I felt the loneliness so much because of the two extremes of life that I lived. All I knew was that I had to keep organising parties and events to keep me from going crazy with loneliness and boredom.

Dave loved the parties I organised but never questioned why I had so many. Every week I arranged dinners out or in and made sure that within our circle of friends someone was planning the next gathering for us all to attend. Knowing I had something to look forward to each weekend kept me going.

I eventually realised I was beginning to have bouts of depression. I'd never had depression before and so put it down to my being alone each evening and some weekends when he went out to play golf or rabbit shooting. Plus I felt being pregnant could cause my depressions.

I began to worry about how we would manage financially when I finished work at six months pregnant, so before I left my job as a receptionist in Liverpool, I found two bookkeeping jobs that I could do from home. Both paid well and I informed Dave that he must try and get regular work now or find a job somewhere as we now needed his regular income to pay the mortgage. He promised he'd start looking around. (He never did.)

As the time approached for me to leave work, I was visualising my life and dreading being at home alone every day and evening. I'd told Dave I didn't know how I was going to manage the loneliness. Within days of me leaving work, Dave came home with a gift for me, a German Shepherd puppy. It was instant love. I called her Billie. I had a couple of months to train her before our daughter Sharon-Louise was born so she wouldn't be too much trouble. Daily, we walked around the neighbourhood and she was my constant companion, just having her with me each night while Dave was in the pub made all the difference to my depression. My mundane life was beginning to make its changes.

Our friends held the next gathering, a party at their house in West Kirby on the Wirral. On this Saturday evening, we arrived at their local pub with our best friends Jesse and Jack. Jack was a manager for a supermarket and had just been given a brand-new Holden Commodore car. We decided to travel to the pub in that.

Our hosts were in the pub and asked Jack if he would shuttle their guests from the pub back to their home. Of course, Jack was proud to do it in his brand-new car and Dave said he'd do the shuttling with him if he'd let him do some of the driving. They had both already had more than enough to drink and neither of them should have been driving. In those days, people didn't take drink driving so seriously.

Jesse and I, with two more people, were first to be dropped at the party, and Jack and Dave shuttled people over the next hour. Then Dave arrived on his own, his face covered in blood, his suit ripped.

"What on earth has happened?" We all stared in shock. He looked awful.

"We had an accident on the way back to the pub when Jack was driving. I was thrown through the windscreen and Jack was knocked unconscious. We were taken to the Cottage Hospital close by and I've just left him to come and let you all know."

Jesse screamed and became uncontrollable; she threw her hands out, shouting for someone to please take her to him. Our host got his car out and dropped Dave, Jesse and myself at the hospital.

On arriving at this small hospital, we noted a police car was outside the emergency area where Jack was. A policeman stood outside the door smoking a cigarette. We walked into the emergency department and the nurse pulled back the curtain around Jack's bed and allowed us to enter the small cubicle. Jack lay perfectly still as though unaware of anything. The nurse told us that he was still unconscious and to let her know if he regained consciousness while we were there. She had organised for him to be transferred to the General Hospital in Birkenhead and they were waiting for the ambulance to arrive. She then left us all alone.

Jesse, distraught, held Jack's hand and cried and wailed, begging Jack to wake up and speak to her. Worriedly, Dave and I, upset by the scene, looked on. Then Jack's right eye opened as he whispered, "Fer Christ's sake, Jesse will ye shut up! There's nothin' bloody wrong with me but that policeman out there is waiting to breathalyse me an' eel find out I'm over the limit. I'll lose me bloody job! I'll 'ave t'keep this up until ee disappears." Then he closed his eyes again and calmly waited for the ambulance. This had now turned around from an emotional upset to a drama that we all played along with.

We all piled into the ambulance when it arrived to take Jack to the General Hospital in Birkenhead, the policeman following in his car. When Jack was taken into an emergency ward and placed in a cubicle with the curtains drawn around him, the policeman turned to us and said he would inform the Birkenhead division and another policeman would be sent shortly to breathalyse Jack when he became conscious. Jack had heard this on the other side of the curtain and so continued to feign his unconsciousness.

The nurse came from behind the curtain and told Jesse that

he would have to be kept in overnight for observation as he was still out for the count. She had taken the rest of his clothes off him so they could check him over and she handed them to Jesse. He would be going up to the ward in a few minutes and we were allowed to go in and see him before we left. We all three filed into the cubicle where Jack was still lying stock still. He opened one eye when he heard us and whispered, "Is that policeman still out there?"

"No, he's gone," we whispered.

Jack threw back the cover on his bed and jumped out of it, stark naked.

"Come on," he shouted earnestly, "let's get out of this bloody place before the coppers are back."

We started running out of the hospital through the emergency department that was filled with its usual Saturday night activities. People stared as this naked man, holding his penis for decency, followed by three other people who ducked and dived around bodies and chairs and ran out of the hospital main door. We reached the main road and Jack shouted as he veered left, "Aim for the public toilets down the road so I can get dressed!"

We ran as though our lives depended on it until we all arrived at the toilet block. Our adrenaline was running high with the excitement, and we all collapsed on the toilet floor laughing until we thought we'd burst. Jack grabbed his clothes from Jesse and quickly dressed himself as we took the time to calm down until we could walk without laughing. Exiting the toilet block, we calmly walked across the road to get a taxi home.

What a fantastic night!! I wanted excitement and thrills and daring activities and a husband to share the quiet times with in between. But I sat on my own if I stayed home. I didn't want that sort of loneliness, which would be worse when I'd given birth.

When Dave and I married I was twenty-one years old. He was twenty-two. With little idea of birth control, we had our first child almost nine months after the wedding. It fell short of the expected pregnancy period by approximately three weeks, if you counted from the date we got married. My mother panicked and told everybody my baby was premature. People were not to know that we might have 'done it' before the wedding day – she had her reputation to maintain.

Sharon-Louise, our beautiful daughter; arrived as a healthy seven-pounds-two-ounces specimen of perfection on Monday 18th December 1967. Her hair and eyelashes were wispy blonde and if you didn't look too closely it might appear as though she didn't have any. My mother used this as proof to support her story of 'early' arrival.

"She's got no 'air yet because she was premature!"

This was the most profound experience I'd had in my life so far. I gazed in awe at this amazing miracle of nature that we had produced. This tiny hand that squeezed my finger, or touched my face, brought feelings of emotion from so deep within my being that I always found it hard to control the tears.

"There ye go again!" my mother would say. "Yer bladder's too near yer eyes. Ye can't raise the child by whingin' around 'er all the time, yerd better toughen up, me girl!"

So that was it. I had to be tougher for the sake of my daughter. Mum stayed with me for a week until my energy returned. Daily, she made sure I drank two shot glasses full of Guinness, which she said would build up the iron in my blood that I would have lost in giving birth.

"I feel sick even thinking of having to drink that stuff, Mum – it's awful," I moaned each day.

"Just shut up and get it down ye. I want to see you up and about and your routine set with ye baby before I go home."

So daily, I drank this 'stout' that was supposedly so good for me. I reluctantly stood at my front door holding Sharon-Louise as I waved goodbye to Mum one week after I gave birth. I then turned back to look at my home and the quiet life that lay ahead of me.

I was now at home all day with my baby and my dog. Through the week Dave would come home for his dinner, get washed and changed and go to the local pub where he had now made new friends, and I still couldn't cope with the loneliness. I was too far away from my family and friends for them to visit regularly. In the early days of Sharon-Louise's life, my Saturday evenings were at home on my own. Dave still went out as he felt there was no need for both of us to suffer and I foolishly agreed with him. I never wanted to feel selfish. All my friends and family were back in Birkenhead where we had been raised. Dave's best friends were there as well, and he joined them on Friday and Saturday evenings. I always worried about him drinking and then driving for thirty minutes to get home. Saturday he played soccer and Sunday played golf. At that time in my life, I still didn't see Dave as a heavy drinker as all the other guys he knew drank as much as him. I was afraid of him when he drank and found myself behaving in the same way with Dave as I had with Dad. I didn't argue with him at the time and appeased him in any way he wanted just to keep the peace. I dreaded him coming home, not knowing what mood he might be in. Even when he was a happy drunk, I still walked on eggshells because he could switch over so quickly to anger.

We discussed selling the house and moving back to a new housing area on the outskirts of Birkenhead. I needed my friends and family around me for company and Dave needed to be with his friends each evening without the long commute.

Once the decision had been made, the sale of the house happened quickly. The mortgage was still in my name as I topped up my private bookkeeping work. It was 1970 and we moved to another new housing estate called Holmlands. It was in Prenton in Birkenhead and at the end of the estate there was a pub called *The Swan*.

Chapter Eleven

Married to a devious mind with secrets

1970-1979

The house was a new semi-detached brick house on a new housing estate. The driveway was on the right as you looked at it and the front door opened into a narrow hall with the staircase on the right. Ahead, at the end of the hall, was the kitchen and running down the left side of the house was a lounge room in the front with sliding doors between it and a dining room that looked out over the back garden. This garden was a decent size and big enough for Billie to run around in. Upstairs, there were three bedrooms and a bathroom.

Life became easier and happier for me when we moved to this house. All my friends who had young babies and were not working were able to visit me or I could visit them throughout the day. This was wonderful. We all met up at the local shopping centre and arranged days out in the summer at the park and the outdoor baths in New Brighton. Life wasn't lonely throughout the day anymore. Dave was nearer his friends and arranged to see them each night in the pub. I began to realise that Dave saw a different friend or set of friends each evening.

Financially, I had organised more private work to cover our living expenses. I had managed to keep the two bookkeeping jobs I had for the shops in Eastham and added two more bookkeeping jobs, one working for the chemist and a fourth for the sweet and tobacconist, both on Holmlands Drive. I did my work in the evenings after I put Sharon-Louise to bed and while Dave was out. It was still necessary for me to earn this money as Dave still wasn't earning a regular wage and therefore was not giving me regular housekeeping money. His financial contribution was sporadic, but I'd become accustomed to this. It was necessary for him to have his beer money – for his reputation, he told me. Most weeks that was all he earned, he said. (It's amazing how I brainwashed myself!)

Now that we lived nearer my friends, I discovered their husbands had perhaps one or two nights each week out on their own, but Dave was out every night. When I questioned him about it, he thought it was funny and made a joke of it. If he did stay at home, he watched the television and drank his beer. I could never get a conversation out of him without drink inside him and I soon learned it was too dangerous to have an opinion that differed from his. If I pushed my point, he would get angry and violent. I stopped expecting conversation and made the most of the life I was living. My life became two extremes. Dave was either great fun to be with around his friends, laughing and joking (which was the Dave everybody else could see) or he was angry, threatening and verbally abusive (which was the Dave only I saw). I suppressed my feelings and pretended that life was wonderful. I gave everybody that impression because that's how my mother had lived around Dad. I had learned as a child that you don't talk about the arguments in the home and so my friends never suspected what was going on. Everybody liked Dave.

My sister Babs, brother-in-law Mark and nephew Matt lived on the same housing estate and, just as I moved into this house, Babs found herself a full-time job. Matt came to me in the mornings and was with me all day until they both called for him after work. The house became a busy place with people calling from morning until night. This suited me: life was bustling again.

I was so proud of my semi-detached house. My Dad didn't own a car and his visits to our new home had been with me collecting him in my car and taking him home when he was ready. Dad gave advice on decoration of the house, and we were told that he must do the garden. He was a frustrated horticulturist. The first thing he planted was a privet hedge, and the flowers and shrubs were a picture and caught the attention of all those walking by. Dad came to do the gardening and trim 'his' privet hedge most weeks. The garden was Dad's.

Mum gave me her treadle sewing machine to make my curtains and told me to keep it because I was the only one who used it. I had always made Mum's curtains when I lived at home and those of her neighbours and life in this house was no different.

When my new neighbours heard I had a sewing machine, I was making curtains for all in the street. I also made Sharon-Louise's clothes plus bedspreads and my own clothes if I wanted something a little different. I did some repairs and made anything that anybody wanted me to for a small charge. All of this I did in the evenings. Dave started complaining that I had more time for other people than I did for my own family. I was earning the money to pay the mortgage so he benefitted from my work but apart from the extra money I made, I always had to be kept busy throughout the evenings; it helped to pass the time.

One Saturday afternoon, I was about to pick Dad up as he was coming to visit and do the garden. On these occasions we would have dinner together when he'd finish, and I'd then run him home. He rang to ask which bus he should get because he fancied making his own way up to the house. He seemed only to follow instructions that involved directions from pub to pub.

"Get the number two at Laird Street depot, Dad, and get off at the Swan Pub, then walk along Holmlands Drive to get to us," I explained.

"Right ye are," he answered. "Oi'll be 'der when a gets 'der."

I waited in vain for Dad to arrive. Then the phone rang, and I heard the beeps of a pay phone.

"Would ye believe it ave got meself lost," he announced.

"How did you do that, Dad? Didn't ye get off the bus at the Swan Pub?" I asked.

"A happened t'be talkin to an owl dear on de bus an' a didn't see the Swan Pub but just as a looks out the winda a sees the Arrowe Park Pub so that's wheres a got off. And it's here where's I am now and havin' a pint," he answered.

"Okay, Dad. Finish your pint then go back out and get the number six back down the road. You've only gone past by two stops," I instructed.

"Aye, a will when ave finished me pint," he answered. Then as I gave more thought to this instruction I knew I'd never get Dad past the pubs.

"Look, Dad, when ye get off the bus go into the Swan, and we'll meet ye there," I said. "I'll ask my neighbour to mind Sharon-Louise and we'll meet you in the pub later. Let's forget about the gardening today - you can do it next week."

I knew it was a mistake to try to get Dad past the pubs when he wasn't with Mum. I thought it would save us from worrying about him getting lost if we met him in the pub.

The Swan Pub had been an old pub with a new lease of life when the housing estate had been built around it. The owners decided to gut the inside and modernise it. It was painted pink and grey, and the tables and chairs were stainless steel with Formica tops. They were placed in settings of four around this huge area that was much like a barn. A low mezzanine floor at the far end of the room contained a piano and a microphone.

Most of the people that had moved onto this estate were young married couples, like us, and when they visited the pub, they sat in their Sunday best around their small table and hardly spoke to each other. There was no atmosphere in the pub to encourage interaction.

At some time in the future, the new manager must have had big ideas about entertainment in this pub but up until now the piano had never been played. Everybody sat quietly and whispered their conversations.

I asked my neighbour if she would mind Sharon-Louise for a few hours and she was happy to do that. We approached the pub and there was the noise of the piano, singing and laughter. Dave and I looked at each other in amazement.

"Thank God fer that," said Dave. "There's a bit of life in the place at last; they must have engaged a piano player."

We walked in through the door to see Dad standing on 'the stage' with the microphone in his hand. "Der's me daughter everyone – our Pauline. She's the apple of me eye," and I stood, my face red with embarrassment as the whole place looked my way.

"Now yer'll all know dis one," he shouted, "… all t'gether. *If ye Irish, come inter the parlooour, there's a welcome 'ere fer yooooou!*"

And everybody did join in!

Dad had walked into a quiet pub full of strangers and found a piano player amongst the crowd. He'd asked the manager to switch the microphone on and was entertaining these people like they had never experienced before in this pub. He received free drinks all evening and was asked to come back on a regular basis. If the people in this neighbourhood didn't know me before this night they certainly did after Dad had been 'on' at the pub. He was the talk of the new housing estate. It had been years since they'd enjoyed themselves so much. Of course we didn't have that meal I'd cooked for Dad – we couldn't get him out of the pub.

On 10th November of the same year, I gave birth to my son. We named him Gary. He was a big baby and weighed ten pounds four ounces. He was such a handsome child, and I was just as awestruck by him as I was when Sharon-Louise was born.

"Gawd knows how your gunna cope with two kids ye keep cryin' over," Mum commented with a smile.

"I've got you closer now, Mum, so I can sit here cryin' and you can do me work!"

"Ye can bugger off. I've got me own work to do," and we both laughed as she cradled her new grandson and continued, "… though he's gunna be hard to put down – he's a little treasure."

I thought I must be the luckiest person alive to have a girl and a boy. There were three years between Sharon-Louise and Gary and three years between Sharon-Louise and Matt. Between us, we found a great deal of humour in everything we did. Before they went to school, I had taught them all how to read, write and count.

Gary was a quick learner and a willing participant in any of the things we organised to make our life less tedious and to bring some humour to it. He soon learned how to make us laugh and we encouraged him. He became the joker in the pack. We were a happy little group and Dave would come home to a contented family.

Dave loved his children and played with them most evenings until bedtime. This was a time of fun and laughter in our home, and I loved those hours. Dave would then freshen up to go to the pub and I would read to the children. Some evenings they would be trying to go to sleep, and I wouldn't let them because I wanted to know what was about to happen in the next chapter of the book we were reading. The children became 'my life'. I was able to get my Saturday night out with the wild crowd about once a month and that kept me going. Dave thought life itself was wonderful and wouldn't allow me to talk about how unhappy I was with his drinking and not generating any money. If he didn't hear about it, it wasn't happening. If I insisted on talking to him about it in one of his sober moments, he would tell me that he was happy and deserved a drink at the end of his working day. If I wasn't happy then it was my own fault, and I should do something about it.

When the children were older, Saturday or Sunday morning was Dave's time with them, and he took them either horse riding, skating or to the swimming baths, and the world saw a doting father. And he was ... to some extent. The children didn't see him drunk until they were older, and I made certain they didn't hear any upsets that were caused because of his drinking and lack of financial input into the family needs.

Often, I was in bed when Dave came home from the pub. I purposely did this to avoid any confrontations. If somebody had upset him in the pub, he would come home angry, and I would have to suffer his anger. On one evening I had been reading a book that had grabbed my attention and I hadn't noticed the time. I was still sitting on the settee when Dave came home after his drinking, and he was ready for a fight. He would pick on anything to release the anger he was feeling and this night he was accusing me of feeding him leftovers from Gary's plate. I never argued back when he was in these moods, but would quietly try to defend myself by speaking the truth.

"I wouldn't do that, Dave, because I know ye don't like that ..." but his anger built and he began to throw the dining chairs against the wall and started threatening me. His usual behaviour involved pushing me as he growled abuse in my face. Then he would grab the top of my arms and dig his fingers in until they were bruised, holding me in front of his face so I could see the viciousness and anger he claimed I was causing in his eyes. I was cornered in the kitchen and, to get away from him, I ran into the lounge. He picked up a carving knife in the kitchen and ran after me, knocked me off my feet and pinned me to the floor with the knife at my throat. Because my children were asleep, I never cried out. I tried pushing him to get him off me as I lay on the floor. His eyes were vicious and evil as the verbal abuse continued. My throat had constricting and my heart raced. I knew my life was in danger.

I was now extremely frightened of him. This scenario went on for some minutes when he suddenly rolled away from me, struggled to his feet, and tottered into the kitchen to get another beer. This was my opportunity to get to the phone in the lounge and call the police.

"Please help me," I whispered into the phone. "My husband is going to kill me, he's threatening me with a knife, my children are asleep upstairs, please come quickly." I gave them the address and replaced the phone and sat waiting for what he would do next. He still had the knife in his hand and began verbally abusing me again when he walked back into the room.

"I've rung the police," I said quietly as I sat in the corner of the settee afraid of what his reaction would be. He stood looking at the floor, churning this over in his head for a few seconds then he calmly turned and went back into the kitchen and put the knife back in the kitchen drawer. Then he sat down on a stool, placed his bottle of beer on the bench and looked down at it, shaking his head. A supercilious grin crossed his face as though I had done something completely unnecessary.

The police knocked on the door and I ran to open it as Dave remained on the stool in the kitchen. There were two policemen. One took me into the lounge while the other stayed in the kitchen to talk to Dave.

"Have you been physically harmed?" the policeman asked me.

"Not yet," I replied, "but he's threatening me with a knife and if I hadn't called you, he would have hurt me. My children are asleep upstairs, and I'm frightened."

The second policeman came into the lounge after talking to Dave and said, "Everything will be okay now; I've just had a word with your husband, and he tells me that he didn't have a knife and you've been exaggerating all of this. Look, luv, he's your husband and has had a bit too much to drink. You shouldn't be arguing with him when he's like that. Just go to bed and let him sober up. We're patrolling this area and if you have any more problems throughout the night, you can ring again or flag us down if you see us passing. But I advise you to just go to bed and stop aggravating him."

"He's lied to you. He did have a knife and he's going to kill me when you leave!" I stressed. Tears started to flow as I looked at them. The policeman who had been speaking to Dave just looked at me as though I was a child and, shaking his head with disdain, said, "Go to bed, luv. Leave him alone and stop nagging."

The two policemen walked down the hall and out of the front door. As soon as they left, Dave walked into the lounge and ripped the phone connection out of the wall. I moved toward the door to the hall.

"They're patrolling the area," I gasped and ran into the hall. Growling as he followed, he tried to grab me. I ran out the front door to catch the police before they drove away, ran down the short drive waving my arms at the back of the police car for them to stop, but they didn't see me and drove off. As I turned to look at the house again, Dave stood looking at me and then slammed the front door shut. I was locked outside wearing only my night-dress and it was winter.

I wouldn't knock on a neighbour's door for help because I didn't want anyone to know how I was being treated. I was ashamed. My car was on the drive but was locked and I crouched behind it waiting for the police to patrol the area again when I would run out to ask for their help. But they didn't come back that night.

As the day was breaking, Dave came down the stairs and opened the front door and just walked away from it. I painfully uncurled myself from the crouching position I'd been in for hours and went indoors. I ran my hands under the hot water to get some feeling back in them. While doing so, he shoved me out of the way as he opened a cupboard to get a mug. I turned to him and calmly said:

"Now you've gone too far. I want you out of this house today. I'm not taking any more. You contribute nothing to this family, you are a liability, I want you gone."

In response, he pushed his face into mine and growled, "If you don't like the situation, you can fuck off, but I'm staying in this house." He drank his coffee and went to work.

I thought about the situation during the morning and knew without a doubt I would not be able to make him leave.

I packed a few of our possessions and left with the children to go and stay with my parents. The shame of how my husband was treating me stopped me from repeating my story to anyone, not even my mother could get the full story out of me.

"Dave got drunk again last night, Mum. I can't live with him – he frightens me. Can I stay here for a while until I work out what I'm going to do?"

"You can stay for a couple of days," Mum answered, "but these children need a proper home. You can't be dragging them around because you can't cope; it's not fair on them. You've made your bed so you must lie on it like the rest of us had to. You can't make your kids pay the price for you and your mistakes."

Dave came to my parents' house the following evening asking

me to go back home.

"You go back to the house. I'll follow you when I've put the kids to bed, and we'll talk," I said.

Dave left and Mum said sternly, "Sort this out tonight so that these kids can sleep in their own beds tomorrow night."

I followed Dave thirty minutes later, but when I got there, he wasn't home. I sat on my own waiting for him to return, humiliation burning my soul. He'd gone straight from my parents' house to the pub, even though he knew I was following him home. I knew my parents thought we were sorting the problem out and I couldn't face going back and telling Mum he wasn't in the house. I sat on the settee until he came home from the pub at around 11pm. He was mellow when he came in.

"I said I'd follow you, Dave. Why weren't you here?"

"What's the difference ... I'm here now, aren't I! I knew you'd be here waiting for me." He smiled his supercilious smile as he grabbed himself another beer. I was predictable! He knew me better than I knew me, and he'd played me!

He refused to talk about what had happened. He told me I was lying and exaggerating, and he had no memory of the police.

"I'm not arguing with ye! Ye either come back here with the kids or you don't. Stop looking for more trouble by wanting to talk and exaggerate things, which will only get me mad again. Is that what ye want?"

How do I deal with this? I asked myself. *Am I looking for trouble?* I began doubting myself. *Could he have been so angry that night that he may have blanked out what had happened?*

I felt he didn't want to believe he could have behaved that way, and trying to stress that I was telling the truth only fuelled his anger again. Wearily, I said I would come home the following day. The police had told me I was aggravating my husband and exaggerating, my mother had told me I was weak and needed to be tougher and more tolerant for the sake of my kids and not make them pay for my mistakes; and Dave said I was telling lies. There was no support anywhere for me and I felt even if I told the whole truth of the situation, people would believe that I had brought it on myself, that I deserved it. When Dave did remember the way he had treated me, he would always say that I had asked for it. I had a big mouth and was always nagging him about money and his drinking. But I was afraid of him when he was drinking and wouldn't do that. He seemed to live in his private world where he justified his aggressive behaviour toward me, always saying I deserved it.

I was living with a Jekyll and Hyde personality, and I created my life around these two extremes, counting any blessings that came my way and making the most of the times in between the anger bouts. Yet, because Dave said he didn't remember the bad situations he created, I decided to treat his behaviour as an illness. There was good and bad in everybody, and I had to make the most of the good in Dave and learn how to read his moods and protect myself and the children when his bad moods emerged. I continued my life by justifying his behaviour to myself reluctantly – but I had to as there was no other way I could live with this situation.

The house was in my name, and I paid the mortgage. Financially I kept us all – my kids needed a roof over their heads, and I couldn't get him out of my house.

My life settled into a routine, but my mind would often shift into how I could get him out of my life and what I would do when the next situation arose where he might hurt me. I packed a case with basics for me and the kids which I kept in the boot of my car. Money and his excessive drinking was always the cause of the rows as the children were growing and their needs became more expensive. If he gave me any money on a Friday, he would always ask for it back by Tuesday at the latest, and so he still wasn't contributing to the housekeeping.

As far as the average man in the neighbourhood went, I classed Dave as a half decent man. He was a generous person 'out there', always the first to order a round of drinks in the pub, so usually bought the last as well. What 'the lads' thought of Dave was important to him. It was the men in this area that talked about how 'tight' somebody was.

"Ee could peel an orange in 'is pocket" was a familiar expression used for people that didn't join in with the pack. If you smoked and didn't hand your cigarettes around at the bar, you were talked about. If somebody was down on their luck, Dave would be the first to slip them a five-pound note with the words, "Give us it back when yer've got it."

The problem was, Dave wanted to be liked so much by the 'lads' that very often he would give them his last five-pound note and would then 'hit' the credit card. I soon realised that if he gave me any money for housekeeping, it was off a credit card. A credit card to Dave was free money. When his credit card demanded payment, he would tell me in an aggressive way that I had to pay it off for him, so he still wasn't giving me any housekeeping money but was building debt instead. I began to read him as more complex than I had first thought. I became aware that he was a gambler and would lose money on the horses or at the casino and then get more money off the plastic card, perhaps always thinking that he could replace it before the statement came in; but of course; he never could. It seemed he'd been gambling like this in the casinos and betting shops all through our marriage and I was completely unaware. We started having massive rows (when he was sober), which always fell on Dave's deaf ears. He was in serious debt and had used the house as collateral for his credit card debt. The house wasn't in his name and yet had been used for collateral. I had no understanding of how the banks could do that. I had to think of a way out of this situation.

Trying hard to choose the right time to get him to listen to me, I would say, "Can't you see, Dave, that you're gambling your kid's security. The banks can step in at any time and boot us all out. You've got to stop this, Dave."

"You're the one that's good with money - you can sort it out," he would reply. Sometimes he laughed about it and then went to the pub. I was still working my bookkeeping jobs which covered the mortgage and family needs and only a small amount more. That small amount was now being used to pay off his credit card debts.

Like me, my next-door neighbour, Maureen, had two small children. We decided to start a clothes party business from home. We could share the business and mind each other's children. We were both hard-working women and had an eye for business and the project grew in no time. It provided both families with all our clothes and a substantial income. We needed transport for this growing business and were able to buy a station wagon each out of the proceeds. For the first time since I was married, I was now feeling financially comfortable and able to cover our needs and even create a savings account.

Dave's one-car garage was known by all as the place to take your car for repair. I couldn't do the accounts for him as he didn't have a head for business and wouldn't keep receipts or invoices. His customers were told he only dealt with cash (which he pocketed and used for his drinking and gambling). The community all took their cars to him for repairs, and he would only charge what they could afford. 'Old people' would offer to pay, and if he liked them, sometimes he would reply, "Don't you worry about it, luv, it's on the 'ouse." They would come back with homemade cakes and biscuits, and we would always have a steady supply of these. It seemed his outgoings were more than his incomings. He was spending what he earned on drinking and gambling and when he lost he drained a credit card. He gave me nothing and I was left trying to pay for all the family needs and his credit card debt. The arguments would be fierce, but I couldn't make him stop.

The 'lads' in the pub all thought Dave was the big businessman and he needed to live up to this reputation. He would get in a financial mess but always knew I had been saving money and he would pressure me to 'bail him out again'.

The clothes parties became a huge success. Maureen and I were booked by clubs and large gatherings and our every waking moment was spent organising them. We kept telling ourselves we would have more time when our youngest children were at school. When this time arrived, it was a large enterprise that needed premises. We had the money to do this and sat down with our husbands to discuss the future of our business.

Dave wanted no part of it and didn't agree with us continuing. He wanted me at home "where ye should be, an' stop this bloody galavantin' around." I knew that his ego was dented with our success. He wouldn't acknowledge that I was also keeping him in his way of life.

We sold the business as a going concern. Maureen bought a hairdressing shop with her 50%. I knew I had a good business brain and began searching for some business interest to put my money into and make it grow.

In the local paper, just at that time, the council were offering free plans to build a business unit on a new industrial estate they were opening near Woodside Ferry. It was to be called The Priory Industrial Estate. They wanted only one of each business and opened it up as a lottery. I completed the application after speaking to Dave about it and all he said was, "It's up to you." I gave it lots of thought and felt it was worth putting my money into. Once it was built I could either sell it and make a profit or Dave could run his workshop from it. The council called me – I had been chosen and 'won' a unit space with plans. The building needed to be completed within the next six months.

I asked the bank to loan me the balance of money to build it. Dave still worked in his one-car workshop. Even if I could get him to hand some money over from what he earned, the return would not be enough to cover the extra payment for the building. I used my considerable profit from the clothing business to start the build and the bank promised a loan for the balance if I could find another job that would meet the requirements for repayments.

"I'm getting another job to cover these payments, Dave," I said. "I need your help now to work with me and look after the kids and get them to school in the morning until we've paid this loan off. Then when you've seen them off to school you are free to oversee the building of the industrial unit. Are you okay with that?" He agreed.

I found another job in Lever Brothers, the soap powder factory in Port Sunlight. I worked on the production line from six in the morning until two in the afternoon filling soap powder packets. The money was excellent. The building of the workshop had to be supervised by Dave during the day and I worked to pay for the materials and the builders.

At the time I was looking for jobs, I'd also applied to a promotion agency for work. One week after starting in the soap powder factory I was also offered a promotion job. It was full-time but unsupervised. I was given garden outlets to visit where I erected advertising material and took orders for the product. I needed all the money I could get to quickly pay off the loan for the workshop and so I also accepted this position. At the end of my 6am until 2 pm shift each day I would run to the ladies' rest rooms where I would put on my makeup, get changed and jump in the car to race through eight hours work in four over the afternoon before the outlets closed. The agency never found out that this was how I had done the work and, when the promotion was finished, they gave me more work and a bonus.

Both our Mums worked a roster and were at my house daily for the children coming home from school and cooked a meal for us all. In the evenings, I would catch up on housework, read the children their stories and then sit down to do the shops' bookkeeping accounts and the paperwork for the building. I would get to bed around midnight to be up again at five a.m. to go to the factory. Dave would see the children off to school and then go and supervise the building and do any work in his workshop if he had any. During all this time I missed playing with the children but kept consoling myself it wouldn't be for long.

Dave decided he would like to move into the workshop and run a proper business from it. I encouraged this as long as he allowed me to do the accounts.

"Then when you move into the workshop and build the business, Dave, the business can pay the loan off. I can stop all these jobs and run the office from then on. I'll have just one job and can start after I've got the kids to school and finish at 3pm so I can be home for the kids. That will be a dream after working all these jobs," I told him.

Dave moved into the workshop and employed his friend as a painter and his brother as a labourer. I began instructing how to gather his receipts etc and I'd do the accounts from home until the workshop was making money then I could put my plan into place and work less hours. But he simply took no notice of this instruction.

This manic work phase doing two full-time jobs and part-time accounts, plus looking after my family, had to stop. I still needed to work to whittle away at the large loans we had, and so I found a full-time job as a representative for a car battery company. The salary was excellent and covered the two pay packets I was giving up. I still did the bookkeeping for the shops at night but through the day I was now working less hours.

My job provided me with a good income, and I was able to steadily chip away at the loans. We were still arguing about Dave pocketing the cash from his customers for his habits but now he was telling me he had no money to give me because he was paying the wages out of what the workshop produced. My assumptions were that, although Dave was still running a charity, he had a bigger business, so he was now able to pocket even more cash. I tried to explain to him that I could wind back and not work as hard if he would run it as a business that would provide money to help pay all the debt we had, which included his gambling debts, but again he ignored me.

Family life was not normal in our house, and I saw little of Dave except at weekends. He took little interest in my work. It provided us with a good lifestyle, but we didn't talk about it. All we seemed to do in between Saturday nights was argue about his drinking and gambling and his debts. He was still contributing nothing to the household expenses because he said he was paying wages for staff. If I insisted on organising his book work to find out why he wasn't making a profit, he would viciously defend himself.

"And don't you dare come down to that workshop lookin' as though you own the place and makin' a fool out of me, d'ye hear me? Stay away or yer'll be sorry!"

After the arguments, he would go into a silent period which could last for weeks. Eventually I would start to talk to him again because I couldn't stand the silence.

I told myself that Dave loved us all, I felt I knew that. He became abusive when he got drunk but said he never remembered it the next day. This was 'blind anger'. He would accuse me of exaggerating and my mention of it would cause another row. His only reaction on being faced with his behaviour was anger. I couldn't make him talk coherently about this situation, and the silences would start all over again. It was a vicious circle. I brainwashed myself into this lifestyle – keeping the peace when he was sober and living in fear when he was drunk. He spent little time with me but threatened me if I tried to leave. I couldn't live with him, but he wouldn't let me live without him. I could also see he couldn't let me go! Me working as I did provided him with his financial lifestyle. I was his cash cow! He still produced nothing to keep his family.

After another night of violent anger from Dave, I dragged myself around the following day trying to lift my spirits again. I took a sick day from work and collected the children from school and put all three in the back seat of the car and drove to the nearest supermarket to collect my groceries. The kids were full of high spirits. As I pushed the trolley around the shop floor, they threw sweets and biscuits and chocolate bars into it along with toys and games and I became frustrated with them. Going through the checkout I had to keep saying "No, not that. The kids have thrown that in without me noticing, sorry."

The kids seemed to instinctually understand that I was not fully alert and so they ran around the car park as I packed the groceries into the boot, and I had to stand screaming at them to get them into the back seat of the car. When I drove out of the car park onto the main road, they were fighting in the back seat.

"Will you stop this!" I kept shouting. "If you do that again I'll stop and smack you all!"

They took no notice of me and were physically fighting in the back seat as I was driving, when an elbow hit me in the back of the head.

"That's it!" I shouted as I slammed my foot on the brake. I opened the driver's door and got out, opened the back door, and grabbed Matt who was closest to me and dragged him out of the door. I smacked the back of his legs and made him stand against the car while I dragged the other two out and did the same to them.

"Now get back in that car and I don't want to hear another peep out of any one of you!" I shouted as I pointed at the car. Once they were in, I slammed the door and turned around to see a bus stopped behind me with a trail of traffic after it. The bus driver was leaning on the steering wheel waiting until I had finished.

"Nice one, luv," he shouted cynically as he shook his head in disgust. My face was burning. I had stopped in the middle of a busy main road and was holding up all the traffic as they witnessed me smacking my kids.

My hectic life of working these jobs to cover the mortgage payments for both the house and the workshop was taking its toll. It gave me no time to give thought to how I would organise the workshop to either make it a profitable business or sell it. I knew I had to face this now and make Dave face up to me selling it as it wasn't making money.

On Saturday at the end of this burn-out week, I decided that weekend was the time for Dave and I to speak of the future of the workshop. I had already decided it had to be sold as it was only supplying his gambling money. The kids were all around at my sister's house and Dave was out playing golf, so I picked up the spare set of workshop keys and drove to the industrial estate to look through the office. I stood before the building in shock … it had another name over the door! I didn't want to believe what seemed clear to me. He had sold the premises and I was still paying the bank back for the build.

Driving home, I fought within myself, trying to keep calm and make plans of what I'd say and do now. I even prayed "Please, God, let him have placed the money into a bank account."

When Dave returned home from golf to eat his meal and go out again, my words began to choke me as I began the conversation.

"Why is there another name over the door of our workshop?"

"Because I've sold it."

"When?"

"A couple of months back."

"Where is the money?"

"It's gone, woman. Okay!! It's bloody gone so shut up and get out of my face."

"Are you telling me you have gambled away all of that bank loan that I am working around the clock to pay? The bank loan that is in my name?"

His anger rose to fever pitch but so had mine! "I want you out of this house *NOW*! Get your things and get out of here!" I shouted – but he did his usual, grabbing me by the top of my arms and shouting abuse in my face. Then he threw me back against the kitchen door, grabbed his keys, turned and went to the pub.

How can I get rid of this man? I was stuck in a financial trap and my naivety had caused it. *Why hadn't I faced up to who he was years back?* I wanted to run away, but where to? I wanted to scream, but didn't want to upset the kids. I needed someone to hear me and comfort me, but I was so ashamed of his behaviour toward me and I couldn't even go to my sister, my parents or my friends and tell them. I was so ashamed of myself. This was all my fault!

I packed his clothes in a case and put them outside the door for him to pick up when he came home. I put the deadlock on the doors front and back. He arrived after 11.30pm and, as he was not able to get in, he smashed the window beside the back door, put his arm through and unlocked the door. Now his anger had built to that of a wounded bull!! I had been sitting on the lounge in the dark waiting to hear him come and go with his case. But, once he was inside, he burst into the lounge, grabbed

117

me by one shoulder and punched my face. The blow knocked me to the couch. Then he threatened he would kill me if I ever did that again. I wanted to be dead that night. I didn't contemplate suicide because I wouldn't leave my kids, but I just remember feeling 'I want to be dead'. That punch was the final insult and had now drained the 'life' out of me. I saw no way out of this life I had blindly walked into. This was worse than being in a prison. *Will I ever be free?* I sank into total despair.

My job was now extremely important as I had at least four years to work and pay off the loan. I was also paying the mortgage on the house and was the primary bread winner for my family. I contacted my boss and asked for a week's holiday as I had some family business to attend. I visited the doctor but could only say we fought because he drank heavily. He sent me to a psychologist as I was suffering from depression. I now felt I had to tell my parents, his Mum, and my sister that Dave had sold the workshop and had gambled the money he received. These people had all been helping me as I worked to pay for an asset which was going to be of value to my family once it was paid off. I had to tell them I still owed the money to the bank as it was in my name and so I still had to continue working.

Immediately my mother told me she and Dad wouldn't be minding the children any more through the week. She had been helping me so far as she felt my family would benefit.

"If I continue minding the kids, Pauline, the only person that is benefitting is Dave and it's time that man faced up to his responsibilities," she said. "I'm not putting myself out to help that man gamble and drink the way he does."

Over the next months, Dad also stopped calling to do my garden and lawns. I didn't ask why - I instinctively knew he would feel he was helping Dave if he did them, so he stopped. Dave's mother said very little but offered to still mind the kids if I needed her.

Apart from my family, I told no one about Dave's activities and not another person about him punching me. I was ashamed of how I'd been treated. My best friend Jesse wouldn't be fobbed off as she noticed the swelling on the side of my face that I was covering with makeup. I eventually told her the full story. She pleaded with me, "You've got to get out of this marriage, Pauline – it's dangerous. He'll kill you one day and then what would the kids do. You've wasted all these years thinking you were building your future and look where you are now? It's only going to get worse. This life is not a dress rehearsal - you must get out!"

"You tell me how, Jesse? Wherever I move to he will follow. He contributes nothing but is living freely here while I pay the loans and mortgage and feed us all. I'm his cash cow; he won't let me go."

She took me to her lawyer who immediately placed a restraining order on Dave and then sent him divorce papers. When Dave opened the envelope, that supercilious smile crossed his face, and he ripped the papers up in front of me. Then he grabbed me by the throat and pressed his fingers deep until I gasped for air, all the while growling into my face what he'd do to me if I tried to get a divorce.

That night I saw he wasn't averse to killing me.

Over the next weeks, I suffered his vicious anger firstly because I'd involved Jesse who was married to his friend, and secondly, becaue I thought I could get away with reporting him to the police and involving a lawyer. It was hard hiding it all from the kids now and I did tell them that Daddy had been naughty and sold our workshop without telling me, so I wanted him to go. They began crying. "Don't let Daddy go, Mum, he's sorry - please let him stay." But they were too young to understand the repercussions I was suffering. My life was hell but I had to work through it until he calmed down.

This was still the 1970s in England, and a man's world. The

laws benefitted the men and not the women they assaulted.

I collected the children from school on a couple of days through the week as I adjusted my work schedule, and I asked his Mum to do the other days. I fell into a routine and merely plodded along paying the debts, working to keep a roof over my kids with a leech on my back that was bleeding me dry. I did brainwash myself. I was in a situation I could not get out of, and I felt I had to work to keep my spirits up and not be depressed constantly – I had to accept my lot and work around it.

Babs and Mark sold their house and, with Matt, went to live in New Zealand. I'd had Matt with me for so long, I had a period of depression again. He had been my third child and the kids and I missed him terribly. Plus, I missed having my sister living close to me. Although I never told her 'the whole truth' of my life, she would 'look' at me, and I knew that she knew. I couldn't really hide it from her properly even though at times I would defend Dave by telling stories of some of the good things he did for his kids. She would just 'look' at me. I couldn't convince her that he had any good in him. She had no time for him.

My mother never casually visited my house again but insisted I take the kids to see her once a week.

"I want you to be vigilant, Pauline, because I know he may still harm you. I've always said you need to tolerate your lot once you have kids but I'm now worried he could kill ye one day. Ye dad went to see 'im down at the garage and told 'im if one hair on your head is touched in anger that 'eed kill 'im. Ye Dad told him to get out of your house and leave you alone. But Dave told ye dad that it was none of his business and punched 'im on the shoulder and told 'im to get out of his face."

Hearing this made me so upset that he would actually harm my dad.

Once my sister and her family had left for New Zealand, I threw myself into a hectic work routine to avoid sinking too far into a depression. I began decorating my home and every room was redecorated over the next couple of years. Dave had never been someone that had conversations with me so I didn't miss any relaxed chatter, plus now I was relieved as he left each night for the pub. I didn't feel lonely anymore - I kept busy around the house. While he was out, there was no tension. He still contributed nothing but arrived every night to eat his meal and then to sleep in my bed after returning from the pub. The silence between us was now going into months and it suited me.

One Sunday morning, at 6.45 am, the doorbell started ringing in loud wails, long drawn-out piercing screams that woke the whole household.

"Who can that be at this time of the morning?" I muttered as I grabbed my housecoat and ran down the stairs.

When I opened the front door, my mother stood there in a state of collapse, supported by her neighbour. A cold chill ran through me.

"What's happened?" I said as I grabbed her and manoeuvred her into the lounge and onto the couch. I looked down at her and again asked, "What's happened, Mum. Tell me!"

She just stared at me, her eyes round like saucers with fear. Her face was white. I looked at her neighbour. "Please, tell me what's happened."

"It's ye father, Pauline. Am sorry t'be the one t'ave t'tell ye luv, but ye Mum found 'im dead in bed beside er this mornin," said the neighbour.

Horrified, I looked at my mother, who was still in a state of shock, staring up at me with fearful eyes, shaking her head as though someone would wake her any moment from her nightmare. "Oh Mum!" was all I could say and sat down and put my arms around her.

"I'll go now, luv. Ye know where I am if there's anythin' ye want me t'do for ye. I'll leave ye with ye grief, luv. An' let me say now 'ow sorry I am. 'ell be badly missed … ee was a lovely man," and the neighbour left.

Mum's eyes stared and seemed to be pleading with me to wake her up. I sat beside her and put my arms around her. She placed her head on my chest and we sat for some time saying nothing. There was absolutely nothing going through my head – nothing!

Eventually Mum said, "And we only bought his new suit and shoes yesterday," and I then had a vision of Dad in his suit and shoes. He always wore a shirt tie and jacket/suit if he wasn't at work. He didn't own any casual clothes. His new suit would have been a shade of grey with a stripe or, for a change, could be dark navy; he had never bought a different color, and his shoes would be black lace-ups and highly polished. He only ever bought clothes that were the latest version of his old ones. This made it difficult to compliment him on his new clothes as we mostly never noticed they were new.

"Make us a cuppa, Pauline luv."

"Oh yes, Mum," and I stood to walk down the lounge toward the kitchen, and only then did the emotions kick in – *BAM*!! The first one was anger!

I couldn't speak to him before he left!! I can't live with that!! I want him back NOW!

This anger screamed through my head and affected every nerve in my body. As I walked, my feet bounced on the floor with this powerful anger as it surged through me. As I made Mum's tea, the next emotion began: a fierce compulsion to go to their house. I could somehow accept this situation in their house. *I need to go right now. Right now!!!*

I took Mum's tea to her and said, "I want you to stay here for now, Mum, while I sort everything – I'm going to your house and will pick up the things you'll need."

"Yes, I'll come with you," she said.

I didn't want that. I felt I couldn't do what I needed to do to accept this situation if she was with me, even though I didn't know what that was, so I said, "No, Mum it's too soon."

"No, Pauline, I'm coming with you – I know where everything is and what I need to bring." She was so determined, I knew I couldn't change her mind so said, "Okay."

As I opened her front door with my set of keys, I noticed our family home smelled only of Dad, and not Mum. It was also cold. (Over the years I had discovered that smells were my spiritual connection.) Mum walked behind me down the hall and, as I opened the lounge door, Dad's chair was right there in view in the left corner beside the fireplace … and he was in it! I blinked and he was gone. Then Mum hung on my arm and from behind me said, "I am suddenly so tired, Pauline; I need to lie down." Her legs began buckling beneath her.

Navigating her around the door to the settee behind it, I sat her down. I placed cushions at one end and lay her head on them, then gently moved her legs and placed them on the settee. As I looked down at Mum, I could see she had immediately dropped into a deep sleep – her face muscles had relaxed, her breathing was shallow, and her eye lids had no movements. It seemed like hypnosis – a snap of the fingers and she was UNCONSCIOUS.

Surprised at this, I looked at her for a few more seconds then turned, closed the lounge door and went to sit in Dad's chair. I then looked past the lounge door back to Mum and the door opened – Dad was standing there looking at me with his beautiful Irish smile and twinkly eyes. I began to smile, my anger and angst immediately dissipating.

I said, "I'm sorry, Dad. I became angry because you'd left without me speaking to you."

"I know that, darlin', dat's why I'm here."

123

I poured out my love and admiration for him – thanked him for all the things he had done for me and how proud I was that I was his daughter – I recalled so many things I needed to thank him for! Then, when I had exhausted my thank yous, he said "Ye Mah will take this badly … I want you to tell her that I'll be walking beside her until we are together again."

"I'll tell her, Dad."

"I must move on now, Pauline. My love is locked in your heart and always will be so I'll never be leavin' ye – G'bye, darlin'."

"I'll always love you, Dad. G'bye." – And he shut the door.

And just as he did Mum woke up, sat up straight and planted her feet on the floor again. "I feel so much better for that sleep, Pauline," she said as she stretched her arms above her head. "How long was I sleeping for?"

I looked at the clock and then looked at my watch to check the time again. It hadn't even been five minutes. I became confused.

"Not long, Mum," I said, but Mum could always tell when we were covering something up. "Have ye something to tell me, Pauline?"

I slowly nodded. "While you were sleeping, I was talking to Dad."

Unsurprised, she said, "Oh, were ye, luv. What did he 'ave to say?"

I repeated word for word our conversation then said, "Dad said to tell you he'll be walking beside you until you're together again." She drew in a huge gulp of air.

"Oh, Pauline, that was our private pledge to each other for whichever one went first." Then she began to quietly cry for the first time that day, and I sat beside her and wrapped her in my arms and cried with her.

Eventually I said, "I don't know though, Mum … I'm not

sure now if I dreamt it or imagined it. You see, he was wearing a brown suit and shoes." She pushed me back and smiled through her tears.

"He's done that to let you know you weren't imagining it. They're his new clothes – they're hanging in his wardrobe."

I sat looking at her for a few moments unbelieving! Then I went upstairs and opened Dad's wardrobe door, and there was the brown suit and shoes I'd just seen him wearing, with the price tag still attached. He had changed his colour choice for the first time in his life!

If psychiatrists are right, that in times of shock we can manufacture happenings that aren't real, then how did I know about my parents' private pledge to each other – and his brown suit and shoes?

Dad was only sixty-five when he died of thrombosis, in July 1977. The following month Elvis died and then in October Bing Crosby died, one of Dad's favourite singers. We all acknowledged there was a new singing trio now for the spirit world.

It took me a long time to get over the death of my dad. I tried to do the garden work when I had time, but it now looked neglected without him. Every time I looked through the window I was reminded of him and my days were full of depression. I worked hard at my job to keep my mind off my problems and missing Dad.

Dave and I had come to a compromise that he could do what he liked with his own money providing he cut up his credit cards and never got another. Also, he was never to use the house as security for any debts. If he broke this agreement, I threatened I would tell his brothers and his friends just what and how he had been living all these years.

Dave didn't change his ways and over the next years I became a robot navigating my life around him in an effort to keep us safe. I accepted that this life I lived would be worse if I tried to fight him so I gave up. But I was never relaxed and would search cupboards and drawers often to see if he was trying to hide bank statements. During these busy years, the children had grown, and I could see that, as they were heading toward teenage years, we were going to need a bigger house so they could spread out.

I began to search for a larger house that would perhaps need some work done on it and would therefore be in my price range.

Dave didn't want this move, but I didn't care if he wanted it or not. I secretly hoped if he didn't want it he could go and live elsewhere but, in retrospect, he needed his cash cow. He was being kept for free so why would he walk away! I went ahead with my plan. He was back working in a small one-man garage still pocketing whatever he made which covered his alcohol and gambling. His drinking pals thought he was the big businessman and Dave played up to that. I had started my marriage being afraid I would end up like the wives of these men and now realised that my life was so much worse than those other women.

For this reason he got away with the physical and financial abuse he put me through as I never fought about it. In despair, I would say nothing the next day as it would only start rows and fighting. There were people in this world that had to face worse problems than I was subjected to, and I would feel guilty when I heard of these people soldiering on without complaint.

In thinking of the environment I'd been raised in and the stories I'd heard of these women who supported their husbands suffering PTSD after the war, I would feel guilty when thinking how strong they were and how they got on with their difficult lives. I decided I must do the same and not accept defeat.

Now the children didn't need so much of my time, I needed to have some purpose in my life and doing up an old house would keep me occupied and give me a sense of achievement. Work was always my saviour. I had to keep pushing on.

Chapter Twelve

A face in a painting

1979

I visited real estate agents around the area I wanted to move into and told them of my budget and needs. My two closest friends, Jesse and Jenny, lived in Prenton and I decided it would be lovely to live close to them. Each weekend I drove around looking at houses, and many times I stood looking at one particular house near where they both lived. Why it kept standing out to me I wasn't sure. I could see it needed some renovation and I knew I would love to do it, but at that time it wasn't on the market. Then the phone call came from the real estate agent.

"I've found your dream home." It was the two-storey Victorian semi-detached brick house I'd been looking at. The double gates opened to a short drive, which led to the free-standing garage and out houses. A path forked off this to the right leading to the front porch. There was a door to the porch, which, once opened, allowed the caller to stand under cover to pull the doorbell. The front door opened onto a large entrance hall, with a magnificent dog-leg staircase coming down the wall in front, descending to the left with a small landing; it then ran half-way down the left wall where it turned again to finish with a sweep in the centre of the hall. On the landing where it turned to run down the left wall, was a beautiful stained-glass window, which caught the morning sun and scattered beams of coloured lights around this truly impressive room.

The walls were lined with timber panels to three quarters of the way up and finished with a display shelf which was held in place with intricately carved finials. This magnificent, graceful, impressive example of early craftsmanship was entirely painted … in British Rail Yellow. *What on earth possessed someone to abuse this masterpiece?*

Mildred, the housekeeper, currently owned the house and was a pleasure to deal with. She had inherited the house on the death of her employer, Mrs Martin, who had died only days before. Mrs Martin had been born in the house, had lived all her life in it, and had died in it.

Seeing past the abuse, I could envision this hall back to its former glory and, as I stepped into it with the real estate agent, I let out a sigh of delight.

"Oh! It's beautiful," I said.

"I'm so glad yer like it," said Mildred. "Me 'usband will be pleased, ee's just finished paintin' it. We thought we'd jus' give it a lick o' paint t'smarten it up before we put the 'ouse up fer sale."

I stared at Mildred. The modern additives of this beautiful home had been continued throughout each room. She followed me around the inspection with commentary she felt would help sell this house to me.

"The dining room had "a big 'ole in the wall with old wooden seats each side of a tiny little fire grate (an Inglenook fireplace) so we boarded it up and put in a really good gas fire that takes no lookin' after," she informed me. The lounge fireplace had been ripped out and replaced with a "nice modern tile job that's nice an' easy t'clean". The kitchen and morning room had been knocked into one '"cos we lived most in ere ye see, so it was easy t'watch the telly an' cook at the same time, an' we knocked that wall down t'that wee room (the butler's pantry) so's I could see which bell's ringin' from me chair 'ere by the telly."

The bells, as Mildred called them, consisted of a mahogany wood panel on the wall that had two rows of little brass bells with the room names, plus the front and back door, written in brass lettering above each bell. There was a bell pull in each room and one at the front and back doors.

There were also a series of out-houses with pieces of antique furniture thrown in them in various stages of decay. The five bedrooms each had a fireplace in them, which were all boarded up. The bathroom had never been altered since it had been installed so was in a very poor state and desperately needed modernising. The carpet was well worn and needed replacing, and the décor was original in some rooms whilst obviously 'Mildredrised' in others. It needed a great deal of work and tender loving care to bring it back to its former glory and I was eager to take on the challenge.

Dave wasn't happy with my choice of house. I, on the other hand, was looking for another project – life was too predictable and monotonous for me. Dave was busy with his social life, the children had theirs, and besides, this wasn't just a home for us to live in, it was an investment. Once I had renovated it, it would be worth so much more than we'd paid for it. I'd always done the painting and decorating around the house since we were married, and it was something I now enjoyed doing. This was something my father had taught me to do and besides, it kept me occupied in the evenings . If, when it was finished, I found it hard financially, I could sell it for a profit – I decided *it's like money in the bank*. I couldn't believe my luck – within one month we moved into my dream home.

Mildred and her husband were a lovely couple. They helped us shift our furniture in and insisted on calling in now and again to see if there was anything about the house that might need explaining or that they could give me some help with. Mildred became a friend.

Mildred and Charles were moving into a smaller house and didn't need all the furniture that Mrs Martin had left. They had sold any pieces of value but made me an offer – if they paid for a rubbish skip, would I tip what I didn't want into that. I was only too eager to do this, as I could see that a lot of what she was leaving could be saved and restored.

We moved into the house on a Saturday and the children thought it was great fun ringing the bells in every room. The front and back doorbell sounded the same as the other room bells and so each time a bell was heard, there would be a race to the butler's pantry to see if it was the front or back doorbell or one of the children playing in a room.

"Will you cut it out!" I kept shouting, hoping they'd soon get over the novelty, but I often joined in the fun of the bells, and we worked out signals for what we wanted. "'cos I'm the lady of the house, if I want breakfast in bed in the morning, I will ring the bell three times," I laughed, "or if I just want a cup of tea I'll ring once."

"Yes!" said Gary and Sharon-Louise. "If we just want a drink at night when we're in bed, we'll ring it once, but if we don't feel well, we'll ring it twice."

We all thought the bells were lovely and I took each of them down and polished them until they shone. I revarnished the plaque and we all pointed the bells out to every visitor.

The attic was my favourite place when we first moved in. I spent my time sorting through old papers and magazines that littered the floor, but I felt like an intruder, reading through private letters and official transactions for three generations of an entire family. It was exciting to me, but it also seemed wrong. It was a peculiar feeling. Amongst the debris was a small painting – approximately twelve inches by eighteen inches – of a woman in her late teens or early twenties. She had a very pleasant face, slim and what seemed like thin, short, blonde hair. The most extraordinary thing about this painting were her eyes. They had been painted so perfectly and directly in the centre of the sockets, that no matter which angle one looked at the painting, her eyes seemed to look back at you. It was obviously an amateur painting, but I felt it must have been somebody that had lived in the house, so I thought it should be brought down and hung on the wall.

"What for?" grumbled Dave when he saw it. "We don't know the woman and it's not even a good painting. Get it off the wall!"

"But perhaps she lived here," I said. "And she might like to see how we progress with the renovation." I smiled. "Anyway, please leave it there until Mildred calls. She might know who it is. I just feel that it should be hanging on the wall."

"You're crazy, you are," Dave snapped and tried to ignore the painting that seemed to peer at everyone that came into the room. "It gives me the willies," he often said, but I took no notice. It was going to stay there, at least until I found out who she was.

On the first Wednesday in this house, I was woken by the sound of a bell. I looked at the clock. It was 5.45 a.m. *Who on earth is ringing the doorbell at this time of the morning?* I thought.

Getting out of bed, I looked through the bedroom window down at the porch where it was possible to see any visitors if there were any. Nobody was there.

That's funny! If it's one of those two messing about with the bells at this time of the morning, I'll have a few words to say to them.

I grabbed my dressing gown and marched down to Gary's room. Gary, being the practical joker, would think it was funny to do this. I opened his door ready to tell him off, only to see him fast asleep. I looked around the room and everything was in its place. It obviously wasn't him. I closed the door and walked

131

down to Sharon-Louise's room. She was fast asleep. Closing the door, I thought *I must put a heater in that room, it's freezing in there.* I looked into each of the other bedrooms and there was no sign of anything unusual. I went downstairs and looked around the house and found everything in order. Eventually I stood looking at the bells in the butler's pantry, wondering if perhaps I had imagined the sound of the bell.

After some minutes, I went back to bed and snuggled back down for another hour, deciding it had been my imagination. We'd all been playing around with the bells so much over the last few days that I must have been dreaming of them.

Nevertheless, when Dave awoke, I told him about being woken at 5.45 a.m. by the doorbell. "Yes, I thought I heard the doorbell," he said, then drank his coffee and went off to work. The kids also confirmed they had heard a bell ringing in the night. I knew then that it was neither a dream nor my imagination.

That evening, I rang Jesse and told her about this incident and what a peculiar feeling I had about it.

"It's probably the paperboy," she said.

"But I haven't ordered a paper yet," I replied.

"Oh, you know what these little buggers are like. Because your bell is so unusual, he probably rode down your drive just to give it a pull. It was probably the highlight of his mornin', wakin' somebody else up," she said.

"Yes, you're probably right. Well he'd better cut it out because if he does it again, I'll give 'im a thick ear."

I then put the matter out of my head.

The following Wednesday morning I was awoken again by the bell at 5.45 a.m. I immediately nudged Dave. "Did you hear that!" I said.

Dave shifted in the bed.

"Did you hear the bell going, Dave?"

He pulled the covers up under his chin and said sleepily, "Yes Paul, go an' see who it is."

I jumped out of bed and hurried to the window again. *Little devil*, I thought. *I'll catch him.* The porch was again quite empty. The front gates were closed. I opened the window to peer down the road to see where the paper boy was. *He must have moved pretty fast*, I thought. He was nowhere to be seen. I closed the window and did the rounds of the house. Everything was just as it should be. Again, I stood looking at the bells in the butler's pantry. *This is weird. One of those bells definitely rang. It had to be the front doorbell.*

I made a cup of tea and sat thinking how I could find out who was ringing the bell at that time in the morning.

I'll get in touch with the local newsagency and explain what is happening and perhaps they would put a flea in this lad's ear.

Waiting until 6.30 a.m., I rang the shop and explained that perhaps one of their boys was playing a prank every Wednesday morning.

"Not our boys, luv," said the owner. "They're not even 'ere yet. Our boys don't start 'til 6.30 a.m."

Dave got up for work and again confirmed that he'd heard the doorbell. Gary and Sharon-Louise both came down the stairs and said they too had heard the doorbell ringing that morning.

That evening I mentioned to Dave that I thought it was a bit spooky, but he had a logical explanation for it. "I think it's a short in the electric wiring."

"I thought the bells weren't electric?" I answered.

"No," said Dave, "but the bell pulls probably run along the same track as the electric wiring and it only needs a break in the cable, and it will set the bell off."

I knew Dave was trying to find an excuse as much for himself as me because if there was anything spooky in this house, he didn't want to believe it. Any talk of something spiritual made him angry.

The following Wednesday morning I set my alarm for 5.30 a.m. Settling myself in the butler's pantry, I made myself a cup of tea and waited, determined not to take my eyes off the bells until I saw which one rang. The hands of the clock were just descending on 5.45 a.m. when one bell began to ring. *OMG!!!* The shock as it went off set my nerves jangling.

It's the front bedroom! Sharon-Louise's room. I ran out of the butler's pantry and scaled the stairs two at a time. Grabbing the door handle of her room, I threw it open. A cold blast of air hit me. Sharon-Louise had been asleep in her bed on the other side of the room away from the bell. And I'd just woken her.

"What's happening?" she said sleepily, objecting to her sleep being disturbed.

"It's kksy, luv. I'm just putting you in the spare bed for a while." I carried her into the spare bedroom and tucked her in, then went back to her room where the temperature must have been two or three degrees. I looked around but there was nothing except the feeling I was not alone. I picked up her blanket and placed it around me and sat on the bed.

"It's all right," I began to say, "we are going to look after your house – you'll be pleased with it when I've finished, I promise you. We won't harm anything; we'll put it back just the way it used to be when you lived in it. I want my family to be happy in this house and with you still around you could frighten them, so please, would you go now. You can move on, I promise you I'll look after your home."

I sat talking like this for a few minutes until the temperature of the room started to rise again.

Walking out of the room and down the stairs, I felt I was in a trance. *What made me do that?* I wondered. As I made a cup of tea, I knew I would have to see Mildred. I needed some answers. At 7.30 a.m. I rang Mildred and invited her around for morning tea on Saturday.

That evening I convinced Sharon-Louise that one of the other bedrooms would be better because her little room was too cold and so we spent that evening before her bedtime moving her into another room.

After the children were in bed, I tried to talk to Dave and explain the feeling in the room, that I felt I wasn't alone there.

"You exaggerate everything you do," was his reply. "I've told you, it's the wiring. I think you should have the house rewired cause if it's bad, it could start a fire. You'd better get that done first before anything else." Then he growled, "an' get rid of that bloody paintin'." He took it down and placed it on the floor facing the wall. I waited until he went to the pub and walked over to the painting and turned it around to face into the room again.

"Sorry about that," I said to the painting. "He doesn't understand," and hung her back on the wall.

Mum hadn't seen the house yet and was coming to visit during the evening on Friday while Dave was at the pub. I'd mentioned the bells when I'd telephoned her but not with any significance. That Friday evening I explained to Mum the happenings of the bells since we'd moved in. She listened attentively, then after a few minutes she stood, straightened her spine and held her head high with her eyes shifting around before she answered;

"I can feel her presence, Pauline. It's a female and yes, I think it's the old dear that used to live here." She stopped talking then and walked around the ground floor of the house before she said, "She herself is not to be feared. She was a good person and can't settle until something is completed that is keeping her here on this spiritual plane. I can't quite make out what it is that's keeping her here, only that she's givin' me the impression she needs to tidy up this earthly problem so others will not be hurt; she will then move on. If you aren't able to help her to complete her life here and she's still around in a month or so, I'll come over and chat to her and help her move on."

Saturday morning arrived and Mildred came bustling in. "Oh, it's luvly t'come back inter this ouse again," she said.

I had started to strip the awful British Rail Yellow paint from the hall woodwork, and I'd discovered Charles had worked for British Rail so must have acquired the paint at a 'bargain price!' Mildred seemed disappointed that "all er 'usband's ard werk" was being eradicated. Still, she tried not to show too much disappointment and settled herself down in the morning room and started to talk about her new house and how easy it was to clean after the years she'd cleaned Mrs Martin's house.

She was a joy to listen to. Her new posh 'ouse was a real step up in the world for her.

"It must have been hard for you," I said, "when Mrs Martin needed twenty-four-hour attention. You couldn't have a day off, could you?"

"That's right, luv, it was 'ard. It's just as well I'm a strong woman, cos she wouldn't move out o' that little front bedroom an I 'ad to run up an' down them stairs all day an' all night."

I felt something stir in my gut.

"I wanted er t'go in the front parlour, I could ave put a bed in there fer er, an' fer me, but no, she still ad all er faculties right t' the end ye' know. 'Don't put me downstairs, Mildred luv,' she said to me. Oh, she knew all right. So, I ad t'run up an' down, up an' down, day an' night. She would ring that bell an' I'd be off. She wouldn't ave anyone else look after er either, y'know. I tried t'get er 'ome 'elp just so's I could ave a bit of a break like, but she wouldn't ave no one else mess wiv 'er'."

"How long did that go on for, Mildred?" I said.

"Oh, nearly seven years, luv. I was real tired at the end an' I said to er, 'Look, Mammy,', cos that's what I used t'call er, ye see, 'Look, Mammy, I've got t'ave a bit of a break with me own family. I'll get me sister in t'look after ye just for a few days.' I nagged fer ages till she said okay, an' I got our Hilda t'come an' take over while me an' Charles an' the kids went t' Rhyl fer seven days. But it didn't werk out, did it? I only went on the Saturday an' our Hilda rang me on the Tuesday mornin' and said, 'Look, our Mildred, yer'd berra get back ere, she's goin fast. I don't think she's gunna last the week.' So, I was back on the train an' left Charles an' the lads down there, but it was just as well I came 'ome cos that night a' could see she was a gonna. I sat with er all night till she ventually went t'sleep. She talked that night about bein' a little girl ere, an' all about er past. She didn't ave any pain, she jus' wanted t'talk to me, an' I could see tha' so I didn't mind lettin' 'er rabbit on. When she went t'sleep I tucked er up an' I ad a bit of a kip in the chair in 'er room. Well! She woke up an' didn't see me an' rang that bell an' I said, 'It's okay, Mammy, I'm 'ere!' as I wrapped my arms around 'er. She jus' looked at me an' said, 'Oh Mildred, luv,', an' that was it. She jus' died in me arms. I'm real glad I came 'ome when I did."

I felt my chest go tight and a tingling sensation ran right through my body. "What time was that, Mildred?" I asked.

"Oh, it was exactly quarter t'six, luv. I remember that cos the nurse that used t'call an' see er said when it 'appened, I ad t'know the exact time t'tell the doctor, fer the death certificate."

Mrs Martin had died in Sharon-Louise's room on a Wednesday morning at 5.45 a.m. I was stunned for a moment and didn't know what to say next. I got up from my chair.

"Another cup of tea Mildred?" I needed to do something for a few moments. Mildred chatted on about Mrs Martin, or Mammy as she called her, and I listened while I made another pot of tea. Before I sat down again, I went to the lounge and fetched the painting I had found in the attic.

"Look at this, Mildred. Do you know who this is? I found it in the attic."

"Oh! My lord, it's Mammy as a young girl. She did that 'erself. In 'er younger years she fancied 'erself as a bit of an artist, she did."

That seemed the final link. Yes, Mrs Martin was still in the house. I didn't know enough about this sort of thing, and I didn't know how I was going to release her to the next spiritual plane; I only knew I had to try. I felt no fear about her spirit being here. Mum had told me she was not an evil person, and it must have been a happy house, so somehow I knew, when the time was right, Mrs Martin would depart. Mum also said there'd be a reason for her lingering for a while. I had to find out what that was.

Paint scrapers were left in the hall beside the phone and if anyone was talking on the phone, I asked that they scrape the yellow paint off the walls as they chatted. It was a massive job and a slow procedure, so I had a couple of projects on at the same time. The out-houses were cleared out, mainly by Dave, and the furniture that I felt could be saved was collected in one corner for the day I had enough money to get an antique restorer in. There was a large wooden cupboard in the out-houses that Mildred and Charles had used to store paint tins and tools. The two doors to the top half of the cabinet were hanging by one screw and they had, at one time, had glass in them. The shelves were covered in paint and had various uniform shaped notches cut into them which obviously had been purposely created for the use of this cabinet. The bottom cupboard opened to a series of narrow drawers, which Charles had kept screws and nails in, and they were lined in green felt which was well worn. The whole thing stood about eight feet tall. Dave kept saying he was going to take the axe to it, but I kept pleading with him not to.

"I think it could be done up, Dave. Please don't break it up. We need all the furniture we can get for this big house. If it was done up, perhaps it could go in the hall when it's finished. Plus,

I think it could be valuable." But the out-houses were Dave's project as he talked about a pool room being created there and he was impatient to clear this area. I knew I would have to move fast, or it would be firewood.

That night I rang an antique restorer and asked him to come and have a look at the out-house cabinet to see how much it would cost to restore and if it was worth it. He arrived the next night with his son and was intrigued by the piece of furniture and said he would love to have a go at restoring it.

"I'll look through my books and let you know more about it, but the wood is definitely ebony," he said. "It'll cost a hundred pounds to restore it." I told him to take it there and then. I didn't know where I was going to get the money from, but I would think of something. The restorer rang me back a few days later and announced it was a gun cabinet, built around the late 1700s in Germany. He was enthusiastic about bringing it back to its former glory. This spurred me on to get this awful paint off the woodwork in the hall where I thought I'd place the gun cabinet when it was restored.

That weekend I gathered the best of a few of the pieces of furniture and antique bric-a- brac that had been left in the out-houses and took them down to an antique/secondhand shop. I was most surprised at the prices I got for some of them, and I managed to get the full one hundred pounds it would cost to restore the gun cabinet. Dave hadn't noticed anything missing from the pile in the corner and hadn't even asked where the cabinet was after it was removed. This made it easier to stash the money without his knowledge, avoiding him asking for some of that cash.

Six weeks was the time it would take to restore the cabinet and I worked hard on the house in this time, clearing the front dining room and stripping the wallpaper off the walls. I also uncovered the beautiful inglenook fireplace in there. This was done under the watchful eye of Mrs Martin. I had hung her painting on the wall in the dining room where Dave couldn't see her. It became a normal procedure for me to talk to Mrs Martin. I knew she was still around but doing no harm and I kept her informed of all that was going on around the house.

"Well, Mrs Martin, I've sent your gun cabinet off to be restored. Where do you want me to put it when it returns, eh?" I would look at her painting and chat away like that as I worked in the room and on many evenings when I was alone. As I was stripping the paint from the hall walls, there appeared a large dark shaped area on the wood panelling. The gun cabinet had the same shape along the top of it so had obviously sat there during its life in the house, and I climbed down from the ladder and walked into the dining room.

"So that's where you want ye cabinet to go eh?" I said to the painting. "That's okay with me," and Mrs Martin would just look back.

I continued happily scraping paint and decorating the dining room over the next few weeks. The bells had stopped ringing on Wednesday mornings because I had asked Mrs Martin not to do it.

"I know you're here now, Mrs Martin, so there's no need for that racket every Wednesday announcing your presence and waking us all up," I told the painting.

While I worked, there were many times a feeling would come over me as though somebody was breathing and looking over my shoulder and the hair on the back of my neck would rise and I would begin to talk to her. "Well, what do you think of it so far eh? Am I doing it to your satisfaction? You'll let me know if I'm not, won't you?"

I had accepted Mrs Martin into my life, and she gave me a curious sense of companionship.

Moving into this house meant my friends Jesse and Jenny

lived within walking distance of me. Our houses were all from the Victorian era in England and we had each bought houses that needed renovations. At least once a month on a Saturday we haunted the junk, secondhand and antique shops in Liverpool city looking for bargains to restore and place in our houses.

On this Saturday, we were at the end of an unsuccessful trip to Liverpool and decided to visit one last shop before we went home. As we walked in, Jenny said, pointing, "Look at that!"

It was a fire surround that stood about five feet high, of solid oak with the uprights being carved bull's heads with rusted brass rings through their noses. The mantle shelf was almost five inches deep and the whole thing was covered in dirty green peeling paint!!

Jesse and I couldn't see the beauty in this immediately, but during the time we watched Jenny haggle until she was happy with the price, it began to grow on us.

The shop owner knew us and said, "The guys are leaving shortly for your neck of the woods should I throw it on the truck now?"

"Oh yes, please" said Jenny. "John may not be home but just leave it leaning up against the side of the garage."

"Will do, luv, but tell yer 'usband he'll need another burley bloke to help him get it indoors as it took three men to move it into the shop."

We went for an early dinner and sipped our first glass of wine as we listened to Jenny's excited chatter about how she would restore the fire surround. We then drove home, and all walked through Jenny's gate to look at this fire surround again just as John her husband came out the front door. "Did you buy this fire surround, Jenny?"

"Yes, isn't it wonderful? When I've restored it, we can put it in our front lounge!" Jenny said with great excitement.

"No, we can't, Jenny. I've never seen anything so ugly. You'd better ring them and tell them to collect it on Monday – it's not coming into our house. I'm going for a pint with the lads, cover it over before the neighbours see it. You are definitely losing it, Jenny!!" And off he went.

Jenny was so upset as we walked into the house and down the hall to the kitchen where she opened a bottle and poured us each our second glass of wine. We sat around the kitchen bench consoling Jenny until Jesse said, "I wonder what it will look like in my hall?"

"Oh yes, Jesse. Let's get it over to your house before John comes home then he won't nag me all weekend."

So, we swigged our second glass of wine and went out – hauled this heavy fire surround onto our shoulders and began tottering toward Jenny's gate.

"No, we can't do this, Jenny. It's too heavy for us," I shouted. "It took three men to lift it into the shop remember – we can't do it."

"Oh yes we can. Women can do anything, Pauline. Where's ye gumption?" Jenny said as we shuffled along tripping over each other's feet. Then Jenny shouted, "STOP! We need a marching song to keep us all in sync. When I shout 1, 2, 3 lift, we begin singing – Hey Ho – Hey Ho it's off to work we go." And the laughter began. Singing like the seven dwarfs, we took off along the street to Jesse's house.

"Put it down, put it down," one of us would shout as we stopped for breath and screamed with laughter, then off we'd go again.

"Hey Ho! Hey Ho!" until we eventually reached Jesse's gate. Just as we opened it, her husband Jack came out of the front door.

"I've been listening to you lot coming down the street. What on earth are you up to?" he said with a smile.

"Jenny bought this fire surround, Jack, but John didn't like it so I thought we'd have it and replace the one in our hall," Jesse announced.

"Well, you thought wrong, Jesse. That is not coming into this house."

"But it's solid oak, Jack."

"I don't care if it's solid gold; get rid of it – it's not living in our house. Don't you dare take it in … I'm going for a pint with John."

We all now felt dejected as we leaned the fire surround against Jesse's gate and walked behind her into the kitchen. She opened the fridge and took out a bottle and poured us all our third glass of wine.

"Men!" we all decried them and their lack of vision, that they can't see a thing of beauty until its restored. We sipped our wine as we discussed how useless men were and eventually, I said, "Perhaps it will look okay in my dining room!"

"Yes, let's take it up there," they both agreed, and we swigged the last of our wine before we took off once again.

Now we were beginning to think this was a great game as we carried this very heavy fire surround along the footpath to my house, a little more squiffy now but singing all together. "Hey Ho – Hey Ho, put it down, put it down," we screamed with laughter.

Jenny again shouted, "Okay, on the count of three. One two three … lift. Hey Ho! Hey Ho! It's off to work we go, Dee dum dee dum dee dum … Hey Hooo! Hey Ho!"

The journey had now become part of the fun as we eventually walked through my front door and straight into my dining room and placed it against the chimney wall. We all collapsed onto the dining chairs. We were quiet for a few seconds, so exhausted that our faces were blood red with the strain and sweat poured down our faces. Once I recovered, I went to the kitchen and poured us each our fourth glass of wine.

We all sat quietly looking at the fire surround until Jenny and Jesse found their voices again and began saying how wonderful it would look when I'd restored it. But by now, I was peering at it and trying hard to visualise it restored and in place. I didn't like what I saw, so eventually announced:

"I don't like it – it's ugly and I don't want it."

They both turned and stared at me then we all burst out laughing. We were choking on this laughter when Jenny shouted, "Why didn't you stop me from buying it – it's the ugliest thing I've ever seen!"

Nobody wanted the fire surround, so we swigged our fourth glass of wine and off we went again to put it back beside Jenny's garage for the dealer to collect the following week.

"Hey Ho, Hey Ho, drop it, drop it." Between screams of laughter, Jenny tried to keep us in step and constantly shouted "on the count of three," as we weaved our way back to Jenny's house. It was now nearly midnight – bedroom lights were coming on and net curtains were peered around, neighbours wanting to see what these three women were noisily doing carrying an old wooden fire surround through the neighbourhood.

Were we embarrassed by our behavior? – No!

Would we have done it if we hadn't had all the wine? Probably not.

Are we sorry we did it? Never.

We still laugh about that night, and we can take that memory with us to the grave.

(So go out and do something silly – it's worth it!)

Jesse was almost as keen to see the return of the gun cabinet as I was. On the day of its scheduled return, she arrived with a bottle of wine. "I've brought this around to toast the return of Mrs Martin's gun cabinet," she said.

Everybody that knew me now referred to the gun cabinet as Mrs Martin's. We sat in the dining room at the front of the house looking through the window and opened the bottle of wine.

"We'll just have one glass each now," said Jesse and we sat in front of Mrs Martin's painting and placed the cork firmly back on the half bottle of wine.

We chatted for some time until the noise from the truck engine came from outside and we both looked through the window. "It's here!" I shouted; and the cork immediately popped out of the bottle. Jesse stared in shock and amazement.

"It's alright," I laughed. "It's Mrs Martin letting us know she's celebrating with us."

The gun cabinet was carried into the hall and placed where Mrs Martin had indicated it once sat. It was a truly impressive object and the man who had restored it came with it to see my reaction to his work.

"What a beautiful job you've made of it!" I exclaimed. And that was true. He had restored the cabinet perfectly according the picture he showed me. But the gun cabinet dominated my beautiful hall. There was no doubt it was a magnificent example of early craftsmanship, and a truly impressive piece of furniture, but it was far too big and black and ugly for this hall.

It stood there, dark and depressing, dominating my beautiful hall. Black and shiny but ominous – it had to go. No wonder Mildred and Charles had put it outside.

"But where will you put it then?" Jesse asked.

"I've got no idea," I said, "and I'm not sure I can get rid of it because Mrs Martin has been looking forward to its return."

Dave came home and stared in disgust at the huge, black, dominating piece of furniture.

"You can get rid of that. I'm not having that in the house. It's bloody awful," he shouted.

That night while Dave was out, I went into the dining room

to talk to Mrs Martin. "Well, I've restored it for you, Mrs Martin, but you must admit it is a bit over the top, isn't it? I need to know if you'd mind if I sold it and it went to a good home, somewhere it could stand in splendour in a much larger hallway than this and be appreciated for its beauty. I wish I knew how you feel about this because I don't want to upset you if I sold it, but I think it's got to go." I sat and stared at Mrs Martin and turned the situation over in my head. I then rang Mum.

"Stay focused and confident, still accepting Mrs Martin around you. I believe that cabinet is somehow part of the resolve to release Mrs Martin. Feel no fear and be open to anything you feel while you're around that cabinet and she'll come up with the answer soon," was all Mum said.

Dave came home from the pub that night and I began to tell him I would get a valuation on the gun cabinet.

"I'm not sure about selling it though," I said dreamily. "I mean, it belonged to Mrs Martin, and it has more right to be in the house than us."

Dave exploded into one of his rages.

"I think you've gone crazy altogether now, woman. What do you mean it's got more right to be here than us? What a stupid statement. It's our bloody house!" he roared as he stepped toward me. "You'd better stop this Mrs Martin business – all the lads in the pub know about it. You're making me a laughingstock. Now, get a valuation and get rid of the bloody thing." He said this in anger right up close to my face, which would normally be the start of one of his vicious attacks. A table lamp that had belonged to Mrs Martin, which now sat on the table beside his chair, began to flicker on and off. We both went quiet and stared at it for a while. I could feel Mrs Martin's presence and I felt he could too. His anger took a turn of direction as if he knew Mrs Martin was watching him.

"You see … the wiring needs doing in this house," he

muttered and left the room and went to bed.

Staring at the lamp, I said "What are you trying to tell me, Mrs Martin? Are you agreeing or disagreeing with Dave? I still don't know what to do."

I sat quietly making plans for the next day. "I'll ring a valuer, but I'd better ring an electrician as well to shut Dave up."

The antique valuer could not come to see the gun cabinet until Saturday, but the electrician said he could come and check the house the following evening and give me a price for rewiring.

Just as I arrived home from work, the electrician arrived at the front door. "Whara luvely 'ouse" he said as I let him in the porch door. "Where's yer lecky box, luv?"

"It's under the stairs in the hall there," I said, pointing to the electric cupboard beside the gun cabinet.

"Jesus Christ, what a bloody monstrosity," he said in shock. "I'm sorry, luv, it's probably a family heirloom or sumthin' eh. It's a luvely bir of furniture to be sure, but never made fer this 'ouse, eh! Mus be bir 'ard t'live with!"

I knew it had to go. I just hoped Mrs Martin understood.

The electrician checked the wiring and announced, "It's lucky you called me, luv. The stuff in this 'ouse is ancient. Ye could 'ave a fire anytime. Yer don't 'ave t'accept my quote, luv, bur I'd get this lot done as quick as yer can. I'll werk out yer quote an' ring yer t'morrow."

That sounded expensive, I thought. *Still, to be on the safe side I'll ring a couple more electricians and get more opinions.* They all said the same, that the wiring was dangerous and should be replaced right away. The quotes started to come in and the average cost of replacing the wiring was fifteen hundred pounds. This was a huge amount of money to have to find and I began thinking I would have to get another loan.

Saturday morning arrived and the antique valuer rang the doorbell. "Good morning. Pendray's the name, from Antique

Valuations. This is my assistant, Graham."

I asked them in. The gun cabinet now looked so ugly to me, I was embarrassed to be asking an expert on antique furniture to be even looking at this monstrosity. He ummed and ah'd and scratched his head.

"Has anybody else given you a valuation on it, luv?"

"No," I said. "I've got no idea how much it's worth. I'm not even sure if I even want to sell it. I've recently bought the house and that cabinet belongs to it, you see. I just thought I'd better find out if it was worth anything," I stuttered through various explanations of why I might sell it and why perhaps I shouldn't sell it and knew I was sounding like a complete idiot. I was worried about Mrs Martin because the dining room door was open and she was hanging there listening to every word. Mr Pendray lowered his head with his hand under his chin obviously thinking it through, then looked up at the ceiling, then straight at me for a few seconds until he said:

"Look, luv, I've been looking for one of these to send to a client in Germany. That's where this cabinet was made. I'll give yer fifteen hundred pounds for it if yer'll sell it to me an' let me take it here and now," and he produced a wad of notes from inside his jacket.

My jaw dropped. I stared at Mr Pendray in total shock.

"Well, what do you say?" He smiled for the first time.

I regained my composure and walked straight past him and into the dining room and looked at Mrs Martin hanging on the wall. "Thanks, Mrs Martin," I said. "Now I understand," and I kissed my fingers and placed them on Mrs Martin's lips.

I turned to Mr Pendray who looked totally bewildered. "It's yours." I smiled and threw my arms around him and gave him a hug. My mystery had been solved and I had to hug somebody.

Mr Pendray and his assistant lifted the gun cabinet into his van and I immediately rang the first electrician.

"You've got the job if you can do it right away," I said. "I've got the money."

Mrs Martin had paid for the rewiring. The cost of restoration of the cabinet was paid for by the sale of pieces of antique furniture and bric-a- brac that were left in the house, and the wiring was paid for by the sale of the restored gun cabinet.

Over the next few days, I realised that I didn't feel Mrs Martin anywhere. I often went to look at the painting, but her eyes didn't seem as penetrating. I couldn't feel her looking over my shoulder anymore and I felt that Mrs Martin had completed her task and had moved on.

I missed her.

Chapter Thirteen

Battles won and lost

1980 - 1982

The job I held with Exide Batteries paid me very well. I had been
with them now for approximately eight years and had won many
awards for top salesperson and other achievements. My boss
was a great guy who took an interest in me as a person and,
without knowing too much about my marriage, he somehow had
an instinct when things were going wrong for me. I was excited
about my 'new' house and asked if I could add another customer
so I could earn more money to do further renovations.

"Leave it with me," he said. "I'll sort it."

I was well known in the industry and well liked. I had my
regulars that looked forward to my visits and chats.

Phil was the company's biggest customer; he owned five large
service stations. They wanted him to be well looked after and so
he was given to me and, of course, I waited on him hand and
foot. I had even been invited to his 40th birthday party.

"Bring your husband," Phil said. "It's this Saturday at 7pm -
here's the address."

"Yer not goin'," Dave said when I told him. "You're invited
as well, Dave; I must go as he's our biggest customer." We
argued about it all week as I couldn't back down. I had
convinced him I had to be there but there was no way he would

let me go alone, so eventually he reluctantly agreed to call in with me for an hour and then we'd leave. That was okay with me – an hour with Dave around people he didn't know was long enough. He would be uncomfortable and so would I. But at least I would have attended and with my husband which would get out around the industry. My many industry awards had been at dinners which I'd attended alone. I knew people were beginning to think my husband was imaginary.

Dave started drinking at the pub at lunchtime. He came home irritated. As I drove to the party, he began making statements …

"I suppose he's ye boyfriend, eh! Is that why you need to be there? Are ye 'avin' an affair with him?"

"Don't start that, Dave; he's a customer and Exide don't want him upset in any way."

"Don't start pullin' the wool over my eyes, ye know. Nobody makes a bloody arsehole out of me in front of people." And on he went building his anger as we approached the house.

Phil welcomed us in and we were shown into his games room that had a full bar down one side of the room. He stepped behind the bar and asked what we would like to drink. "Thanks, Phil. I'll have a gin and tonic if you have that," I replied.

"And you, Dave?" he asked, smiling at Dave.

Dave hesitated and I looked at him, at his vicious grin and the scowling eyes. *Oh my God*, I thought, *this is going to be a short visit.* My anxiety soared!

"A pint!" He spat his request as though it was an order.

Phil poured our drinks as he began a conversation and even asked Dave what his work was. Dave didn't answer but leered at him. Phil placed his beer in front of him and Dave swilled some of it and stepped backwards away from us down the bar. Phil and I began chatting and we both tried hard to involve Dave, but he would pick up his beer, have a drink as he stepped backwards and placed it back on the bar further away from us again. He was taking himself out of our chat zone. The glass was beginning to be banged back down on the bar and just as I felt I had to plan to get him out quickly, it was too late.

He picked up his glass and threw it against the wall at the back of the bar. In two swift steps, he reached over and grabbed Phil and head butted him, growling, "Nobody makes a fuckin' fool out of me, mate."

Phil's guests all moved quickly and grabbed Dave, held his hands behind his back as they frogmarched him to the front door. He fought, swore and attempted to free himself, as he abused everyone there. I kept apologising to everyone around us but of course it fell on deaf ears as Phil stood staring in shock. I grabbed my bag and coat and followed the crowd as they opened the door and threw Dave out, then they turned to see me and threw me out after him.

Our car was parked against the walkway on the main road, and I ran toward it as I retrieved the keys from my bag. As I opened the driver's door to get in, Dave was there and immediately grabbed me and flung me out of the way and into the centre of the road as he slid into the driver's seat. I ran around the car and opened the passenger door as I listened to him screaming, "Give me the fuckin' keys".

I sat in the passenger seat then handed him the keys as he leaned over me and opened my door and started kicking me to get me out of the car. I hung on to the door handle, trying not to fall onto the road. He began driving as he continued to scream at me to get out and kept kicking at me as he was driving. The car veered all over the road, and I knew we would have an accident if he carried on. Horns sounded as drivers became afraid. Then suddenly he stopped the car, clambered out and ran around to my side of the car, where he opened the door, pulled me out and threw me onto the grass verge and kicked me. Then he got back in the car and drove off. My coat and bag were still in the car. I began to walk home in high heel shoes, my spirit now entirely broken.

As I walked, I churned through various plans in my head. If I left the house with him in it, I would still be responsible for the mortgage on it as it was in my name. I thought of transferring the house into his name and walking away. It would mean taking the kids with me as he couldn't be trusted to care for them properly. Could I transfer the house into his name and then leave him there? If I lived elsewhere with the kids, would he leave me in peace? I knew he wouldn't as it still meant he'd lost his cash cow. He would crash his way into wherever I lived feeling it was his right. I knew I couldn't escape from this man. I walked like a zombie. It took me more than three hours. I felt dead inside.

Eventually I arrived home and let myself in with the set of keys I had hidden in the out-houses. I slept in the spare room. Sunday morning, we both ignored each other. Talking to this man was futile. He wasn't mentally sound enough for reasoning. I dragged myself through my day.

My name would now be mud in the industry. Exide had been such a good job and now I knew I would have to resign. I walked into my boss's office on Monday morning and he had already been informed of what had happened.

"I'm sorry, Bill, but I'll have to resign. I would suggest you go out to see Phil and tell him another will be looking after him and please tell him how sorry I am."

He came from behind his desk and wrapped his arms around me. "You've been the best sales rep we've had in all the fourteen years I've run this franchise, Pauline. Of course, I understand you wouldn't be able to face them all now and I'm so sorry. I do think you should divorce that man, but that's your choice. I hope you get your life sorted properly, Pauline. You don't deserve to be treated as you are."

I gathered my possessions from my desk and walked away

from the best job I'd had so far in my life. And now how would I meet my family financial obligations without that job. The mortgage on my house had been given me by the bank based on the large salary I earned. Now I had no income.

Mentally, at this stage in my life, I shifted into acceptance. Fighting in the past had been futile. Having no way out of my situation rested heavily on my soul. Constantly talking to myself to avoid depression, acknowledging there were others in this world worse off than me, I had to just get on with it. But talking myself through these times to avoid depression was becoming futile.

I picked up some work doing the accounts for a couple of shops close by on Woodchurch Road. I once again told Dave he must now contribute as the mortgage needed to be paid. He began giving me a small amount each week but I knew he had probably taken it off a credit card. He had got away with that disastrous night at Phil's house only because I wasn't fit for fighting any more.

I became depressed and used my holiday pay to live on for a while as I tried to heal my mental health. Over the next two months, I spent every waking moment redecorating my house. As each room was completed, my spirits lifted a little. Dave never missed his nights out with his drinking pals and his weekends were now spent playing golf both days. All of this suited me. I didn't want him around me as I worked on my healing. He had started to mix with a wealthy group of people. He still gambled and now was frequenting the casinos more and I knew the plastic card was taking a hammering. Daily I waited for the bomb to drop, revealing how much his debts had climbed to. My holiday pay soon ran low even though I was trying to stretch it out.

I couldn't row with him anymore, as the only person that suffered from that was me. Warily, I tried explaining to him that he had an illness, and he must face up to it as his children and I were the ones suffering, not him. Even as I stated this I could see he wasn't listening.

A letter from New Zealand arrived from Matt who was coming home for a visit and this lifted my spirits somewhat. I began to plan for his stay. Ringing around my family, I announced that Christmas this year would be at my house, and it would be a large celebration for Matt's homecoming.

There would be seventeen of us and my dining table wasn't big enough, but Mum had an old gate leg table in her attic that we dusted off and put at the end of my table. It was slightly wobbly, but I placed cardboard under a couple of the legs and when the sheets were placed over the tabletops this couldn't be seen.

Christmas morning was always a routine that never changed. When the children had opened their presents, we would begin visiting friends and family and having a glass of Christmas cheer with them. This year, we collected those that needed a lift to my house and arrived home at 11a.m. Dave and the children entertained our guests as I busied myself in the kitchen cooking dinner.

At 3p.m. the meal was ready. The table looked lovely with my best china and crystal and Christmas decorations around it. I placed the vegetables in serving dishes and the turkey looked magnificent with little chef hats on the legs and holly around the serving plate. When I had finished placing it all on the table, I opened the lounge door and shouted, "It's out."

"Hurray!" they all exclaimed, and I looked at Dave who began to totter toward the door. He had been handing out drinks to our guests one by one as they entered the house and had one with each of them at the same time. As he swayed into the dining room, he decided that the table was slightly out of line and attempted to move it to straighten it up. The table closest to him was the old trestle table and, as he dragged it 'straight', it collapsed!! And because I had put a large sheet over both tables to make it look uniform, the sheet pulled the dishes from the other table as well and the whole dinner crashed onto the floor.

"No!" I cried as I saw what was happening. The silence in the house was deafening. All our guests stood staring at the dinner that was now on the floor smashed into broken pieces of china and crystal. Not one person moved a muscle, including me, as we didn't want to believe what we had just witnessed. Nobody could think of the right thing to say to me. Looks of disbelief went from the floor to me and back again. I stood like a statue staring at the floor. Dave kept lifting his shoulders and 'umphing' now and again with a pathetic grin on his face.

I picked the turkey up from the centre of the mess because I thought I could save that and turned and walked into the kitchen, closed the door and leaned against it.

How am I going to feed seventeen people? I thought as jumbled ideas began racing through my numb brain.

"Let me in, luv," my mother shouted from the other side of the door. "Let me in, Pauline."

"No, I'm all right, Mum. Leave me alone for a few minutes while I think how to feed everyone," I shouted back. "Could you please ask everyone to help clean up the mess."

"Are ye all right, luv?" she asked again.

"Yes, I'm fine, Mum - just clean the mess will you and put a clean sheet on the table again. I'll open some tinned vegies."

Standing for approximately two minutes to calm myself down, I then flung myself into action. Mum came in and gave me a hug. I fought with myself to not cry; I knew I had to keep thinking rationally.

"Use the every-day dishes in that cupboard, Mum" I said, and we once again put out a dinner on the tables. The turkey was delicious and, when everyone could see that I had survived the disaster, the jokes started to be bandied about and the disaster turned into an afternoon of laughter that everyone said would stand out as a Christmas day they would never forget.

When Matt went home, I began working again at Lever Brothers in Port Sunlight on the production lines. I needed to keep our heads above water with all the debts Dave was incurring. I had always been a healthy person with a great deal of energy, but my health was now beginning to deteriorate. My days were spent with work and my nights were working at home and living in fear as my body began to break down.

In my exhaustion, I visited the doctor who sent me for tests on everything. The results came in one by one and one morning I wearily opened the post which held a letter from the hospital.

"I've got cancer," I mouthed the words and looked at Dave as I sat at the kitchen table with the letter from the hospital in front of me. Looking at it again, it said, 'cancer of the cervix' and I was being admitted next week for a cone biopsy. Dave stood looking at me and was quiet for a few moments, then said

"Well, it's not such a big thing these days, is it? They'll do the operation and cut it out and that's that! Look at me muther, she had cancer of the lung and she's okay now. There's no point in getting all bloody morbid about it," he said, slightly irritated.

I felt so alone. Here was something I had no control over and the one thing I needed right now was for someone to put their arms around me to share the helplessness and fear that had struck my soul. Everybody thought I was tough and could cope with anything that came my way. Now and again and at times like this I found it hard being me. I couldn't think past those words 'cancer of the cervix'. My eyes kept coming back to the words on the paper in front of me.

This can't happen to me. I'm Pauline, I'm invincible. This sort of thing happens to other people, not me.'

I had no tears, I didn't feel like crying. I was waiting to be woken up! I still wanted to believe that the hospital had made a mistake.

"Are ye goin' to ask me muther to stay while yer in hospital?" Dave eventually asked.

"Yes," I replied. "I'll call in and see her tomorrow," and in the distance I heard my children laughing as they approached the kitchen door. Quickly folding the letter, I placed it in my bag and said to Dave, "and don't say anything to the kids yet."

"Yer'll be alright, luv. Look at me. A couple of days rest in 'ospital will do yer good anyway," Dave's mum said, trying to comfort me. "Don't worry about the kids an' Dave. I'll come an' stay."

No sympathy there either, I thought. Perhaps my inner panic was overreacting to this news. A small operation, a week's rest and I would be back on my feet. Others were thinking this wasn't such a problem.

My mother's face squashed those thoughts when horror and fear struck her eyes. I couldn't bear that. Poor Mum, I had to make her see that it was nothing to worry about. Forcing my laughter, I said "Mum! Don't worry so much. Honestly, it's nothing these days. They see a slight chance that there might be something and they take you in and sort of scrape it away. It's a type of precaution really. It's not confirmed that I have cancer. Please don't worry, Mum, because I'm looking forward to the rest. I'll have a whole week in hospital and then I'll have two weeks off work. We can have days out when I get home. It'll be like a holiday to me."

I continued in this manner until her face regained its colour and I had talked her through her panic and assured her that there was nothing to worry about. "I'd like to say I'd mind the house and kids while yer in hospital, Pauline, but I won't be under the same roof as that man - ye know that, don't ye?"

"Yes, I do, Mum. Don't worry, his Mum said she'll stay with

them all."

By the time I was leaving, she had rallied around and so had I. I had done such a good job on my mother that I went home feeling 'I'm ready for this rest'.

For the next few days, I reorganised things around the house ready for Dave's mum to take over and packed a small suitcase. I went into The Women's Hospital in Liverpool the following Monday.

It was a teaching hospital, it said on the admission form. What that implied didn't sink into my mind with all I had to organise for my week away from home.

I was admitted firstly into an examination ward with eight cubicles that had narrow half beds with a back rest attached and curtains right around the bed, which was placed in the centre of the cubicle floor area. I was then asked to take off all my clothes from the waist down and put on a gown that tied at the back and only reached my hips.

"Sit on the bed, dear, lean back, and place your feet in these stirrups," the nurse directed. I complied. "The surgeon will be along to see you shortly," she explained and left me dangling.

The surgeon's voice could be heard in the other cubicles. The time ticked on as I dangled in the stirrups and gazed around the cubicle looking at the curtain all around me. *If I wasn't strapped up like this, I could read my book*, I thought, but my book was in my bag which was behind me.

As I lay back on the bed, I pushed the stirrups further up my calf to behind my knees which was more comfortable, my legs were dangling properly now. The minutes ticked by, and this gave me time to relax into this position and not feel the nakedness of my crotch so much, which was being bared to the world in a fashion that was not at all ladylike and had embarrassed me when the nurse first connected me to this contraption.

Swinging my legs around now I was reminded of the swing rings in the local park that I used to play on when I was a child. Slipping my bottom further down the half bed until it hung over the end, using the base of the bed to hold my back, and the back of the bed holding my head which forced my chin onto my chest, I dangled my arms over the side of the bed and decided that it was quite comfortable if I allowed the contraption to take my weight.

I could meditate in this position, I thought and dangled around quite enjoying myself now. *They could do with some music in this place to cover the surgeon's voice, he's booming everybody's personal history out for all to hear*, so I mentally blanked out his voice, and the minutes ticked by.

Slipping into a deep meditative state I was unaware of the time and where I was, when suddenly the curtain in front of me was swept aside and seven young men including the surgeon began peering straight into my nakedness. I stared in shock and wanted the floor to open up and swallow me. Quickly I shifted back up the bed as the surgeon began to introduce himself and each of his team, one by one. I wasn't listening, I was so embarrassed. He prodded and talked as though I wasn't there, and they each peered into my crotch. He said something about tying my tubes at the same time and I nodded, hoping if I agreed to everything they would quickly disappear. My face burned right throughout this time with them all. They eventually left. The examination must have only taken ten minutes, but it was the longest day of my life.

The ward I was admitted to had twelve beds in it and another woman was being admitted at the same time. We were both placed next to each other near the door as we had operations scheduled for the next day.

Flora, the other woman, talked in a very loud, wealthy, high-pitched voice that could be heard all over the ward. Flora was having her tubes tied because she didn't want to have children. She made a point of telling everyone in the ward that she was from fine stock, was paying privately for her operation and was disgusted that she had been placed in a public ward simply because she wanted that particular surgeon. Maggie, a patient in the bed opposite me, commented when Flora had left the ward to go to the toilet

"A don't know 'oo she frigin well thinks she is - 'er fanny must be surrounded by frigin mink. She can ger' off 'er bleedin' 'igh 'orse," and the laughter began.

Next morning the curtains were drawn around our beds as we were prepared for our operations by having a shave, with Maggie shouting she was putting a bid in for the mink as the curtains were drawn around Flora's bed. We were all trying hard not to let Flora hear but Maggie's wit continued and it was impossible in the end as the whole ward was in an uproar with poor Flora not knowing what it was all about.

Five minutes before we were trolleyed away, Flora took out her false teeth and her face collapsed. I quickly looked over at Maggie who had already seen the procedure because she was rolling about her bed laughing, moaning and holding her stomach where her stitches were. The belly laughter that was vibrating from Maggie was infectious.

"Ahhhhhh" she laughed trying to get her breath.

I was fighting to suffocate my laughter, but it was impossible, and it burst out in front of the sister who had come to give us injections.

"What's tickled your fanny?" said the sister and Flora looked at me and smiled. Flora's smile without her false teeth was something to behold and I thought I was going to choke on my laughter. Maggie had witnessed this and was rolling about on the bed by this time, shouting "Oh!! Frigin 'ell, I don't believe it." She was shaking and choking; we were uncontrollable and the more we laughed the more Flora smiled and the worse we became. We couldn't tell anyone what it was about – we couldn't even speak!! The sister put it down to pre-op nerves and gave me my injection while she laughed along with us but didn't know what she was laughing about.

"When you wake you will feel pain in your stomach," said the sister to both Flora and I. "Now this will be from the air that is trapped because you've been opened. If you can, try and bear the pain until it passes of its own accord, it's better for you, but if the pain is too much then let me know and I'll give you a laxative," she announced.

I awoke sometime later to Flora's moans. "The pain's unbearable," she shouted in her high-pitched duchess voice, spluttering through her toothless mouth. "I can't stand the pain any longer," she wailed.

"That doesn't bloody surprise me," I heard Maggie say. "She probably 'as an injection t'get 'er bleedin' toenails clipped."

As I lay there with the dummy in my mouth from the anaesthetic I began to laugh again at Maggie's comments. I literally did "spit the dummy."

The nursing sister arrived and drew the curtains around Flora and placed a laxative in her back passage. She was then lifted on to a metal bedpan. Within seconds the "wind" escaped into the bedpan and rattled it like a tommy gun, vibrating around the quiet ward. Flora shouted over the top of this noise in her high-pitched voice, "Oh! How awful! I'm so sorry, ladies. Oh! I'm so sorry," each time her farting ripped and rattled into the metal bedpan.

Maggie screamed with laughter all this time and shouted, "A said she was all frigin piss an' wind."

Flora made the most of her operation and removed her pillows and took her teeth out to make sure she looked ill when the doctor and her visitors called. We decided Flora lacked attention and being in hospital was the best thing that had happened to her for some time. I, on the other hand, missed my kids and having Dave's mum at home who would fuss over me for a few days, I was anxious to get out. Every day before the doctor's rounds I would put my make-up on and do my hair. Flora wouldn't do this in case she looked too healthy.

After three days, I plumped up my pillows and tidied my covers and sat up straight and folded my hands in front of me, waiting for the doctor to arrive. Flora took her pillows away and lay flat in a 'poor me, I'm still very sick' position. Maggie looked over and saw us both

"Oh Christ! Look at those two!" she screamed. "Worzel Gummidge and Aunt bleedin' Sally!" and she roared with laughter again. These two characters were popular on TV at the time, dressed as a scarecrow and a painted doll. I could see what she was laughing at – the scarecrow would be Flora who wouldn't comb her hair as she might look too healthy and, for me, my complexion was still very pale after the anaesthetic, and I'd put a bit too much blusher on my pale cheeks trying to look healthy.

"Oh, for God's sake, shut up, Maggie," I said, but not really wanting her to. Her laughter was infectious, her comments hilarious and, by the time the doctor arrived, I was kneeling on the floor leaning over a chair holding my stitches around my stomach, convulsed with laughter. My mascara had run into my painted cheeks giving Maggie more fuel for her wit.

"I don't think there's much wrong with you," was all he said as he smiled.

On Friday, I was given the results.

"We've taken the neck of the womb away and tied your tubes as a precautionary measure," the surgeon informed me. "Your periods will probably be heavier in the future, and I would like you to have regular checks for us to keep an eye on it, but it might never flare up again." He assured me I had nothing to worry about and so I never worried. I had too much living to do to be worried about what might never happen.

I was released after a week of laughing that was better than any medication or any holiday I had ever had. A whole week of being cared for and not having to worry, and it hadn't cost me a penny! It was all on the National Health Service.

I decided a 'Maggie' should be planted in every hospital ward.

Dave's mum stayed with me for another week, and I enjoyed the fussing she gave me. It was lovely to be on the receiving end of somebody caring for me and I wallowed in every minute of it. When she left, I began catching up with all the accounts and happenings of the last few weeks.

As I was checking to see if Dave had done anything in the out-houses while I was away, I firstly found a letter from the bank acknowledging the change of title on the house. I could see he had his name placed on the title with mine and was then able to use it for security in borrowing money for gambling. I found statements from various places demanding payments immediately and these had been hidden in drawers in old cupboards. Frantically, as I gathered them together and totalled them up, I could see this was the end. I was drowning under the debts Dave had gathered. My head was in so much pain, my stomach began churning and tying itself into a knot. My spirit knew this was the beginning of the end and a big change in our lives.

My temper exploded as soon as he walked in the door. I screaming at him about what he had done, and he had bellowed back that I was a Liverpool fishwife. "Now shut your face, shut up! I'm not listening to any more of this!" he growled as he pulled me towards his face, forcing me to look into his eyes so I could see the loathing and hate there. My usual fear wasn't ignited. He then threw me out of the way and stormed off to the pub to drown his sorrows for having a wife like me.

In the hall, I sat hunched on the bottom stair with my elbows on my knees, my hands holding my scalp together as it felt it was about to burst. My jaw set solid, my back teeth clenched and my lips pressed tightly together to suppress the sobs. Every muscle in my face and body quivered with tension as I fought to control this fierce emotion that was trying hard to suffocate me.

My brain visually created a performance on a stage! Above and behind this scene I was starring in, floating in the air as you would expect a ghost figure to be, was myself as a younger woman. I was slim with Irish green eyes that reflected my bubbly personality and I had thick curly auburn hair.

I stared at this scene, knowing that my ghost figure was the person I wanted the world to see, but this person on the stairs was the real person that nobody knew. I was at last seeing the person I'd become. My eyes were haunted and wet with tears and my mascara had run in rivulets down my cheeks. My auburn hair was tousled and unkempt after running my hands through it in exasperation.

What had happened to the young woman I used to be? The years had gone by, and my lifestyle had taken its toll on me. I didn't recognise the person I saw sitting on my stairs.

I'd been screaming, "How could you do this again? How could you gamble your kids security away?" And, as my mind ran over the confrontation we'd just had, I thought *My God! I really did want to kill him.* The realisation of this emotion at the height of my anger pulled the plug on this powerful energy, and it drained away leaving me feeling lifeless and beaten. I was totally exhausted with work, worry and the constant fighting.

Within days, another statement arrived in the mail for two thousand eight hundred pounds. As I totalled all of these statements together, I noted it was approximately how much we'd get for the sale of the house – *my* house, that I thought I'd sell for a profit if I couldn't manage the payments, was now being sold to pay off his debts.

Dave had won. He had pushed me right over the edge. The only answer was to sell the house to pay off his debts and I knew that when I did that, I would leave him. I pitied him for the affliction he had, but I was the only one trying to deal with it, whilst he was having the life he wanted with an inexhaustible supply of money for him becoming a mountain of debts for me. He would never face that he had an addiction, and I could now see at last that without facing the problem he had, he would never recover from it. Dave's addictions had destroyed our lives.

I had to make some major decisions. *How will the children cope without their dad around?* I thought about my own father and suddenly I had a great deal of respect and admiration for my mother who had never split the family up although Dad had drunk the same way as Dave. But Dad didn't gamble like Dave! *Would Mum have left if he had?*

The children came in and I tried to chat to them and pull myself out of this depression, but I knew this time it was going to be different. This was the end of the road – my lovely home that I had worked so hard for would have to be sold to pay off Dave's gambling debts.

I looked at the children and my heart ached for them. Their lives were about to be turned upside down. I had wanted so much for them, and I'd fought and worked hard to give them some security, but we were now penniless.

For some weeks, I lived my life in an emotionless void. Floating through my days and spending my evenings with pen and paper trying to work out various ways of saving a little of the money at least to start afresh. *What can I do?*

I called in the real estate agent to value the house. My hard work on the house had increased its value but I could see that with agent and lawyers' fees there would be nothing left after paying his gambling debts, which would clean us out after the sale of the house. We would have to rent.

New Zealand, I felt, was the perfect place to start afresh. I wanted to be near my sister and nephew again. I had made my decision to go before I told Dave.

"Placing your name on the house title and the bank manager doing it without my permission is against the law and I could fight you and him for doing that and you could both end up in jail. But I can't be bothered fighting any more. I'll sell the house and clear your debts and then I'm going to New Zealand with the children. You can carry on with your lifestyle here in England as I refuse to live with it any longer. I'll be applying for a divorce." I stated this in a quietish flat voice. There was no emotion in it. I was matter of fact as I filled the kitchen sink with water. He stood looking at me.

"Now you're going too far. Okay, I'll stop the gambling now and I mean it this time."

I turned and looked at him with steely eyes, waited at least thirty seconds then said, "I really don't care whether you mean it or not now. The divorce will go through quickly and the house will be sold but we won't be getting any money from it as it will all go to pay off the debts you have. You are a selfish man. So, you can do what you like from now on. It's over. I would prefer it if you left the house now, but when have you ever listened to what I prefer, so be ready to move somewhere when it's sold because you're not coming with me."

I sold my house and, after paying off his many debts, I was left with seven hundred pounds.

A Big Rubber Knocky Down Dolly

I've decided to trade me man in
For a big Rubber Knocky down dolly
Cos I know it would be much more use to me
Than this selfish insensitive Wally

If I just had a knocky down dolly
He could stand at the end of me bed,
My frustrations and trials, would be all satisfied
With a smack to the back of his 'ead!

He wouldn't create any work for me
So never again would I crack,
I could punch 'im, an' stick 'im, and karate kick 'im
He'd fall over, and just bounce back!!

He wouldn't be comin' 'ome drunk,
Bein' angry an' scratchin 'is belly,
No more snorin' an' poutin', no coughin' and shoutin'
No rugby and golf on the telly!

I've thought very 'ard 'bout this trade in'
And listed the credits to savor it.
Me man scraped to 4 – I couldn't think of any more,
But the dolly got hundreds – the favorite

I might 'ave to make up the difference,
Cos trade ins are rubbish for treasure,
So I'll throw in 'is golf clubs, 'is car and 'is club subs,
An' p'rhaps the beer fridge for good measure

So I can't wait for Monday morning
When I'll drive to the warehouse with Wally,
Then I'll trade in me man just as fast I can
For a big rubber knocky down dolly

Chapter Fourteen

Leaving Merseyside

1982

My face burned, my nerves jangled, my temples felt like they were bursting as I stood in line straight-backed. With my jaw set firm as I stared at the back of the heads of those before me at the check-in desk at Heathrow Airport, I repeated my mental checklist like a mantra – passports … book to read … sleeping mask … ear plugs … change of knickers … toiletries … phone number for when we arrive. *At least the flight looks as though it's on time so this drama with Mum isn't going to last forever. Poor Mum,* I thought as I acknowledged her distress. *It must be hard for her saying goodbye to her precious grandchildren who will now grow up in New Zealand.*

Guilt now added to my consciousness as I witnessed my mother's slight, five foot one inch frame shaking and vibrating with this unashamed outpouring of grief. One by one and over and over Mum would grab her grandchildren and press them into her ample bosom as she showered them with kisses. Then, as the time marched toward our departure, she began throwing back her head and quietly wailing into the air which made the hair on my neck stand on end. The pain in Mum's face matched the pain I'd seen there when Dad had died in 1977. *How can I do this to my mother?* My gut lurched and squirmed. I wanted to be sick! *It's too late, I can't backtrack now.*

Forcing myself to turn in her direction, I shouted, "I'll send for you Mum in 12 months, I promise," then pleaded to lighten the depressing atmosphere, "then you'll see us all again and have a lovely holiday." But Mum's eyes met mine and I could see she was silently saying, "I might not live that long, Pauline."

Over the last five years since Dad's death, Mum had aged. This strong little woman that had held the family together was now weak and sometimes pathetic. I had so admired her throughout her life, but she was now a hypochondriac. She wore her broken heart on her sleeve for all the world to see. She seemed to constantly look for sympathy. Rather than recovering, we felt she had grown worse day by day.

"I'm defyin' medical science by breathin'," was her favorite cry. My patience was often tested as I tried to support her through her grief, but at times I wanted to shake her and scream "Stop this, Mum!"

As children, we were sometimes afraid of Dad when he was drunk, but we still thought he was funny and loved him. And so, I tried to understand Mum's reluctance to accept Dad's death and move on. Dad had been a truly one-off individual, a little funny five feet two-inch Irish leprechaun who should never have touched alcohol. Without it, he could charm the birds out of the trees, but drinking alcohol brought out the devil him. Consequently, we really loved someone we really feared. Over the last five years I was hoping she would snap out of this depression and be the strong dependable mother she had always been. The decision to leave England had been made more difficult because I knew Mum might never survive this separation. Her grandchildren had become all she lived for. Eventually, I had talked myself into believing that our lives couldn't be placed on hold until she recovered. She might never recover! And this scene of pain was now ripping me to shreds.

The airport was packed to capacity. Passengers stood crushed together around their cases as they stood in line before the check-in desks. Some already nervous passengers squirmed and shifted from one foot to the other as they heard and witnessed the scene this small family created, and no doubt blaming such distressing behavior as the reason for their own anxiety. A woman wearing her Sunday best hat and looking more like she was off to have tea with Her Royal Highness remarked under her breath:

"Disgraceful ... they shouldn't be allowed to carry on like that," just as a businessman who stood reading his newspaper, shook it in a deliberate manner and nodded in agreement.

I felt numb and so very, very tired, and wished we could just walk through the departure gate and be in New Zealand without the flights and fights that were sure to ensue between me and Dave. My gut knotted when I thought of him getting stuck into the free booze as soon as the plane became airborne.

A wave of nausea washed over me as I questioned my decision to take the family so far away from their roots. *Are we doing the right thing leaving England? Can a better life really be waiting for us all on the other side of the world, or will it be the same old same old?*

Dave had filled a plastic bottle with whisky and was swigging it like water. His alcohol consumption showed on his once handsome face: his skin was rough and pitted and his nose was getting bulbous. He already looked rumpled and dishevelled in his jeans and sweatshirt as he leaned on my shoulder. I turned and looked into his face, saw that his brown eyes were beginning to fog over, and the whisky smell on his breath was pungent. Quietly I uttered, "Don't drink any more, Dave – you'll get plenty on the plane."

"Eh!" he snarled. "This is me medicine. A don't like flyin' an' this helps me, okay?" He grunted loudly and continued gulping his elixir of choice.

Embarrassment washed over me as I deliberately avoided eye

contact with anyone and turned to face the check-in desk again. Closing my eyes, I prayed silently, *Please let us on the plane before he's completely comatose.*

I looked over at Sharon-Louise, who was now fourteen years old, and Gary, who was eleven, their faces buried into their grandmother's neck and mascara-smeared clothes. Sharon-Louise had spent all morning donning her clothes and makeup and now her mascara was splattered all over her eyes and ran down her painted cheeks. White lipstick had been kissed off and pink lips showed through white face paint. Purple lacquered hair had been carefully teased up to resemble a cock's comb but was now bent at a jaunty angle. I pondered if it was an improvement on her earlier attempt. She was a pretty girl with a neat, size 10 figure that should have allowed her to look beautiful in anything she wore.

Today, once again, I squirmed over her choice of clothes – a faux black leather mini skirt, no more than twelve inches of cloth in total and barely covering the necessities, was stretched like a pelmet above black sheer tights. On her feet were yellow five-inch-high heels sporting bows on the pointed toes. A pink T-shirt topped this ensemble with PRINCESS SEEKS FROG in sequins across her breast.

Gary's attire was also in keeping with the latest fashion and followed the trend of the Bay City Rollers: thick black-soled Doc Martin boots, red and yellow plaid pants with a denim jacket over a black T-shirt. He had such a handsome face, a younger version of the Dave I had fallen in love with, but now his face was swollen, red and wet with the tears he shed over the thought of never seeing his grandmother again.

To make sure I looked the part to travel on a plane to my new life, I had visited George Henry Lee's, a posh shop in Liverpool. For the first time in my 35 years, I bought a wool suit. I chose a colour that suited my auburn hair – grey and light green tweed with a pleated skirt that finished neatly at knee level. The white shirt under the box jacket, I felt, gave me a sophisticated look. Grey two-inch heels finished off this sober ensemble. When Sharon-Louise saw me dressed in this attire, she remarked, "Oo the bleedin' 'ell got you ready?"

I pursed my lips and knitted my brow as I looked into her face. "This is the start of our new life, Sharon-Louise, so watch your language from now on, will ye."

I was relieved to see we were next in line, and it was nearly time to curtail the airport performance. "Come on you lot!!" I shouted. "Say your last g'bye to ye Nan."

Mum had been moving along with us all from outside the rope barrier. On hearing my words, she issued a resounding tearful encore that only relented when I stepped forward to initiate my final farewells.

"Ta-rah, Mum," I said, acknowledging the pain in her eyes as I began hugging her. "I luv you, Mum," I said as I fought back tears.

"Yer'll probably never see ye mother again, Pauline. I don't know 'ow ye could do this to me. It'll probably kill me," she cried as she pushed me away. Quietly howling and gripping her hands to her chest, she gave an academy award performance of a heart attack. Once again, I thought, *One of these days, Mum, you're going to cry wolf.*

Our bedraggled foursome stood before the check-in desk. I held the passports and flight documents as, one by one I lifted our thirteen pieces of luggage off the trolley and onto the scale beside the attending officer, who was clearly not impressed with us at all. Dave's arms were now around his children, using them as crutches by leaning heavily on their shoulders. His eyes were blurry and he wore a drunken smirk on his ruddy face. He thought he was fooling the young woman into believing he wasn't drunk. Sharon-Louise's face resembled a clown as she chewed gum with an open mouth and kept turning and waving to her Nan. "Tara Nan – I luv ye."

Gary struggled under his father's weight but smiled through his tears and waved with his free arm to his beloved grandmother. Gary was the more sensitive of the two children, and I knew this stressful farewell would be tearing him to pieces. Yet I also knew he looked forward to the whole adventure of going to live in another country, an outdoor life that suited the athlete in him. He'd been chattering for weeks about joining a rugby team and eventually becoming an All Black. Camping weekends, fishing, and bush walking were on his agenda, but right now these thoughts were the last on his mind as I witnessed on his face the torture he was going through.

My anxiety levels were at an all-time high as I fought to subdue my tears and worriedly chant my new updated itinerary mantra in my mind after handing the cases over, checking the special list of five things to remember now: passports, tickets, money, two kids, one drunken husband! – though I wished I could leave the last worry off my list.

Finally, all the luggage was checked, and boarding passes issued. I turned to my family and now, forcing a smile, shouted "That's it!!", and waved the papers in the air. "Come on, you lot, we're on our way – Eh, Up New Zealand, here we come!"

I turned to look at Mum. "Ta-Ra, Mum," I shouted and, although my throat was constricting and choking with the tears I was suppressing, I beamed a smile, hoping her last vision of me smiling would help. "I luv ye, Mum!" I blew a kiss, took one last look at the people of my birth country, then like an actress, I threw back my head, squared my shoulders, held the boarding papers in the air, turned and strode out leading this motley crew through the airport security and toward the boarding gate.

The seating area at the gate was packed with passengers and only an odd vacant seat was scattered here and there. I chose one that had my back against the window. The rest of the family sat on the floor. Surveying all those seated at the gate, my radar was up as I scanned the enclosure to ensure Dave wasn't upsetting anyone, yet still trying hard to give the impression I wasn't with him. As he nursed his near empty plastic bottle of whisky and sat with his back against a wall, the whisky fumes drifted under the noses of those near to him. A woman close to him peered with disdain, turned to her partner and whispered behind her hand. Another gathered her children together, moved across the lounge area and sat them on the floor. This left a vacant seat beside where Dave sat on the floor, but I had no intention of moving into it. I needed distance between me and Dave and tried hard to give the impression that he had nothing to do with me, yet my face burned with embarrassment.

It was time to board. I looked over at Dave nursing his now empty plastic whisky bottle like a comforter. His eyes were closed, his chin had dropped to his chest and he was beginning to snore – and he was unconscious. I fought with the idea of leaving him where he was, perhaps accidentally forgetting him, but knew his kids wouldn't let me do that.

"You two pick ye father up and I'll see to the papers," I instructed with a sigh. The children had to heave Dave's arms around their shoulders and approached the flight attendant at the gate. She gave one look at him in this condition and announced with disdain: "He's not allowed to travel in an intoxicated state. Can you stand over there please," and indicated to the side of the lounge.

"Look, dear," I pleaded, "he's only drunk and he'll be unconscious now for at least nine hours. I know him well enough. He won't be a problem – just let us on the plane cos he's getting pretty heavy for the kids."

"I'm sorry, rules are rules. If anyone is in an intoxicated state, they must not board the plane – you three can get on but he can't," she snapped as she looked away and began to ring for help.

Within minutes, a strong Liverpool accent came from a tall handsome steward that arrived in response to her phone call. "Frightened of flyin' is ee, luv?" He smiled at me as he cocked his head toward Dave.

"Terrified," I answered, "but I know him, and he'll be unconscious now for the night. We've got to get on this plane, my luggage is already on it," I begged as I stared into the young man's eyes.

"What's his name?" he asked.

"Dave."

"Come on, Dave," he shouted as he grabbed him under his arm pits and lifted him off the ground. Moving his grip down to Dave's waist, he then placed one of Dave's arms around his neck in the way a fireman would give a lift. Dave stirred slightly, enough to move his legs and pat the front of the steward with his free arm.

"Okay, mate – yer' all right, mate," he muttered in a drunken slur as the steward almost carried him down the walkway and onto the plane. I was consumed with embarrassment as I walked leaving distance between me and Dave, still attempting to give the impression to those around that he had nothing to do with me.

"My name's Brad," he said. "We've got a pretty light plane tonight, only half the seats are booked so ye can spread out. I'll give ye four seats each and ye can put the arms up and lie down and get some sleep. I'll put Dave in his seats," and he proceeded to take off Dave's shoes and lie him horizontally across the seats near the window. He tied him in with two of the seat belts and placed a pillow under his head. "You can sit here." He indicated four seats in the middle of the plane in line with Dave's. "Keep an eye on him, won't ye, if he stirs in the night, he's your problem, okay? I'll get a bucket in case he's sick."

"There's no need for the bucket, Brad – he won't part with a drop of what he drank – he's too bloody mean. Don't worry, if he needs the bathroom, I'll sort him. Thanks for that, Brad." Humiliation washed over me as I looked at Dave in his comatose state.

"Okay, kids, one of you in front of ye mother and one behind her. Ye can all have four seats and when ye lie down put the seat belts on like I did with ye Dad. D'ye understand?" He smiled.

Sharon-Louise stood holding the back of her four seats; she stretched up to her full five-foot six inch plus, with her yellow stilettos, and arched her back throwing her PRINCESS SEEKS FROG breasts out. "Am really tired, 'ow do ye put them seat belts on?" she enquired seductively. She wasn't aware that her face at that time resembled a clown or a zombie and would have had any man running for cover. Brad looked at Sharon-Louise and then winked at me.

"Okay. I'll show ye how to do it," he smiled as he helped her into her seats.

"I don't wanna go t'sleep yet," Gary said as he stood in the aisle.

"That's okay, luv. Come and sit with me until you're ready, then when you're going t'sleep I can help put those seat belts across you," I told him.

Gary slipped into the seat beside me, and I smiled at him and then leaned over and grabbed him and gave him a slobbery hug and a kiss as he started to laugh.

"What's that for, Mum?" he chuckled.

"That's 'cos I luv ye and I'm excited cos we're on our way. You're happy, aren't you, Gary, about going to New Zealand? It's an adventure ye know. Other kids in your class would be so jealous. You are happy, aren't you?" I studied his eyes for the truth in his answer.

Gary stared at me as he thought for a few seconds. "I'm sad right now, Mum, about leaving everyone, especially me Nan, but I am excited," he answered, and I knew he had spoken the truth. I sucked in a deep breath as I sat tall in my seat and smiled into Gary's face, then I let the air go from my mouth as I looked ahead, relaxed my shoulders and grabbed his hand in mine. *This is it,* I thought as the plane began to taxi toward take-off. *We made it, were on our way,* and the plane tipped back and took to the air.

Gary began listening to his music on his headphones as I opened the book I'd brought with me. Dave was completely unconscious when I turned to stare at him. *I'm not strong enough to get away from this man,* I thought. *I really don't want him coming with us,* but he'd used emotional blackmail on the kids who had cried that they wanted their dad to come with them to New Zealand. I kept fighting for over two months against him coming but he got his way again. The appointment I had made for the interview in New Zealand House applying for a resident visa, had been my secret and yet he knew it was happening and followed me there.

"How did he find out about these things?" I asked a lawyer when I began my attempt to divorce. He opened them in front of me and ripped them up, threatening me with what he'd do if I tried that again. I sat thinking of those rows and the promises he wouldn't gamble again, knowing full well he wouldn't change, but I became the villain in the house as the kids and him ganged up on me. All three of them genuinely cried that they wanted to be together in New Zealand.

The smiling face of an air stewardess came into my view as she said, "Penny for them?" and woke me from my memories as she leaned down and looked into my face.

"Oh, I was miles away!" I answered as I straightened in my chair and looked up again into her friendly face.

"Would you like a drink? It might help you sleep."

"Yes, that would be lovely, thanks. I'll have a gin and tonic please." The stewardess poured my drink and handed it to me and then turned to look at Dave. "No, he doesn't want one, thanks," I quickly said with concern. "Please don't wake him!"

"Yes, I can see he's had enough. I won't be waking him, don't worry." She smiled and gave me a conspiratorial wink. "Enjoy your drink in peace," she said and moved the trolley on down the aisle.

"I need to go to the toilet, Mum" Gary said as he pushed his tray table up.

"Ok, luv, you know where it is," and I stepped into the aisle to let him out. As I stretched and turned around, I noticed a man waiting to pass me.

"Oops, sorry," I smiled but his angry response was "I hope that sorry is for the bloody racket your husband is making with his snoring. Nobody will get any sleep around these seats," he growled. "I'm going to ask to be moved," and his angry face stared down at me as I sat back in my chair. Embarrassed and flustered now, I picked up my drink and had a good swig of it to settle me but I really felt like crying. *Guilty by association again!* I thought.

Gary was back and, as he moved past me to his seat, he said, "Mum, you can hear Dad's snoring right down to the toilets!"

"Oh dear, I don't know what to do about it, Gary," I said. "If it bothers you when you're trying to sleep, luv, you can have my ear plugs."

"No, I'm used to it. I can still go to sleep without them. You bought them for you, Mum, you use them." He was always considerate and caring, not wanting me to know he was upset about anything, trying in his own way to make things right for me. As I looked over the back of the seats in front of me where Sharon-Louise slept peacefully, I thought, *Nothing disturbs her — she loves her dad and won't be drawn into decrying him in any way.*

Gary settled back in his seat and placed his headphones back over his ears as he changed his music and flicked open a magazine on New Zealand camping sites. Once again, my mind began to wander as I recalled various events.

Churning over my wedding day in my mind, my Irish sense of humor kicked in once again as I replayed the scenario of sitting in the General Hospital, my traditional white wedding dress covered in blood after my cousin had crushed a glass in his hand and cut the artery in his wrist. Smiling inwardly, I turned to look at Gary. He moved his earphones away from his head and smiled back.

"What's so funny, Mum?"

"Did I ever tell you about my wedding day, Gary?" I laughed and began the story for him. He left his earphones around his neck as he settled down smiling, knowing he was about to be entertained. Even though he had heard the story many times before, he loved listening to me tell these funny stories. I could always embellish a yarn and bring humour into it and Gary and I sat squealing with laughter as I played it out again for his benefit, exaggerating and mimicking the various reactions from those that had witnessed this debacle in the hospital!

We were now two hours into our flight and Gary wanted to sleep. Moving to the row behind us, I lifted the arm rests as I secured the seat belts across him the way Brad had instructed. "Are you cold, luv?" I asked. "Do you want a blanket over you?"

"Yes please, Mum. Am not cold but a can't sleep without something covering me."

Tucking the blanket around him, I leaned over and murmured into his ear, "When you wake up, Gary, we'll be in Singapore. You dream about that, luv. Sleep tight cos I want you to be wide awake and take in all the sights; it's going to be lots of fun, you'll see. Ni Night, luv." I kissed him on his forehead and stared into his young face momentarily, then patted his bum and whispered, "I luv ye, Gary."

"I luv ye, Mum!"

Sharon-Louise was fast asleep and already dreaming of the adventure she was on. *She does have a pretty face,* I thought as I stared down at her. *If only she'd realise it and stop plastering that muck on it.* For all her loud ways and façade of toughness, I knew Sharon-Louise had a big fat heart but found it difficult to show sensitivity. I collected a blanket from beside her and tucked it around her and under her chin. She stirred as I leaned over her.

"'night, Mum," she murmured. I kissed her forehead.

"I luv you, Stink," I said as I gently pushed her hair away from her eyes. Stink was a nickname we had given her as a baby and although she forbade anyone to use it on her ever again, I knew that she still loved hearing it when no one else could hear. It was an endearment that made her feel loved. With closed eyes, Sharon-Louise smiled and snuggled down into her blanket and slipped back to her wonderland dreams.

The lights of the plane dimmed, and everyone settled down to sleep. I looked over at Dave. He was lying with his head back and his mouth wide open, snoring.

He won't change, I thought. I had checked to see if New Zealand allowed gambling in the country and was told they didn't, but my sister already lived in New Zealand and had told me saying they could find places to gamble if they were serious. I didn't want to think about this too much and would face it when it started again.

"Would you like another gin and tonic?" I heard as the stewardess leaned around the back of my seat.

"Not just yet, thank you. I haven't finished this one." I settled down, intending to finish my drink and then try to get some sleep.

"Mum!" Gary interrupted my thoughts.

I stood up and peered over the seat at him. "Yes, luv? Do ye need anything?"

"I need a drink of water please, Mum."

"Won't be long, luv I'll go and get you one."

I eased out of the seats and walked down to the galley to collect the water and as I turned to return to my seats, I could hear Dave from almost twelve feet away. His deafening, penetrating, resounding snoring grated on my nerves. Embarrassment washed over me as I wished with all my heart that he wasn't with us spoiling our adventure. Walking back, I listened to him wheezing and coughing and clearing his throat. I could also see that we had the last occupied seats back to the galley – other passengers must have all asked to be moved away from his snoring. Gary drank his water and I settled him back to sleep and returned to my seat. My temples were now tight, and my nerves vibrated with every loud explosion from Dave's mouth. Passengers walking by going to the bathroom held their hands over their ears and frowned. My anxiety rose: my throat constricted, and swallowing became difficult. Inwardly, I fought to calm down, but my face felt hot, my temples tight. My whole body vibrated with jangled nerves. I needed something to do. So I stood again and slipped back into the space behind my seats to check on Gary once more. Agitated, I fussed and tucked his blankets around his chin and stood watching him for a short while as I calmed myself down, and then began to smile. Drinking in his innocence, I thought, *I love my kids*, and then I looked over at Sharon-Louise, who was still smiling in her sleep. *Somehow I got it right with these two.* I smiled back at my daughter's sleeping face.

Returning to my seat, I sat back, gave a sigh of resignation, and settled with a new assessment of my situation. I was now calm again. *What is perfect?* I thought. *This move might only be five out of ten but it's a new beginning. From here, I start as I mean to go on.*

We were leaving England with seven hundred pounds after

the mortgages and Dave's numerous credit cards had been paid off. I had purchased all the household items we had with cash which meant they hadn't been repossessed; they were safely packed into a container along with some antique pieces of furniture I had bought specially to sell when we arrived in New Zealand which would help us financially.

Dave was an alcoholic, a gambler, and a bully, but there was something about him that made me feel sorry for him. He didn't have a good upbringing as his father had died when he was only four leaving his mother with four boys to raise. She had brought her alcoholic brother to live with them to help financially, but their uncle beat them all until each one of them was old enough and big enough to beat him back and win. Therefore, I felt Dave believed that was how to get your own way: you beat people into submission. You make them afraid of you. And in his world, you can love those people that are frightened of you because they try to please you. His uncle still lived with his mother and often she would say she should never have brought him into her home to live. He drank and smoked and had no pride in himself at all and was the most belligerent person I had ever met. He also wanted nothing to do with the boys or their families when they married. There seemed to be no soul in the man. He lived from social paycheck to social paycheck and merely drank his money away.

In my early married years with Dave, throughout the nights, I took many beatings. I would suppress my cries, preventing the kids from hearing what was going on, and I always walked out of the bedroom door each morning with a smile on my face. I never wanted my children to know how their father had treated me. I wanted my kids to have a normal life with loving parents and so hid what I could from them. As a child , I had felt fear when I heard my mother taking countless beatings and so I was adamant I would never let my children hear anything like that. I was determined to raise my kids without that sort of fear, and I felt it had worked; the children loved their father and simply felt he was a loveable drunk.

Once it became clear that I had made a mistake in marrying him, I had to learn how to navigate my life around him, because I had tried all I knew and couldn't make him leave my home (a home that I paid the mortgage on). I felt my only choice was to accept him, as he wouldn't be eliminated from my life: I supplied the means for him to get the money to live in the way he did. Without me, his lavish life wasn't possible. I was his source of income.

I couldn't get support from anywhere that would help me to become free of him. Two lawyers had to be cancelled as I received beatings every night and my life was hell when he found out I was trying to divorce him. Some advice from the first lawyer was I must not leave the family home as he can then claim it and fight for the children that way. He could keep the house and kids and fight for me to pay the mortgage for them.

I had gone to Mum who told me I'd made my bed and I must lie in it. "These kids need their own roof over their heads."

I'd called the police on many occasions and every time they told me to stop nagging him and leave him alone when he's drunk. My friends were embarrassed with the fighting on their doorstep when he found out I'd ran there and he'd followed me.

"You've got to divorce him, Pauline, and unfortunately we can't have you running here as the neighbours will be thinking this fighting on our doorstep is me and John."

I ran once to the Women's Refuges, but I felt I wasn't in their league either; women and children hiding away and frightened. I looked at my children and didn't want them reduced to that sort of life and environment. I would not move out of my home as it was me that was paying the mortgage and me and my kids were entitled to live in it. He paid absolutely nothing toward the mortgage or our living.

And so, after all these years of living around Dave, I'd learned what kept the peace and kept us all safe, so our lives were lived around placating this man.

Thinking of the many other people in the world that had problems, I concluded that nobody's life was perfect; he was a life problem I had to navigate. He was a heavy financial burden I could do without, but my kids wanted him around. He loved his kids even if he didn't show it a lot and, until they left home, I'd have to tolerate him as best I could. I received my pleasures from my children, grabbed happiness where I could and so made the most of what I had.

I stepped out of the toilet after changing into a light dress that would be more comfortable to sleep in just as Brad, the air steward, appeared before me.

"How are you coping? Do you want a bit of company for a while? The crew are having a few drinks at the back of the plane here and I think ye deserve to unwind a bit, don't you?" he asked, smiling his handsome smile.

"That would be lovely, Brad – thanks so much," I said and followed him to where the crew were sitting. "What would you like to drink?" he asked.

"I'll have a gin and tonic if yer askin," I said, smiling.

The crew were all Liverpudlians and the wit and humour that was bandied about over the next few hours had me almost wetting myself with laughter. They told me all about New Zealand and advised where to visit and all agreed that it was a beautiful place.

"Have you ever been in the cockpit of a plane?" Brad asked.

"Never," I replied with excitement.

"Come on, let's sit you in the captain's seat, eh!" and I followed Brad through the plane and up to the cockpit. It was empty!! *Oh, my God!*

"Where's the pilot?" I uttered in shock. "What's going on,

who's flyin' the plane for God's sake?" and Brad began laughing.

"It's on automatic pilot: it's flying itself right now." He chuckled. "Go on, sit in the captain's seat and I'll take your photograph with an instamatic camera, and you can show your kids tomorrow how you flew the plane takin' them to their life in a new land." This was exciting. I sat in the pilot's seat, frightened of touching anything but smiled my best photograph smile and had my picture taken flying the plane. I sat staring at this photo with excitement when I got back to my seat and couldn't wait for the kids to wake up to show them.

"What d'ye mean ye 'ad a party last night with the crew?" Dave growled through gritted teeth as he heard me. "What went on while I was asleep, eh?" He glared at me accusingly, waiting to see a chink in my defense.

"You've got such a filthy mind," I said as I stared him down. "The crew invited me to join them 'cos they felt sorry for me having to put up with a drunk like you. I had to move thirteen pieces of luggage and take the responsibility of getting my kids onto a plane, which included you, and you were about as much use as a chocolate fireplace. No! Worse than that … you were a bloody liability so don't you try accusing me of anything to start a row," and the kids looked on. Riled, Dave threw off his blanket and moved toward the bathroom.

His jealousy was a constant fear for me. He would imagine me flirting when I was only trying to be friendly. When I was out with him, I would never make eye contact with men fearing he would misinterpret my friendliness.

"Are you all right, Mum?" Gary asked, snapping me out of my reminiscences.

"Yes, I'm fine, luv, just slipped into a bad memory there." I smiled as I kissed him on the nose, needing to bring the joviality back to the moment. "So, what do you think?" I smiled as I showed the photo to them again. "I look pretty snazzy, eh, flying the plane. I'll bet few kids can say their Mum flew the plane on the way to their new life, eh!" I chuckled.

Sharon-Louise began chuckling out loud "Yer a bloody hero, Mum."

"What have a told you, Sharon-Louise? – stop the swearing," I reprimanded with a half-smile.

"Okay, okay, but a still feel a bloody hero is better than just saying a hero – it's more!" she laughed as she raised her arms in the air. I raised my eyebrows and said, "Okay, you win – it is more," and we all laughed. Gary now smiled but fear showed around his eyes as he watched his father walking back from the bathroom. Sharon-Louise couldn't always pick up on her father's vicious moods, but Gary nearly always did these days.

Singapore was hot and humid during our two nights' stopover. Dave started drinking soon after he woke in the mornings and didn't want to go far, so most of the time was spent ducking in and out of air-conditioned shops and bars to be able to breathe.

Gary looked awful and found it hard to get his breath. I called a taxi early for our return to the airport in Singapore for the second leg of our flight as I felt I might find an English-speaking doctor there. Gary's face looked ashen, and he now had pains in his gut. I thought he may have food poisoning.

The doctor said, "It could be asthma," and asked Gary to breathe into a machine, which immediately helped his breathing, and his face regained its colour. "Get him to a doctor in New Zealand as soon as you arrive," he told us.

Dave was in his usual state of alcoholism and had found a drinking partner and the two of them sat on the Singapore airport floor sharing a bottle of whisky, drinking it like water.

My concern for Gary was shared with Sharon-Louise but Dave had no idea what was going on as he was drunk again and weaved toward the check-in desk leaning on his daughter. Frantic with worry, I kept checking Gary, watching him struggle to breathe and praying we wouldn't be stopped again from boarding the plane because of Dave. But they did allow him onto the plane; nobody tried to stop this drunken man from boarding, which was a huge relief for us all. Again, the plane was only half full which enabled us to each have four seats and sleep the last leg of our journey.

Still in my heightened state of anxiety, I watched Dave snoring and was repulsed and disgusted, but happy not to be sitting with him throughout the journey. *Nobody will know he's with me*, I reasoned as I sat alone in my four seats. Gary began to breathe easier and slipped into sleep. Dave and Sharon-Louise slept, and I pushed the arm rests up, grabbed a pillow and blanket and settled into a fretful semi-conscious sleep until we were woken for breakfast and prepared to land in New Zealand.

At 6.30am, the plane was approaching Auckland and we gazed in awe at the view from the small plane windows onto Manukau and the surrounding islands. The morning sunshine sparkled on the clear azure blue waters and scattered shimmering diamonds across gently rolling waves, as they kissed the shorelines of velvet emerald green hummocks edged here and there with tiny touches of white surf.

"Wow!" we all sighed in awe.

"It's like a picture!" Sharon-Louise slowly murmured in wonder.

For a brief period, Gary's worried face was transfixed, then he slowly remarked as he tried to breathe, "England is like ... black and white ... but New Zealand is like ... colour." He had been trying to work out how to explain this vision before his eyes and we all agreed he was right.

Excitement built as we collected our luggage and walked out through the small airport where my sister Babs, her husband Mark and my nephew Matt met us.

Gary tried to be enthusiastic but was still struggling to breathe and they immediately took us to a doctor who revealed that Gary was indeed suffering from asthma. He had never had anything like that when we lived in England and I worried and became deeply disappointed that he had contracted this as he landed in this new country, spoiling his excitement.

"It can be activated through stress," the doctor informed us. He gave him an inhaler which immediately helped his breathing.

Stress I thought. *This journey has been stressful to my son.* It was my idea to come all this way across the world and I was now blaming myself for Gary's illness.

Chapter Fifteen

A fresh start

1982

We arrived in Bucklands Beach, which was a magical part of Auckland, New Zealand, on a tiny peninsular with quiet streets of many styles of houses, some wooden, some brick and tile, all neatly kempt with blazes of colour splashed around clipped lawns. Expanses of freshly mown green playing fields undulated over and around hills and swept down to sandy beaches. The water lapped lazily against the shore, crystal clear blue skies smiled above our heads and my family fell in love with this beautiful part of the world. That is apart from Dave, who kept comparing everything with Birkenhead and complaining, "But there's nothing here! Where're the local pubs and the golf course?"

Babs, Mark and Matt were excited with our arrival. Seeing them all again made my heart ache with pleasure. I hugged Matt for minutes as I embraced my long-lost number two son. Babs explained she had put Sharon-Louise and Gary each in a bed in the house and Dave and I were taken outside and were shown our bedroom for the immediate few days, a very ancient caravan in their garden.

"Who do they think we are?" Dave remarked when we were left to look over it, "A gang of bleedin' gypsies?" But Babs and Mark couldn't have been more hospitable. They invited other Merseysiders they knew from around the area and hosted a

Welcome BBQ in our honour in their garden.

For the next couple of days, they showed us around the area, pointing out various houses that were up for rent. I had a budget in my head and once I'd worked out what the rental rates were and what we could get for the money, I settled for a run-down, old, wooden house on the beach. It had all we needed – three bedrooms, a kitchen and bathroom and was situated looking out over the water toward a small group of islands. It was a magical spot. Babs and Mark had a shed full of basic pieces of furniture, linen, and dishes, that they had gathered for us since I wrote telling them of our arrival. I furnished the place with these until our own furniture arrived.

I scrubbed and cleaned and arranged the old furniture and tried to make the place look homely, but my family weren't impressed.

"Ow long 'ave we got to live in this dump?" asked Sharon-Louise as she stared around our 'new' home.

"Probably only about six months" I answered with trepidation as I waited for the reaction to come.

"Six bleedin' months livin' in a dump!" she screamed. "Some bloody adventure this is turnin' out t'be!"

"Just look out the window, Sharon-Louise. Could we live on the beach in England? If we could, would it look like that? When you come home from school each night, we can have walks along the beach and watch the sun going down over the islands over there. It's magical here. So, the house isn't up t'much, but we need to save some money now t'get a deposit to buy our own and, in the meantime, we can enjoy these beautiful surroundings."

"Oh, whoopsie bleedin' do," was her response. "Wait 'till I write an' tell me mates am not goin' to disco's or anythin' like that but walkin' with me bloody muther up and down the beach every bleedin' night. Yeh! They'll be really impressed."

Dave nodded, agreeing with Sharon-Louise, but Gary looked at his dad and asked, "So can we go fishin', Dad?"

"We'll see, son, we'll see." That was Dave's standard answer to anything. Not even able to commit himself to agreeing to take his son fishing.

"If your dad hasn't got the time, I'm sure Mark and Matt will take you, Gary. You can do anything you want to do here."

I felt a little apprehensive and homesick myself at this point but didn't dare show it. The worry over Gary was the first of my children's health problems that I hadn't shared with my mother; I was already missing her badly, but I was determined to keep the kids spirits up and make this the adventure I'd promised them, and so we began our new life in a shack on a beach at the other end of the world.

Entry into New Zealand meant securing a job for Dave to support the application for residency. Correspondence with my sister at that time helped considerably and she had secured for him sponsorship and a job in a panel-beating company in Penrose, an Industrial area of Auckland.

"Ring them Dave and tell them you're here and ask when they want you to start."

"Bloody 'ell, can't I 'ave an 'oliday first before yer've got me workin'," Dave protested.

"Look Dave, we don't know anyone here and the best way t'do that is to go t'work and meet people. I'm going up to those schools at the top of the hill to enrol the kids so they can start to meet kids their own age next week. As soon as you're all in school and work, I'll be looking for work myself," I stressed.

"We've got to buy a car and uniforms for the kids. I've had the British pounds changed to New Zealand currency and received eight hundred dollars for it. With paying this rent and ordinary living that money won't last us long, so we've both got to work."

This would be the first time Dave would be working for a boss. I knew he felt stressed about it but I wasn't bothered. He wanted to come here with us, so now he'll have to face up to his responsibilities.

The location of the house was the reason I chose it, but I hadn't realised it was the end of a remote beach with no public transport and at the bottom of a hill. At the top of the hill were the grounds of McLean's College that Sharon-Louise would be enrolled in and, on the other side of the hill, was Bucklands Beach Intermediate School for Gary.

If we had to walk along the roads to school it meant walking the two kilometres length of the beach, turning left up a hill to the top where Babs and Mark lived, then left back along the main road. Walking this journey would have taken more than forty-five minutes. Surrounding the back garden of our little hut on the beach was a six-foot high wooden fence with the cross slats on our side.

From the moment we moved in and because we didn't have a car at that time, we scaled the fence and climbed the hill every day when we were going anywhere – this only took five or six minutes. Apart from the schools, the local shops for basic necessities plus the bus stop were at the top of this hill.

One of my biggest problems without a car was collecting groceries and I didn't want to keep asking my sister and her husband for lifts to the shops. But, after a conversation with Babs, I had an ahah!! moment.

"When you're ready to buy a house, Pauline, the Real Estate agents will pick you up and drive you to the property," Babs informed me, "not like back in Birkenhead where you had to meet them outside the house you wanted to see."

I immediately formed my plan. I found a local map and scanned the papers and rang a female agent and enquired about a house in the next suburb. Although I didn't have the money to buy a house, I decided to pretend I was looking, then get the agent to stop at the shops on the way home. My first agent picked me up and drove me around various houses within the price range I had shared with her. After seeing all the properties she had on her books and saying they weren't quite what I was looking for, I asked, "Can we stop at those shops for a minute, if you don't mind, I've got to pick up a few things and it will save me coming out again."

The agent was more than accommodating. "I need to pick up my dry cleaning and get some shopping myself, so I'll meet you back at the car and take you home in about thirty minutes. Is that okay?" she offered.

I made the most of the offer and raced around the supermarket picking up a week's supply of groceries and appeared at the car with the trolley.

"A few things!" the agent smiled when she saw the mound of plastic bags but helped me to put my groceries into the boot of her car and took me home. She even helped me in with all the bags. *What a lovely woman*, I thought. *When I have enough money to buy a house, I'll definitely use her services*, but by the following Friday I needed to shop again and so rang another agency because I didn't want the first one to become aware of what I was doing. She too waited for me outside the supermarket and drove me home.

"The people in this country are so helpful," I announced at the dinner table. "I haven't met a single person that wasn't pleasant to chat to."

Dave eventually rang the company that had offered him a job.

"We're so pleased to hear from you" said his potential boss. "We've got a car here that needs some work, but the engine is good. Would you like to buy it for three hundred dollars?"

"Thanks, I will," Dave answered.

"You can collect it today if you want to and look around our premises but have a bit of a holiday before you start work. How does a week on Monday sound?"

I gave Dave the money for the car and Mark drove him to the workshop to collect it.

"This is exciting, kids!" I smiled. "We can have another week of sightseeing with the car then we'll organise for you both to start at your schools."

We waited expectantly for our 'new' car. Dave pulled up in a very old Toyota Corolla, and the moment Gary and Sharon-Louise saw it they gave it its name; The Crapolla.

Some pleasurable days were then spent driving around the local suburbs and beaches exploring the area.

"From Monday your dad will be taking the car to work each day, so we'd better arrange your interviews at school while we can drive there," I told the kids.

Sharon-Louise and I walked into the principal's office of McLeans College with her reports and papers from the school she had attended in Birkenhead. My children were both bright students and I felt there would be no problem enrolling them. The principal's jaw dropped as she gaped at Sharon-Louise wearing one of her twelve-inch miniskirts in green sparkly spandex, her black T-shirt free of writing, which was an order from me, but she won the fight over high heels as she sported a pair of black patent leather winkle pickers that had only a two-inch heel, so she felt she was meeting me halfway.

"You couldn't wear make-up back home for school and it won't be any different here," I shouted. "Leave it off!"

"Look, Mum, am not going t'school t'day, am only goin' to see if a wanna go to the school. We're goin' to the shops after an' am not bein' seen out without me make-up, okay," she shouted.

"Eyes and lips only!" I shouted, "definitely no Pollyfilla."

Luckily the purple dye she regularly sprayed on her hair was beginning to fade and I had insisted that she put her hair up in a ponytail for the day.

The shocked expression on the principal's face gradually changed to a look of disdain.

"You do understand young lady that you can't wear make up in school?" she asked.

"Yis, I understand," said Sharon-Louise with a patronising air.

"This school has a full uniform that must be worn every day, including the appropriate footwear," she spat her words at Sharon-Louise as she looked over the desk at her high heels. Sharon-Louise sat back in her chair, crossed her arms, then crossed her legs in a deliberate fashion, jigging her foot up and down under the principal's nose to show off her heels and aggravate her even further.

"Is there a shop nearby that sells the uniforms and shoes?" I asked in my best Mrs Bucket voice, trying to break the tension and prevent Sharon-Louise from verbally responding.

"Yes, I'll give you the address. She can start on Monday next. Can she wash that muck out of her hair or is it dye?" The principal aimed the question at me!

"Err, excuse me! I do 'ave a tongue in me 'ead ye know. I can answer me own questions. It's spray on and it can wash off, okay?"

Oh my God, I squirmed.

The principal's face became a mask of repulsion. "Then you had better wash it out before you arrive here on Monday, my lady, or you will be sent straight back home. Do you understand?"

No! screamed through my head. *Don't let her answer that please.* I stood and tried to gather my things, hoping that would prevent a response from Sharon-Louise. But she merely responded with the same expression on her face that the principal had on hers and eyeballed her. I could see how this relationship would continue.

She chose to sit on the bench outside Bucklands Beach Intermediate and wait for Gary and me. "We won't be long," I

197

said, relieved at not having to go through a similar scene with another principal and my daughter. Gary wore his jeans and a white T-shirt with his Doc Martin boots.

"You seem to be a bright young man, Gary," said the principal as he flicked through his reports, and Gary beamed. "You can start school here on Monday and I'll put you in the A class. You must wear a uniform and standard footwear that you can purchase from this shop," said the principal as he handed me a piece of paper with the name of the same shop the last principal had given me.

"Well, that wasn't difficult, was it?" I smiled as we climbed into the Crapolla to go and purchase their school uniforms in Howick, the town centre.

"If you think am gunna wear that bloody pleated tartan kilt fer school yerve gorra nuther think comin'," Sharon-Louise screamed when she saw the uniform in the shop.

"That's the school uniform, Sharon-Louise - you've just got to wear it."

"Then am not goin' t'that school, okay? NO WAY!" she shouted.

"Try the damn thing on, will you." I became aggravated with her and grabbed the kilt that the distressed shop assistant was holding and pushed it at my daughter.

"No; an ye can't make me," she screamed as she pushed the kilt back at me, then she turned on her two-inch heels and stormed out of the shop.

I was exasperated. "Here, Gary, you try these pants on," I said and handed him a pair of grey shorts. Gary stared at them. "I 'aven't worn shorts since year one, Mum. Am not a baby – a want long pants." He was almost crying, and his eyes pleaded with me.

The shop assistant came to my rescue. "In this country, Gary, all the boys wear shorts for school, right up to year twelve. We don't sell long pants for school children. You'll see when you get to school, they'll all be wearing the same shorts. It gets too hot in this country to wear long pants for school," and she smiled a sweet smile and patted Gary's shoulder.

He came out of the dressing room in his new school shorts, stood looking at me, dropped his chin to his chest and began quietly crying.

"Luv, you look great." I hugged him and tried to comfort him and make him feel better about wearing shorts, but I knew I wasn't winning.

"I'll have both uniforms," I told the assistant. "She's got to wear it so just give me her size."

"Now, shoes?" I asked.

"They are next door," said the shop assistant and I paid for the clothes and left. "Come on, Sharon-Louise. I've got your uniform, now you've got to try shoes on," as we walked into the shop.

The ugliest shoes I had ever seen were placed before them both. They had to wear thick, black, rubber-soled leather shoes. Gary's were lace ups and Sharon-Louise's were sandals. Immediately I saw them I was waiting for the verbals from them both.

I looked at my daughter. "A don't believe it!" she muttered in disbelief, as she turned her head and stared out of the window. By this time, she'd had the wind knocked out of her sails.

"If it's any consolation, Sharon-Louise, I agree with you. They are the ugliest shoes I've ever seen. But we've got no choice. That's the school uniform and you won't look any different from anyone else when you wear them. Just try on your size and let's get this lot home," I said, indicating to the shopping bags full of clothes.

Sharon-Louise seemed defeated. For the first time for a long time, I thought she was going to cry. She never cried these days –

well only when she was saying goodbye to her Nan. Tough kids from our part of the world didn't cry – that was for sissies – but right now it looked as though both my kids wanted to fall into a heap and sob their heart out.

"Let's go for a chinese lunch?" I announced as we all climbed into the Crapolla. I wanted to give them a treat to try and lift their spirits again but neither of them would be jollied along. They were quiet as they ate their meal and then Sharon-Louise muttered, "I 'ate this country; a wanna go 'ome." And Gary agreed. "I wanna go 'ome too."

I had a tough job on my hands for the next few days. The kids became dispirited and at home they sat absently gazing out the window saying very little. Dave was sitting on the settee reading the paper. When he saw the kids sulking about being in the country, he added his two-penneth: "Yeh, it's a bloody lousy place. Instead of spending any more money on rubbish like them clothes, yer'd berra work out 'ow much it costs t'go 'ome. 'Cos am tellin' ye this – if I die in this country, you make sure you send me 'ome to be buried. A don't wanna be buried in this God-forsaken hole."

No matter what I did or said I couldn't raise their spirits. Dave had his dinner at his allotted time – just as he used to back home, and now that he had a car he easily slipped back into his routine of eating and heading straight off to the pub.

It was dark outside, and we didn't have a television yet.

"Let's play a game," I said.

"What game?" answered Sharon-Louise as she continued to look at the floor.

"I've got some playing cards," I said with a smile, trying to encourage them.

"No," came her response.

"No, thanks, Mum," answered Gary.

And just then the lights went out. The house was in darkness.

"What's happening?" asked Gary as he remembered where I was and shuffled over to sit beside me on the settee.

"Let's look through the window and see if everyone's lights are off," I said.

We looked out to see the streetlights weren't alight and all the houses were engulfed in blackness. "Babs had told me they often have power cuts around here, so she gave me some candles. Do either of you know where I put those candles?" I asked.

"A think they're in the pantry on the top shelf," said Gary.

All three of us shuffled to the side of the room holding onto each other and followed the walls to the kitchen. By touch only we found the pantry and the candles and matches which were right beside them. We each lit a candle and walked back into the front room and walked to the window. We stood in a row, staring through the window at the water and the moonlight, each with a lit candle in our hand.

In the lounge room was an open fireplace and I suddenly had an idea. Should we go out and gather some kindling from the field at the side of the house and light a fire in the grate?"

Both kids nodded in agreement.

We stood the lit candles on the hearth and left the house holding hands until we became adjusted to the moonlight outside. There was a full moon which emanated an eerie yellow glow and gave enough light for us to see the twigs and kindling as we began to pick up any wood that would burn.

Back inside the house, I took the newspaper Dave had been reading and rolled it into balls for the fire. I placed the kindling on the top and set light to the paper. Immediately the fire ignited and in a very short time I was able to place a decent-sized log on top.

We all sat on the floor staring into the fire, Gary pressed to one side of me and Sharon-Louise to the other. The glow of the fire began to light the room.

Through the window, the moon shone over a perfectly calm yellowish sea and here and there sparkles of water shone like tiny Christmas tree lights switching on and off. "Let's pull that settee up to our backs to lean on," I said, then we all sat back on the floor again leaning on the settee and staring into the flames of the fire to our left and looking through the window at the moon on the water on the right. It was warm and comforting and created a magical atmosphere in the room. "Do either of you remember yer Nan's favourite song for you both?" which I knew they did as I started to sing:

You are my sunshine, my only sunshine,
you make me happy, when skies are grey,
you'll never know dear, how much I love you,
please don't take my sunshine away

We all began to sing it with my encouragement. Firstly, they quietly joined in with me and when the first chorus was over, they began to sing it again this time with gusto. Then Sharon-Louise started laughing. "Do ye remember when me Nan got tiddly and started singin' it sittin' on the front step? She ended up with half the bleedin' street comin' out an' joinin' er."

"Yes, she used to sing it like this remember," I said as I put Mum's soprano voice on, one hand pressed to my breast, and began to sing the song again the way their Nan did. We all began to laugh.

"Worabout that one Gaga used to sing to 'er when ee was alive," and Gary began Gaga's version of Sweet Sixteen and we both joined in.

When first I saw the lovelight in your eyes,
I thought the world held nought but joy for me,
And even though we've drifted far apart,
I never dreamed but what I dream of theeeeeee.
I luv ye like I've never luved before,
Since first I saw you on the village green,
Come to me in my dreams of long ago,
I luv you as I luved you,
When you were sweeeeet, when you were sweeeet sixteen.

Gary and Sharon-Louise both held their chest the way Gaga did and in unison threw their arms up and out at the end and we all fell about laughing. All the songs their Nana and Gaga had taught them were sung out loud as we sat in front of the fire for the next two hours. Then the lights came back on.

"Ooooh," said Gary, disappointed as they looked around at where they were sitting. The magic had gone out of the room. Sharon-Louise didn't ask any questions; she jumped up and switched off the light, sat back down beside me and Gary and continued with:

It's only, a shanty, in old shanty town,
("Just like this place," I laughed over the singing)
the roof is so slanty it touches the ground,
there's a tumble-down shack, by an old railroad track,
like a millionaire's mansion, it's calling me back.
I'd give up my palace, if I were a King,
It's more than a palace, it's my everything,
there's a queen waiting there with a silvery crown,
in a shanty in old shanty town

Throughout the renditions Gary pretended he was strumming a guitar. When they got to the line that said, 'a queen with a silvery crown', Sharon-Louise put a cushion on my head. Repeatedly, we sang song after song from our past. I looked at my two children and smiled to myself. That power cut was a blessing; their spirits were back up again.

After tucking the kids into their beds, I made a hot chocolate which I took to the lounge room window. I claimed the moon as mine – there it was shining over the water and had appeared just when I needed it most to replenish my kids' spirits.

"Thanks, Moon," I said out loud. "Please keep looking over us as we'll need you more I think over the next few months until we're settled."

Then came Monday morning. Dave had left in the Crapolla to begin his first day at work. The children stood before me in their new school uniforms. I hardly recognised them! Sharon-Louise had shampooed her hair which was held in a ponytail and its beautiful auburn shine looked healthy. A white shirt and red plaid kilt with white socks and her black sandals made her look like a normal fourteen-year-old. There wasn't a trace of make-up on her face. It hadn't been easy for me trying to get those clothes on her and, after days of fighting over them, she had accepted defeat. She knew she had to go to school, and she knew she had to wear that uniform.

I had been worried about her development in Birkenhead. Though she was an A grade student, she was mimicking her peers. Discos, clothes, make-up and boys seemed to be all she was interested in at that time. Gary would surely follow the same pattern as the other kids in the neighbourhood and I couldn't see a rosy future for the kids if they stayed in Birkenhead. Sharon-Louise was a stubborn, strong-headed kid and I had to be super strong to steer her in the right direction.

Gary's chubby knees and legs looked pale in comparison to the other kids here in New Zealand, but the sun would now get to his limbs, and I knew it wouldn't be long before he tanned. He wore a grey shirt and shorts with knee length grey socks above his black lace up shoes. They each toted a backpack for their books and lunch box. But their faces reflected their mood. Their shoulders were hunched forward, and their heads hung over their chests. They hated their uniforms and didn't want to go to school.

"Are you both sure you don't want me to walk in with you for your first day?"

"No!" they both answered in unison.

"I'm so proud of you both," I said with sincerity as I surveyed them, "not because you both look like royalty in those uniforms but because you're gunna face all those strangers t'day and show them just who this family is. You're a credit to me and your dad; I want you to know that. You're as good as any one of them in that school if not better and don't you ever forget that." Without conscious thought I was repeating my dad's words. "Now go out there, kids, and let Bucklands Beach know we've arrived." I threw up my hands, laughing, then dropped them around my kids and hugged them both.

They walked to the back fence, threw their backpacks over, climbed over the top and flumped down to the grass on the other side. I stood on the lower cross bar with my arms lying on the top of the fence with my chin on them. They picked up their backpacks and put them back on their shoulders and began to climb the hill which ascended from the back fence at a 60-degree angle.

"Ta-Ra, kids. Have a fantastic day," I shouted, smiling and waving. They stopped, turned, and looked at me without a smile, waved, turned back, and proceeded to amble further up the hill. At the halfway point in the ascent, I shouted again, "Look around, kids, you can see over the top of the house from there ... can you see the water? You'll be able t'see that from your classrooms. *Are you lucky or what?*" I bellowed and chuckled. They both stopped again and looked at me without a smile, looked at the water over the roof tops for a split second, waved, turned back to the hill, hunched over, and continued.

Before we had left Liverpool, I had taken them to the Empire Theatre to see *The Sound of Music*, and as I watched them climb the hill I was reminded of the last scenes. I threw out my arms as I lifted my head and in my finest rendition of Mum's soprano voice I began to sing:

The Hills are alive with the sound of music".

They both stopped, turned, and looked at me, Gary started laughing and shaking his head.

"Mum!" he chuckled. Sharon-Louise stood looking at me, put her hands on her hips and pushed out her chin as she tried to suppress her laughter and shouted, "Fer God's sake, muther, will ye go inside – yer makin' a show of us."

Ha! I had made them laugh and immediately felt better. I climbed down from the fence and returned to the house. It was time for me to dress for my own interview with the largest company in New Zealand, NZ Forest Products. They were looking for a pay clerk.

I chose my wool suit, which I felt was sure to impress and was suitable for an interview. I threw my shoes and bag over the fence and carefully climbed over and flumped down to the other side. I straightened my clothes, put on my shoes and climbed the hill to the bus stop. As I stood waiting for the bus, the rain started; it came down in torrents. There was no cover to the bus stop, and I didn't have an umbrella. By the time I boarded the bus, my hair was plastered to my head, and I was completely wet through. I had to get a second bus, again waiting in the rain for another ten minutes and, by the time I arrived for my interview, I resembled a drowned rat. And because of my wool suit I smelled like one as well. My nerves were taut, and I couldn't relax and be chatty. I was aware of my bedraggled appearance and felt embarrassed. My interview was with the company secretary, and he was from England. I felt that was a stroke of luck as it would have been the only reason he would have employed me.

"You can start next week," he said and the salary he offered was beyond what I had anticipated. I was thrilled. Tonight, we would all have such a lot to talk about. Dave and I both had new jobs and the kids would have new friends.

One by one we related our day across the dinner table. Dave was happy enough with the boss and his workmates but commented they were all "Wet b'ind the ears and needed to learn 'ow t'cut corners an' still get the job done right."

I described the office I would work in and the industry. "It's in Penrose, Dave, near to where you work so we can go together in the Crapolla each day."

Gary said he had made a new friend called Jamie and his school was great and the work was easy, but he didn't like his male teacher. Immediately I was concerned. His schooling to date had always been with female teachers and I felt sure it was Gary's problem.

"Men have a different way of teaching, Gary. Listen carefully and do as he says and you'll get to like him soon enough."

Sharon-Louise never mentioned her teacher but was impressed that the class had both boys and girls. Back home she had attended an all-girls school.

"Some of the boys are really cool an' a fancy a couple of them," she laughed with a mischievous look in her eye. She had sat beside a girl called Clare and they immediately became friends – they planned to see each other at the weekend. "We did the schoolwork they're doing now last year, Mum, so a looked really good when the teacher asked questions an' a could answer every bleedin' one," she bragged.

"I hope you didn't swear when you answered the questions, Sharon-Louise."

"Muther!!" she shouted. "Yerve got no idea, 'ave ye. I only swear in the 'ouse and with you and me friends. A listened t'everyone else and nobody else swore so a wasn't gunna let meself down on me first day. A talked like you do when ye bein' Mrs Bucket." And we all burst into laughter.

Dave went out to the pub and me and the kids chatted on about our day and eventually they went to bed quite happy with their first day and looking forward to the next. I sat looking through the window at my moon. Its warm buttery yellow glow splayed across the gentle waves that lapped the shore. Stars were ablaze throughout the navy-blue sky and electric lights twinkled on the islands in the distance. I sighed and felt contented. We had been in the country for three weeks and this was the first day all my family were being positive about their new life. I stood up and turned off the lights, sat back on the settee and gazed through the window at the breathtaking view. "I think it's all gunna work, Moon." I smiled.

Silently I churned over a few minor problems for another hour, which I mentally shared with the moon , and then I went to bed.

Chapter Sixteen

The lawyer that feared me

1982 - 1983

"Aren't the people in this country lovely! Everyone is so friendly," I commented as I placed our dinner on the table.

"Except Mr Rodgers," Gary said solemnly. "A don't think 'ee likes me, Mum, ee's always tellin' me off for nothin'."

"Of course he likes you – everyone likes you, Gary, you're gorgeous." I laughed as I hugged him and gave him a slobbery kiss on his cheek. "You just show him how clever you are, and he'll be proud of you, just like we are," but it upset me that Gary was having such a hard time with his teacher.

Dave and the children had a whole week of settling into work and school and it was now Monday morning, the beginning of their second week and my first day at work. I left the house with Dave to start my new job in the pay office of New Zealand Forest Products. There were seven clerks – five females and two males, plus the paymaster, Ray, a friendly jovial man in his late sixties. He was short and rather round with a very smiley face. He told me he had worked for Forest Products in the same office all his working life. I felt I fitted in with the team and for the first few days learned what the work consisted of and was given an orientation of the mills. There were seven mills doing three rotating shifts and one mill that did day work only. Although the working hours were 8.30am to 5pm, a pay clerk was required to go in to work at 10.30pm and finish at 1.30am for three nights a week to pay the 3-to-11pm shifts that were finishing their rosters. This work was spread around the office and paid triple time for those three hours. The other pay clerks hated doing the night pays and I assured them I was happy to do almost every one of them as I needed the money.

"If this keeps up, I'll soon have enough money for the deposit on our house," I told the kids.

I was now earning more than Dave and contributing all my money to our joint living and savings. Doing three night pays every week, with my full-time job plus looking after the family, I had little time for any homesickness.

"Dave, I'll need the car to get to work for three nights of the week," I informed him.

"You can run me to the pub every night and I'll get a lift home from one of the lads," Dave responded.

This didn't please me. It would mean his drinking would increase because he didn't have to drive himself. Dave's social life was now in full swing, and he once again thought his money was for his spending only. For the first couple of weeks of his work Dave had given me a small amount if he had anything left over after paying golf fees and beer money. Within a very short time, he'd found a club that ran a TAB, and Dave was back to gambling. *Here we go again*, I thought. Week by week his contribution to the household diminished until it stopped altogether again, and the rows over money began once more.

"How can we get out of this place and get our own house if you don't work with me on this, Dave!"

"I don't want t'buy a bloody 'ouse 'ave told ye. I want t'go 'ome."

"You pleaded to come with us when we were in England, and since we've arrived all you've moaned about is wanting to go home. Stop upsetting the kids with your negative talk," then I added angrily, "So save your money and go back to England, will you!"

"Oh, yerd like that wouldn't ye, me goin' 'ome on me own," Dave sneered his answer. "We can all go 'ome; the kids don't like it 'ere either," he shouted.

"The kids are settling down really well now, Dave, and I don't want you unsettling them any more with your talk about going home. Do you hear!"

Dave snatched up his keys and went out to his club. He had started his 'deep declines', as I called them. He was angry with me and not speaking to me, going about his personal life of coming and going in the house and was irritated by merely being around me. He could keep this up for months.

We would leave for work each day in the same car and the silence was unbearable. Apart from the morning tension within the car, Dave had been playing golf every weekend and taking the Crapolla with him, so when I needed the car on Saturday or Sunday, I had to get up early and run Dave to golf. One of the men in the pay office was selling his car and offered it to me at the price the car yard wanted to give him in part exchange for a newer model. It was a bargain, and I grabbed the opportunity. Having another car would be a blessing. I could also leave home a little later in the morning and not have to leave the kids so early, plus I could start my day in a better mood without Dave.

It was an old Ford Cortina but had been well maintained and when the kids saw it, they christened it The Rolls Canardly.

"Why?" I asked as I smiled at them.

"'Cos it can roll down hills and can 'ardly get up them," they both shouted their response and laughed at me. They never lost their sense of humour.

Weekends were more pleasurable as I was able to run the children to the various sports. Gary joined the sea scouts, and his circle of friends increased weekly. He played rugby for his school and joined a karate class. Sharon-Louise was Miss Popular. Clare became her best friend and together they joined the local basketball team. Clare was almost a permanent fixture in our house and other friends constantly called at night and weekends. The children's social lives began to build up and I was aware that it did not resemble the one they had left behind in Birkenhead. Sharon-Louise quickly accepted the outdoor pursuits rather than discos and never mentioned that she missed that part of her life. Plus, makeup didn't fit into an outdoor life and her swearing diminished, thank goodness.

Raewyn was a friend that worked in Forest Products with me. Perhaps once a month we'd have a movie night and, on the odd occasion, a day out at a market or even a drive to show me more of this part of the country we were living in.

Life had settled into a routine that suited me. Gary had come to terms with his asthma and, with my constant monitoring, we had it under control. Apart from that, both my kids looked healthier and happier than they had ever been in Birkenhead. I was now sure I'd made the right decision to bring us here to live in New Zealand. Dave hadn't changed and had quite forgotten his promise not to gamble and to drink less, but I knew that would happen, so I focused on the kids and me.

Three months had gone by in this house when news came that the container with our furniture was about to arrive. I looked around at the small shack on the beach and knew we would never fit all my furniture into it. So, I began looking for another rental property. I needed to find one quickly as the container would be stored on the dock but only for two weeks, then a storage fee would apply to it.

At the top of the hill on the side of the school fields a house was up for rent that I felt would suit us perfectly. It was a modern three-bedroom brick house with a garage, and it looked down the hill onto the water. I rang the number advertised on the board and was told what the rent would cost. It was almost twice as much as I paid for the beach shack but the beach shack couldn't compare with this lovely new brick dwelling. Earning a substantial pay now meant I could easily afford it and so I decided to take it. I paid the bond and a month's rent in advance.

The container was delivered and placed on the drive of the house and excitedly we opened it and unpacked all our possessions that had travelled all these months from Merseyside. The screams of pleasure from the kids as they revealed various personal objects warmed my heart and we seemed to be smiling all day. The furniture was placed around the house and the cupboards were stacked with my own dishes and linen. I walked around my possessions stroking them here, touching them there, and was reminded of Maureen O'Hara in the film *The Quiet Man* when Maureen eventually got her dowry. *Ha!* I thought, *I know just how she felt*. The antiques I had purchased were housed in the garage ready for sale.

Sharon-Louise and her friend Clare spent all weekend arranging then rearranging her bedroom. In the lounge, I placed a settee here then changed my mind and dragged it there. A cushion on this chair, a vase on that table. Some of the linen I unpacked had belonged to my mother and I kept going back to the cupboard to smell it. This was my mother's home smell. Gary showed off his collection of model cars and Lego to his two friends who had been invited to come around and see his collection, and the entire weekend was spent by all three of us enjoying our home.

On Monday, I contacted an antique dealer who advised me to auction the pieces I had collected as they would realise more money that way. A van collected the furniture and took them to an auction room, which was in a building next to the road where I worked in Penrose. The following Wednesday when the auction was to be held, I was excited as I told Ray what was about to happen that morning.

"Go on," he said, "take a few hours off and see how it goes."

I stood in the back of the auction room and was ecstatic as I heard each item going for far more than I had ever anticipated. After paying the auction fees, I had made more than five thousand dollars. I mentally deducted the cost of purchase of each item, and realised I had made more than three thousand dollars profit. I added it to my nest egg which was now growing rapidly each week as I almost doubled my basic salary each month doing night pays. Dave was living his deep decline, but I'd given up trying to communicate with him. All his money was now used for his addictions and, on this day, he arrived home with a new set of golf clubs.

"I'm buyin' these off one of the lads, so I want the money for them. He wants eighty dollars so get that money out of yer account t'morrow," he barked at me.

"What do you mean you need the money for them? You bought them, you pay for them. I'm saving for the house," I snapped back.

"Don't you make a bloody fool of me, woman. A said ad buy them off him an am not gunna be made t'look a fool 'cos I 'aven't got the money. Yerve got enough money in that bank to cover these clubs. I'm gunna give Gary me old ones so just give me the bloody money," he snarled.

I held off as long as I could but eventually, reluctantly, gave him the money against my better judgment. For $80 it wasn't worth the arguments and disturbing the peace.

My evenings were spent alone when the kids went to bed if I wasn't working, and I would open the drapes and look out over the moonlit water and make my plans. On the nights I didn't have a pay-out, I would try to be in bed before Dave came home. It was safer to be out of the line of fire. He would stumble in through the door most nights and collapse into a chair. I would wait to hear his snoring then would go out into the lounge and take his lit cigarette out of his hand before it dropped to the floor and perhaps start a fire. When I was doing the night pays, the responsibility was passed onto Sharon-Louise. She wasn't to go to sleep until her father was snoring.

Life chugged along in this fashion for another three months until Dave came home one night in one of his vicious drunken moods and I hadn't realised the time as I was reading a book. I saw his eyes and was immediately afraid of him. As he stumbled into the kitchen for a drink, I stood and quietly backed away, then swiftly locked myself in the bedroom. When he couldn't see me in the lounge, he tried to open my bedroom door. Finding it locked fuelled his anger. He shouted now for me to open the fin door as he punched it repeatedly until he put his fist through it. Then he threw himself against the door and burst the lock open.

The onslaught was swift as he physically attacked me. I tried to fight him off as he punched my face then dug his fingers into my neck and wrists. He dragged me into the lounge and threw me to the floor, then collapsed into a chair and, like a child, began crying and sobbing.

"A don't wanna live in this country. Am gunna die 'ere. I hate it." He raised himself from the chair and lurched toward me once again, screaming, "This is all your fault, you bitch!" but he tripped over the coffee table and, hitting his temple on the corner of it, landed in the centre of the room. He lay still for a while as I stood staring, my heart beating fast in my chest. My mouth went dry, and my nerves jangled as I stood looking at him, wondering if he was dead, and trying to anticipate his next move if he wasn't. My body hurt, my face ached and my head throbbed. He regained consciousness and began to crawl around the floor disorientated. He couldn't see me and obviously didn't know where he was. Slowly, quietly, I began to back out of the room, when suddenly he looked up at me, and I gasped in horror – his eyes were grey, hollow, blank, and obviously vacant, and it was his uncle's face. This was the face he had feared all his early life and he had turned into him.

The next morning, I calmly confronted Dave. "I told you that if you ever laid a finger on me again in anger, I would kill you. Well, you were lucky last night that I didn't and I'm not putting up with you any longer. You can pack your bags and get on the plane back to Merseyside. I'll pay your fare. I'll get you the first flight I can, and you can go back to your drinking pals."

"Am goin' nowhere on me own, am stayin' in this 'ouse. Ye can't throw me out 'cos me name's on the lease an' if you don't like the situation, you can move out." He spat the same words at me that he felt kept him safe back in England but I didn't own this house so I could walk away this time.

"Right," I said, "I'll find another house and take the kids with me. Your name won't be on that lease and you're not welcome so you can stay here on your own."

He went off to work and never mentioned the row or my threat over the next days; he merely went through his usual routine of coming and going and not speaking to me. I knew him well enough; he would think if nothing was said it would be forgotten. But this was my new life, and I now had my boundaries. I found another house in a street near Gary's school. It was an older house and, after living as we had in the modern one, it was a let-down to all of us, but the rent was less, and I felt it wouldn't be long before I had the deposit for a home of our own. I calmly told Dave when I would be leaving this house and he ignored me and continued in his usual fashion of coming and going and ignoring me. I arranged for a removal van and, on the morning of moving, Dave said, "Am comin' with ye. Am not stayin' 'ere on me own."

"You are not coming with me; you walk into that house I've

rented, and I'll call the police. You're not welcome I've told you. You're a bully, a gambler and a drunk. You contribute nothing to your kids' upbringing and you're a drain on my money and my health. My sister knows how you treated me last week and she and Mark will be there like a shot and throw you out if you try to walk into my next home. You can save your own money now and go back to England." I said this calmly for him to see I meant what I said. The kids climbed into the back seat of the Rolls as I sat in the driver's seat, switched on the engine, and never looked back.

Dave packed his clothes, threw them into his car and left the house.

The inspection of the house by the owners revealed the damaged door and they informed me that the bond would not be returned. They were keeping it to do the repairs. I knew this would happen but consoled myself with the fact that it was a small price to pay to get Dave out of my life.

My relationship with everyone in the pay office was a good one and I continued to chat and laugh throughout the day, but I knew my bruises were noticed by my colleagues from time to time even though they didn't say anything to me. Dave had moved in with one of his new male friends but nightly he would call at the house after drinking. He would bang on the door demanding I open it and let him in. I wouldn't open the door when I was there but when I was working at night, he would sometimes wake the kids and get inside. I would come home and find him on my settee in a drunken sleep. Those were the nights I never slept at all; I was frightened he would enter my room. Once he was asleep, he didn't often wake but having him in the house again meant a sleepless night for me. He would wake the next morning and leave early to get back to where he lived and change his clothes for work. I was never frightened of him in the mornings.

"I'm warning you, Dave, if you ever do that again I'll call the police. Now get out of my home."

On a night I was home and wouldn't let him in he began shouting and abusing me from the front step then smashed a small window beside the front door ready to put his hand through and open the door. Just then my next-door neighbour came to my rescue, suddenly appearing behind Dave.

"Look, mate," he said to Dave, "since this family moved into the house, I'm sick of hearing you waking the neighbourhood every night when you're drunk, trying to get in. If it happens again, I'll call the bloody police. Get away from this house," he demanded. "If she wanted you here, she'd open the door so bugger off."

Dave went slinking off, with his tail between his legs. He wouldn't stand up to a man.

"Thanks so much for that," I told my neighbour. "I'm sorry about the noise every night; I didn't know everyone could hear it." I felt embarrassed and humiliated again. I was now aware of why I was getting odd looks from my new neighbours when I was trying to be friendly. I must have been the talk of the neighbourhood. Even though he wasn't living with me, his association with me was still a black cloud that influenced what others thought of me.

The next morning, I was late for work as I waited for a glazier to come and fix the window. When I arrived at work near lunchtime, I confessed to Ray what was happening. "You need to get a non-molestation order out on him, Pauline," Ray said as he wrote down a name. "Go to this lawyer around the corner; see if he can fit you in quickly."

I rang the number Ray had given me and managed to get an appointment for the following day. That night I nervously sat in the dark at the close of pub time hoping to give the impression we were all asleep in bed if Dave came calling. He didn't, but I still didn't sleep that night.

The following day I entered the young lawyer's office and explained my situation.

"This paper needs to be presented at court and when it's signed by the judge the police get a copy of it and you can have him arrested if he comes around again," the lawyer explained.

"How long does that take?" I asked.

"A few days," he answered. "And the next thing we need to do is get you divorced from him." I knew that most lawyers thought starting divorce procedures was the next step and as I'd lost money twice before trying to divorce Dave I wasn't eager to start that discussion right now and was worried how much the non-molestation order was going to cost me.

"Let's get this order filed and then we'll discuss the cost of continuing with a divorce," I told him.

"I'll be in touch when it's been through the court," the lawyer announced in an offhand, arrogant manner, making no eye contact with me.

"Ray, would you mind getting some of the others to do the night pays for a while until this non-molestation order is activated?" I asked. "I want to be sure I'm at home if Dave calls and not have the kids feeling responsible for letting him in."

I knew my kids loved their father but neither of them objected to anything I was organising. Without discussing it, I knew the kids understood why we couldn't have their father living with us now. Although I had tried to suppress my pain when he punched me in the last house, I felt the kids had heard the row and they both saw my eye and bruises and said nothing. The next morning they saw the door that their dad had damaged and neither of them even asked what had happened. I still smiled and pretended all was well as I went about trying to organise Dave out of my life. I never wanted my kids to feel fear as I had, and so never explained to them what I suffered silently, but I didn't want to rubbish their father either. I wanted them to feel loved by both their parents.

The following week I still hadn't heard from the lawyer and the nightly visits from Dave began again. He was now tapping at the bedroom windows and the back door. I knew he didn't want my neighbour to hear him as he skulked around the outside of the house, looking for an entry point. I would turn off the lights and sit in darkness never responding until he gave up and went away. I was so tired, my nerves were beginning to fray with this lifestyle. I rang the lawyer's secretary from my desk at work and asked if I could have an appointment at lunchtime. "I'll fit you in for a fifteen-minute slot," she said.

Ray overheard my conversation. "Is that non-molestation still not through?" he asked with concern.

"No, I haven't heard a thing. I don't want to leave the kids yet until I know the order is in place. I still have nothing legal, and I need to be able to ring the police and have him carted off rather than me fighting him. It will make my life so much easier."

Ray walked back to his office and made a phone call, then came back to me:

"I hope you don't mind, Pauline, but I've spoken to our company lawyer, and he tells me you can pick that paper up and bring it to his office. He'll have it filed in court this afternoon. That young man isn't doing his job right if he hasn't filed that paper yet. If it's still in his office, bring it back here."

With Ray's advice and concern I now felt supported as I marched into the lawyer's office. It was lined in mahogany wood with a large, impressive desk in the centre with a seat placed this side of it for me to sit at. He was behind the desk in his reclining leather chair with a window behind him. A file with my name on it was on the left side of the desk beside him as he lay back in his chair which was turned sideways to me as he continued talking to someone on the phone. He arrogantly waved at me to sit down while he continued his personal conversation. I sat quietly for only two or three minutes and couldn't contain myself any longer. I stood up and opened the file with my name on it that lay on his desk and there was the paper I had signed last week. I closed the file and kept it in my hand and was about to put it in my bag. The lawyer, on seeing this, immediately straightened in his chair, finished his conversation and grabbed my hand, twisting my wrist roughly as he tried to retrieve the file. But he didn't know who he was dealing with! I wasn't about to let that file go.

"I signed this last week, and it should be with the police by now," I growled. "Me and my kids are getting harassed nightly while you make up your mind when you'll do some bloody work!"

"How dare you speak to me like that," he shouted, holding onto the file with one hand and pushing at my shoulder with the other, still pulling the file in his direction. "That file is my property, and you can't take it from this office until you pay me what you owe me." He then pushed so hard on my shoulder it was almost the equivalent of one of Dave's punches.

"You've done nothing t'pay you for except cause me more grief!" I shouted , still desperately holding onto the file. A tug of war went on between us across the desk, but I was determined I was going to win. Neither of us would let go of that file. We eyeballed each other across the desk, then his eyes turned as angry and vicious as Dave's used to, and when I witnessed this fear engulfed me. I honestly believed he was going to assault me.

Determined that the first punch would be mine, without conscious control over my right arm, I watched it circle around in slow motion as my fist formed and smashed with vengeance into the lawyer's face. Immediately, blood spurted from his nose. He let go of the file in shock and stood holding his nose and face. Observing his bloody hand, he then looked at me wide-eyed.

"That is assault!" he screamed, looking totally shocked. "You will receive criminal charges for this."

"So, sue me!" I shouted as I turned on my heels, pushed the file into my bag and swiftly marched out of his office and down the hall to reception. This took approximately two minutes. During that time I could hear him shouting into his phone at the receptionist, telling her to lock the door and prevent me from leaving the premises. Ahead of me I saw the receptionist running toward the main door to lock it. So I began running as well.

"Don't you dare!" I screamed as I sprinted toward her as she tried to lock the door. We began struggling in the entrance. I was trying to get out and the receptionist was trying to keep me in. But my strength right now, in my state of fear, was powered by adrenaline and would match any man's. I propelled myself through the door and power-walked through the streets straight back to work. With every step I took, I felt at any minute the arm of the law would grab me.

Obviously shaken and traumatised when I arrived at the office, I related the incident to Ray whose face began to move and show many different signs of emotion as he absorbed the whole story. His twitching face surrounded his eyes, which widened like saucers then kept blinking and clearing. 'Unbelievable' was printed all over his expressions, as his mouth dropped slightly open. He leaned forward over the top of his desk as he focused on me and the story, afraid of missing one word of what I said. In an animated way I demonstrated how the file was used like a tug of war over the desk, how I punched the lawyer's face to make him release it and described the sudden surge of blood, then me running down the hall and threatening the young receptionist, and finally walking back to work thinking the arm of the law would catch me at any time. When I'd finished relatingthe story, I shoved the file at Ray.

"Can you get our lawyer to deal with it then?"

By this time, Ray was sitting in his chair, shoulders rounded and leaning toward me, absorbing every single word I'd said. With his forearms flat on his desk at this point, he threw back his head and erupted into a fit of raucous belly laughter.

"What are you laughing about?" I smirked but became caught up in the infectious laughter emanating from Ray. "I can tell you the whole situation has got me upset and I don't think it's funny," but I began to chuckle as I looked at Ray who was convulsed with this belly laugh, his face a wonderful mask of mirth. I could instantly see how funny this whole incident was and I began to laugh myself.

"Stop it, Ray – this is serious!" I shouted while gagging on my words as we both guffawed and gasped and rolled about the top of his desk. Belly laughter is infectious. Through the glass walls of the office the other pay clerks smiled and all began to giggle at the performance Ray and I were putting on.

"How did you hit him again?" screamed Ray through his red, bloated, tear-streamed face. "Show me!"

"Just like that," I demonstrated again as I swung my fist around and punched this invisible man. "I didn't know I was doing it – honest; it just happened." My tears of laughter released the fear I'd been feeling and, right at that point, it was the best medicine I could have had.

"I'm going to tell the company lawyer all that," said Ray, his face still red and swollen, and eyes wet with tears of laughter. "Please don't tell me I can't relate that incident, Pauline. It's the funniest thing I've heard for years."

"But do you think I'll get arrested?" I asked worriedly. "Will you ask our lawyer that?"

"Pauline, that man wouldn't put himself in court because he knows he's stuffed up. Put it out of your head, love, and don't pay him a cent if he sends you a bill. From what I've heard anyway he'll be too frightened of you – if he sent you a bill you might go back and beat him up!! Ha! Ha!" Then he picked up the file and, with a skip in his step I hadn't seen before, he headed off to the company lawyer's office to relate my funny story.

The paper was filed that afternoon and at dinner time that night the police knocked on my door. "We've got your non-molestation order, Mrs Hicks, and if your husband comes around again just ring us and we'll escort him off the premises."

"Thanks very much," I said.

That night, right after the pubs all shut, Dave turned up on my doorstep. I opened the side window and spoke to him. "I've got a non-molestation order out on you, Dave, so if you don't get off my doorstep, I'll ring the police and they'll arrest you."

"Am not 'ere to argue, Pauline; just let me in so we can talk. I got that paper today in work. You shouldn't have done that – all the guys saw that. Just talk to me," he pleaded in his drunken drawl, which I knew could so easily turn to violence, especially as he'd been humiliated with the police arriving at his workplace.

"I'm ringing the police, Dave," and I shut the window and did.

Dave continued to knock at the door for another few minutes until the police arrived. I peered through the side window and saw the shock on his face when he saw them. "A just wanna say g'night to me kids, officer, and she won't let me in."

"You've been issued with a non-molestation order, sir, and you must stop calling at this house. Your kids are in bed asleep. Come on, give me your keys and we'll run you home."

At last!! I felt protected and slept well for the first time in months. The police had taken Dave home and he had no car to get out again.

The following morning, I saw the Crapolla still sitting on the road and knew Dave would not be going to work that day. When

I came home from work at five o'clock, it had gone. The trouble that must have caused Dave to have to get a bus to the police station to collect his keys and then a bus back to retrieve his car was something I knew he would hate. Firstly, having to face the police after the event would embarrass him, plus Dave was used to an easy life and the inconvenience would be something he wouldn't put himself through too often.

The company lawyer organised a legal separation for me along with filing the non-molestation papers and only charged me the court costs. I went back to doing three nights a week in the pay office and over the next few months my nest egg showed a healthy increasing balance.

After the last incident, Dave rang nightly and, once I had worked out the usual time he would ring, I didn't answer the phone. He put a note through my door to say he had the right to speak to his kids and so I answered his next call and told him I'd allow him to ring only on a Friday night. He arranged a job for Sharon-Louise as a waitress in his golf club on a Sunday and he took Gary with him to play golf, which pleased all of us. I now had a day to myself. He eventually accepted the situation but never failed to snarl at me as he dropped the kids off, saying every time that I would be sorry if he ever found out I was seeing someone else.

Now that I felt I had the police backing me, I could move forward with my plans. I told my sister the whole story about my life with Dave. "I knew something like this was going on," she said.

"Don't fight him on your own, Pauline. You must tell me if he comes back and harasses you and we'll have him locked up."

Chapter Seventeen

Mum's visit to New Zealand

1983

When Dad died, my youngest brother Sam and his wife Pat hadn't long been married and lived in an apartment near our family home. Mum asked them to go and live with her as she didn't want to live in the house on her own. At that time, Babs, Harry – my brother in America – and I had no idea of how bad Mum's hypochondria was, and thought this would be a good move for all of them. Mum would have company and helping them would put her back on her feet as she'd feel some purpose for her life. Sam and Pat could save for a deposit on a house as they both worked and Mum could cook a meal for them when they returned home each night. It sounded ideal but the reality of living with Mum, who was constantly depressed and looking for attention, began to grind Sam and Pat down.

Babs, Harry, and I were sympathetic and felt we should leave it to them both to either stay or go. We all kept saying Mum should snap out of this soon as she'd been such a strong woman all her life – the community even benefitted with Mum's support when she was well, and she had been the bedrock of our home and family. But, as time marched on, we could see Mum settling into this 'poor me' attitude and it became exhausting for us when we visited. We could only imagine how bad this was for Sam and

Pat, living with her day in and day out.

My phone rang in New Zealand. It was Sam.

"Hi, Paul. Pat and I decided we'd have to move out of Mum's house as it's affecting our marriage. You've no idea how depressing it is day after day without a break. We told Mum we were considering doing this and she began crying and almost collapsed. She's really laying on the emotional blackmail, Paul. I don't know what to do. If I stay, Pat is going to leave me and if I go, and Mum dies, I'll never forgive myself."

"Oh, I'm so sorry, Sam. I'm thinking perhaps you put her on a plane to come here for a visit. Perhaps a couple of months and you can both have a break for that time and hopefully Babs and I will have had a chance to chat to her and help pull her out of this depression. I'm going through a tough time myself at the moment, Sam, and I'm not saying it's worse than your situation, but I'd have to think it over carefully. The kids are just settling down without their father being here and that took some time, so I must be careful I don't send them backwards. I'll go and chat to our Babs and we could perhaps share her – one month with me and one month with Babs. I could do with some help right now as I'm working long hours trying to get some money together for a deposit on a house."

"Oh, that would solve the problem for now, Pauline, and hopefully, by the time she comes home, she's easier to live with. Thanks, Pauline."

"I'll get back to you soon, Sam."

Babs and I sat and discussed the situation. We decided she could live with me for the first month and then with Babs for the second month. My intention was to show her how helpful she could be to me and how much I appreciated that help and to try to make her snap out of her 'poor me' attitude. When Mum put her mind to helping someone, her contribution was valuable. I needed to encourage her back to the strong

227

supportive mother that she had always been.

We arrived at the airport to greet Mum from the plane, and she was wheeled out in a wheelchair.

"Oh, no!" Babs and I said at the same time.

Her head was supported by the back of the wheelchair, and her eyes rolled around taking us in. Her first words, uttered in an extremely weak, high pitched fractured voice, were:

"That flight was the worst thing I've ever had to endure. If I'd known how long it was and how bad it was going to be I wouldn't have said I'd come. You're lucky I'm here alive as I thought I'd die on the plane."

Babs, Mark and Matt said their welcomes and that they would see her from time to time at my home over the next few weeks. Before they said their goodbye's, Mark and Matt picked her up out of the wheelchair and placed her in the back seat of my car. Mum blankly gazed out of the window all the way home, not speaking to anyone. Lifting her out of my car and into my home was a struggle for all three of us and her first words were:

"I think I've come 'ere to die, kids. This will be the last time yer'll see yer Nanna."

Sharon-Louise and Gary fought back tears as they looked at their Nanna and then at me.

"You'll be fine in a day or two, Mum, when you've seen this beautiful country. You'll be running around like a two-year-old again."

"No. Don't plan anything to get me out, Pauline. I haven't got any energy. I'll just stay in the house."

"I'm working, Mum, but have been given a few days off next week and we can get out and about then. What do you think?"

"No, luv, 'ave said, I don't want to go out; I might die outside and then were would ye be. No keep me in the house."

"I'm working each day until 5 o'clock and I was hoping you could perhaps cook the evening meal for us while you're here,

Mum. Do some scouse and rissoles like you used to?"

"Oh no, I can't be doin' that, Pauline; I couldn't stand at the stove that long. Ye little house is lovely but put me to bed now luv. I don't want to stay up. I need to rest to get over those days of flying."

So that was it. She wouldn't be talked into doing anything she didn't want to do. Nothing I could say was what she wanted. She stayed in bed all weekend. I went to work on Monday morning and the children went to school. They arrived home at 3.15pm to find their nanna in bed wanting them to fetch what she wanted and then to sit and listen to her negative dialogue. She lay there talking about her day hour by hour and how she fought off death as she thought this was going to be the hour she would die! On and on she'd go describing to the children how death felt as it crept up on her. They started dreading going home.

I would arrive home and cook the meal, but she needed her meal in bed on a tray. She wouldn't come out of that room. Dave still rang each night and even used the excuse of Mum being there to call to see her and to say hello. When he got inside my home, he said he should stay to help with the situation. He brought drink with him and sat in the lounge watching TV and making himself at home again. Once again, he would feel safe knowing I wouldn't throw him out and start trouble in front of my mother. This was not going the way I had planned it. I was stressed over both my mother and Dave, and worrying about how the kids were taking all of this.

The second week went just like the first, but Mum and Dave were piling extra stress on me – Dave with his determination to catch me in a stressful moment and move back in, and Mum crying constantly to bring us all into her room to witness her about to die. I spoke to Babs about it, but she said her turn didn't start for another two weeks so she wouldn't take her yet. I should deal with it better and stop being a pushover!

The pressure I was under was immense. I was in a state of hype day and night. In the third week, I received a phone call from Sharon-Louise when she arrived home from school.

"Nan's about to die, Mum! We came home and she's lying with one leg out of bed saying it was just as well we came home now 'cos she's about to die. She said she won't last until you come home, Mum. What should we do if she dies?" Sharon-Louise was distraught and crying. In the background, I heard Gary crying, "Come home, Mum."

"I'm coming home now, luv. Just sit with her until I get there. She won't die. It's alright, this is her illness," I told them.

I had a brief conversation with Ray, who totally understood, and then I rang Babs for advice. But Babs was at home and ill herself and said she couldn't take her and she might not recover in time to take her the following week when it was her turn, as we had planned.

This news almost blew my mind. I had been hanging in there trying to get through my four weeks and to be told Babs couldn't do her four weeks extending Mum's time with me, sent my mind into a jumbled chaos. As I drove home, I knew that Mum must go home. We must bring her return flight forward and I felt Babs could do that as it was simply organising the flight over the phone. But how was I going to cope from now until then with me ready to have a breakdown, my children in a state of depression, and my husband trying to move back in? I hadn't quite worked it through by the time I arrived home.

Mum was lying in bed and weakly held up her hand as she said: "Thank God you're here, Paul – a think me time's up, luv."

Distraught, Gary and Sharon-Louise grabbed me; each had an arm as they cried in fear of seeing their nanna die.

I took them both into the kitchen and tried to explain to them that she wasn't going to die; it's part of her illness that she only thinks she's going to die. As I tried to settle them down, I knew without a doubt that she had to be out of my house as this couldn't continue any longer. I had made my plan. She was going to spend the next days until her flight home at Babs'.

Walking back into her room I calmly said: "The kids are frightened that you're going to die here, Mum, and I've spent all this time trying to get them settled in this country and you're coming and being so ill has unsettled them so much it's not good for them. They are both depressed and frightened of coming home to find you dead, so I'm taking you around to Babs'. You can stay there until your flight home. Babs can organise your flight if you want to go earlier," and I began to pack up her clothes and place them back in her case.

"I'm sorry, luv. I didn't realise how frightened the kids are. I'll be ok from now on, I'm sure. Don't send me round to Babs', Pauline, I'd rather stay here."

"I'm sorry, Mum. My mind is made up. I'm new in this country, I've had a hard job settling the kids down, I'm working round the clock, their drunken father has smashed doors and broken windows with his anger trying to get back in here. He's now thinking he can move in again to help me cope with you he says! Babs says she may not be able to have you there as she's not well. I'm cracking up, Mum. I can't take any more. There's only Babs and Mark at Babs' house because Matt's at uni; you'll be better off there as they'll have more time to look after you."

All of this I said as I dressed her, putting her dress over her nightie and her slippers on her feet.

"Gary, grab Nanna's case and put it in my car, luv."

"Please, Paul. I'll behave me self from now on, I promise I will."

"I can't do it, Mum; you've got to go to Babs as I just might crack up and hurt you," and I meant that.

I drove around to Babs' house and helped Mum out of the car. I held her under her arm as I walked her up the steps to my sister's back door. Upon opening the door, I found Babs and Mark standing in the kitchen looking at us shocked and perplexed.

"Mum will have to stay with you until you've changed her ticket to go home early," I said as I sat Mum in a chair. "You're both ill, Babs, so you can be ill together. Mum will have company now. But I'm doing my darndest to get back on this roller coaster they call life, and I can't do it with somebody who wants to check out. I'll call and see you at the weekend, Mum. Bye." And I turned on my heel and walked out.

I sat for some time trying to explain to my kids what Mum's illness was.

"It's very sad that she wants to die, and I can't stop those thoughts for her. But I don't want you two being pulled down by Nanna and her illness, so she can stay at your Aunt Babs' until she goes home." They both understood, and I promised we'd call in to see Nanna a couple of times before she went home, but I didn't think she'd be that bad again. How I had just treated Mum must have been humiliating for her and I was not proud of myself for doing it, but at that time I felt I had no choice. I learned from this that you can only help people that want to help themselves. Her behavior was having a negative effect on so many people. That can't be right.

I rang Sam and apologised to him.

"I don't know when she'll be going home, Sam, but I think it will be in the next week or so. I'm so sorry I couldn't stick it out any longer, but it was making me and the kids ill. I totally understand what you're going through now, Sam. I've thought this through, and I feel that she should go into hospital. Perhaps go with her to her doctor and explain her situation. You and Pat are not qualified to deal with a mental illness because that's what this is now. She needs medical help."

Of course, Sam was disappointed that she was going home

but the short reprieve they'd had worked wonders for them both. He promised he'd take her to a doctor when she returned.

"I love you, Sam, and I'm here for you if you are at the end of your tether and want to talk. That's not enough I know, but we've got to try hard to get her into a hospital. I'll give you a letter from me if it will help."

"Perhaps it will, but I'll keep you updated, Pauline. Love you."

"Love you, Sam. Bye."

Mum left New Zealand seven days later. I tried to speak to her before she left about how ill she was, but she was still suffering from humiliation and just kept putting her hand up to stop me speaking.

After two weeks of her being at home, I rang to have a heart to heart with her. She had settled into acceptance. I was apologising constantly and saying if it hadn't had such a powerful negative effect on us all I would have kept her longer, but it just wasn't sensible or feasible. She was ill and she needed to tell her doctor just how ill she was.

"Sam will go to the doctor with you, Mum, and explain some of the things you possibly aren't aware you're doing."

"No, it's okay, luv, I understand. I spoke with your dad last night and he tells me it won't be long now till we're together again. I hope it's sooner rather than later as my time here serves no purpose now."

"Sam and Pat's kids will need you, Mum. You have a purpose there."

"We'll see, we'll see," was all she said.

My phone rang six weeks later. It was Sam.

"Mum woke this morning and came downstairs with the policy box and placed it on the coffee table in the lounge and sat in Dad's chair. As you know, it's the middle of summer here, but she had her winter housecoat on saying she was cold. I asked her why she had the policy box with all the important papers she needed to keep. She said I'd need it soon and would I light the fire as she was cold. I went out back to collect the kindling and coal and when I got back to the lounge, she was gone, Paul!"

"Oh *NO!!*" My first emotion was anger … at myself. *Why didn't I hold on for another six weeks when she was with me? Why didn't I handle that situation better than I did?*

"I'm so sorry you're left to deal with all of this alone, Sam. What can I do from here? I'm not going home for her funeral and I know Babs won't be as well. We've only just seen her, so we'll have our own celebration of her life here with the kids. We'll remember her for how she was and not what her illness did to her at the end of her life. It would be good if you could do that too, Sam."

"Funnily enough, since she came back from New Zealand, she's been a lot better. I think you may have shaken her up and made her see herself as we were seeing her. She's been ready to go since Dad died, Paul. She didn't want to live any longer after he'd gone. She's been pacing herself and just talked herself into dying. The doctor said her heart just wound down and stopped."

Mum's early life had been a difficult one, but we all admired her for how she had handled it and the support she had given to so many.

Not being able to help my mother when she needed it at the end of her life is something I must carry with me. I will always be remorseful to the end of my days.

Chapter Eighteen

And so I built a house - Wells Road

1984

In the local newspaper the council were advertising seven adjacent blocks of land for sale on the side of Gary's school playing field. They were looking for interested parties to register their names for one of the blocks and the names would then be put into a lottery. Immediately I jumped into the Rolls and went around to see what the land was like – it was perfect! Each block was almost a quarter of an acre and sat at the top of the hill at the end of a cul-de-sac. I rang the council and asked for the application papers. On the forms I was asked to state the preferred lot and give a second lot number as an alternative. It was obvious which plot of land was the best and I placed that number on the form and an alternative number for what I thought was the next best. The deposit was something I could afford and so I filed the paper. Although I was excited by this find, I didn't want to tell the kids until I knew it was a sure thing and so I spent the following week in a state of high excitement, willing it to happen.

The following week, my phone rang.

"We've had eleven people interested in the seven plots of land and the lottery was drawn, picking out seven of these people, and your name was drawn out. You will be allocated one of the plots, but now we do another lottery for each plot. We'll ring you in seven days. Please be ready with your payment as you are given only two weeks to come and pay your deposit or it is passed in and given to another applicant."

At that point, I needed to visit my bank manager and explain my situation. He could see from my salary deposits how much I was earning. After looking at the amount I had saved as part payment of the land, he announced, "This isn't a problem – we can give you a mortgage to cover the balance of what you'll need to buy the land." Only then did I tell the children.

"We're going to live even closer to your school, Gary. Come and see the land where we'll be living."

We were all so excited at the prospect of building a home on this land that nightly for a whole week we walked around our first choice of land, mentally claiming it.

"I want me bedroom on that side of the land overlooking the water," Sharon-Louise stated as she lay on the grass. "Me bed will be right 'ere and I want long windows so I can look out while I'm lyin' down."

"We might not get this plot of land – it might be another one," Gary informed her.

"No, it's going to be this one; I can feel it in me water," she giggled. "I don't even want to think about us getting any other one."

Silently we willed this land to be ours as we waited for seven days for the result of the lottery. I knew we would have to be very lucky to get that plot of land. The phone call came on the following Tuesday morning.

"The lottery has been drawn and you have your first choice of plot." We received our wish. That night we went back to the section of land that was now ours and all three of us danced in a circle holding hands, squealing with excitement.

My financial situation was now paying rent for the house we

lived in and a mortgage for the purchase of the land. I knew I would have to work fast to get a house on the land and compound these two payments. Once again, I sat before my bank manager.

"You can see what I earn each month and could easily pay a mortgage to cover the cost of buying a prefabricated home that I've seen for $40,000. Would you lend me the money to buy it? I've already worked it out and what I pay for rent would be the same amount of money I would pay for borrowing $40,000."

"Mrs Hicks, I can see how much money you earn, but it's obtained with overtime. We can't use that to determine your ability to repay another loan. Even if I did lend it to you, the margin is so tight that if you didn't get your overtime in, you wouldn't be able to repay it. Your budget shows that your living expenses are very low and unrealistic. I don't feel we should lend it to you. It would put you under far too much pressure."

"I'm not under pressure paying rent and that is dead money. I have never missed a payment; you can see that from my statements. It seems stupid to me that I can't have a mortgage for the same amount of repayment that I already pay out in rent. I am a person of my word; I promise you that the repayments would never be missed. Please trust me; I can do this. I won't let you down. Please," I pleaded with the bank manager. I was determined to leave that bank with a mortgage for the prefabricated house I wanted.

The bank manager sat looking into my eyes for a short time. "You are a very determined woman, Mrs Hicks, and I admire you. I also believe that you won't let me down," he said as his eyes began to smile. "I'll approve the loan." And he extended his hand. I beamed a smile that took over my whole body, grabbed his hand and automatically leaned over and excitedly kissed him on the cheek.

"Well, that's the first time I've been thanked in that way," he chuckled.

I strode out of the bank with a grin across my face that I couldn't contain. With my back straight and a skip in my step, I returned to work and related the story to Ray.

"I nearly didn't get it, Ray, but I persuaded him I could make those repayments and that the overtime I do is guaranteed."

"Yes, your overtime is safe, Pauline, but when you told me you were going to ask for a loan for the house, I knew without a doubt you would get it or die in the struggle." Ray laughed as he shook his head at my enthusiasm.

The wooden prefabricated houses I'd seen in brochures were built in a yard and then transported to the erection site. The cost included connecting it to the services. I chose the cheapest house the company built that had three bedrooms, a bathroom, a kitchen, and a laundry room. They also gave an option of decorating the house yourself as it sat in their yard and to save costs, I chose to do this. It would take eight weeks to build it.

I was now working from 8.30am to 5pm during the week plus doing three night pays from 10.30pm to 1.30am and at weekends I visited the yard where I painted and decorated the inside of our new home. Ray often praised me for my hard work and on the odd day when I was doing a night pay, if the office was quiet he would let me go home at 3pm to be there for my kids when they came out of school. I felt that the excitement of all I was accomplishing kept me from being tired. Sharon-Louise and Gary had their new friends to keep them occupied and, at this time, I hardly saw them with all the work I was doing.

"It won't be forever, kids," I comforted. "When we get the house on the site and move in, life should be a little easier."

I chose a very light cream for the walls of the interior of the house and painted all the woodwork and ceilings white. Every Saturday and Sunday morning for seven of the eight weeks I was up at my usual 6.30am and went to the yard to paint my home.

Almost right on schedule, the day arrived for the house to be delivered to the site. It would be transported along the roads through the night and had to be off the public highways before 5.30am. "It should arrive at your site about 4.30am, Mrs Hicks," I was told.

My alarm woke me at 3.30am that morning and I packed a bag with food nibbles and drinks and crept into the kids' bedrooms and shook them both awake. "Come on, sleepy head, our house is arriving this morning and we're going to see it put on the site."

"What time is it?" Sharon-Louise complained sleepily as she looked at the clock. "Am not goin', Mum; am too tired," she objected and tried to settle back into her sleep. Gary was already dressed in his track suit and stood beside me, eager for the excitement and experience of this new adventure. "Put your jacket on over your tracksuit, Gary. It could be cold out there," I told him.

"Get up, Sharon-Louise," I said as I threw her covers back. "You'll be sorry you missed it if you don't, now come on." She grunted and lazily pulled on her pea green tracksuit and placed her fluffy pink slippers with the bunny faces on the front on her feet. She grabbed her duvet and put it around her shoulders and followed us out to the Rolls.

We arrived at the site and parked the Rolls on the side of the main road. Ahead of us, the road was straight as it climbed to the top of a small hill and then descended out of sight until it met the main highway. We all climbed into the back seat of the car, with me in the middle. I opened the bag of food and drink and while we ate, we quietly watched the road ahead. When the food was finished the kids began to get restless.

"Where's this bleedin' 'ouse," Sharon-Louise complained. "Ow much longer 'ave we got to sit 'ere in the dark like a gang of bleedin' grave robbers!"

Gary and I chuckled at this statement. "What do you think your Nan would do?" I asked.

"She'd be singin' like the friggin' Salvation Army by now," cried Sharon-Louise and we all began to laugh.

I started singing one of Mum's favourite songs as I placed my arms around their shoulders and with the words of Jim Reeves I began

I luv you because you understand me
Every single thing I try to do
You're always there to lend a helping hand dear
I luv you most of all because you're you
No matter what the world will say about me
I know your luv will always see me throoo-ooo
I luv you for a hundred thousand reasons
And then I threw my arms into the air for the last line
But most of all I luv you 'cos your yooooo!!

And brought my arms down around my kids shoulders again and pulled them into my chest as I kissed their heads and we all huddled up laughing.

We began to remember songs that suited the occasion as our little threesome sat in the dark of the night in the Rolls at 4am in the morning, singing fit to bust.

"What's that?" whispered Gary as he pointed up the road, and we looked ahead at an arc of white light that was lighting the sky over the brow of the hill. We opened the window but couldn't hear anything, yet the arc of light slowly grew larger and brighter, as it began to ripple upward and outward and spread into the dark sky.

"This is bleedin' eerie," Sharon-Louise muttered. Wide-eyed, we watched the growing white arc until precisely in the centre there appeared a single red flashing eye, followed slowly in the shape of an arrow by two more, then two more as this arrow of red lights pointed high into the arc of white light creeping into the navy-blue sky. Not a sound could be heard.

"It's our house," I whispered as we sat in awe, watching this magical spectacle. The A frame roof line of the house had been strewn with red lights forming an arrow and, as the top of the truck appeared at the brow of the hill, we could see the outline of the roof of our new home surrounded by the arc of white light and then the navy sky. Two huge yellow lights began to emerge – the headlights of the truck – as it then began to descend the hill, creeping toward us. Slowly ... slowly ... and with hardly a sound, this huge truck majestically sailed down from the sky, as though it was a magic carpet descending, with its prize possession safely tied to its back.

"It looks like a spaceship," Gary quietly murmured, and I smiled in his direction, he was mesmerised. I then looked at Sharon-Louise. For the first time ever, she was stuck for words her face ablaze with wonderment, her eyes wide and her mouth mimicking a goldfish breathing.

All three of us sat transfixed on the scene developing before us as it moved nearer and nearer, lighting up the sky all around. I was suddenly overwhelmed with my accomplishment and began to quietly cry. *I created this magic*, I thought, and felt it resembled a huge birthday cake being ceremonially delivered to us on the back of a truck.

It stopped on the road beside the building site and had been followed by a van with four men, who would place the house on the site and connect the services. We were woken from our dream state with the bustle and interaction of the workmen and the immediate cut of the gentle hum from the quiet engine of the truck.

Sharon-Louise slowly turned and looked at me as she pulled herself back to reality

"Bleedin' 'ell, muther, when ye do it ye do it in style, don't ye!" She laughed as she threw her arms around me and kissed me. "A can't wait to write an' tell me mates back in Birkenhead about 'ow we got our new 'ouse," she chuckled, and Gary stared at me with pride with a few tears in his eyes and then hugged me.

We all stood on the side of the road as we watched the workmen slowly roll the house off the truck and along the land to where I had indicated it should be placed. As the day dawned, people began to gather around to watch the procedure. Thirty minutes before school started, almost every child in both the children's classes seemed to surround us. Our excitement built through the morning. The whole procedure took almost four hours and eventually the foreman turned to me with my new set of keys and said, "There ye are, luv. There's ye new house."

I had told Ray I'd be late, and I'd let the kids take half a day off school. For a few short hours we walked from room to room soaking in what we thought was the beauty of our new home. I couldn't remember if I had ever been any happier.

The house sat about four feet above the ground and, after I had related the entire story to Ray and my colleagues when I arrived in the afternoon, Ray told me:

"When you go home, Pauline, measure the distance from the bottom lip of the door frame to the ground and I'll get the lads in the workshop to make you a set of wooden steps."

"Thanks so much, Ray." I smiled: he was such a helpful person, and I appreciated his support.

The removal truck was booked for the following Saturday, and they moved our possessions into our new house that all three of us were so proud of.

The entire land the council had sub-divided was about two acres on the side of Gary's school's playing fields. We were the first to 'build' and move into our home. Consequently, the house looked more like a posh farm shed sitting in the middle of a meadow. But to the toffee noses in the district, it resembled a wooden caravan, and we were the gypsies. The houses surrounding the area had been well established and it became obvious to me that they did not like my little wooden house spoiling the pristine view they once had. I knew I had to be patient. *By the time I've finished this house they'll be envious.*

Over the next few months, Ray began giving me at least one early finish each week, so I was at home when Sharon-Louise walked toward the door followed by Gary who threw down his backpack and burst into tears. "What's up, luv?" I asked as I tried to comfort him.

"It's that Mr Rodgers, Mum. We were doing a project on the computer and the first to finish got twenty house points. I finished first and put my hand up and he came over and tripped on the cable and pulled the plug out of my computer and then said I was lying, that I hadn't finished and made me stand up in front of the class for them t'see what a liar looks like."

My anger began to rise, and I was aware that I had been defending that man to my son and could now see Gary was being bullied by this teacher. Sharon-Louise looked at Gary and her face took on a vicious scowl.

"That's it," she shouted as she grabbed her cardigan. "I've 'eard enough about that man an' 'ee deserves to have a smack in the jaw an' am gunna be the one to do it!" With that she turned and strode through the door.

"I'll deal with this, Sharon-Louise. You stay here with your brother. If anyone's gunna smack him it's gunna be me," and I propelled myself out of the door, marched across the school fields and into the classroom where Mr Rodgers was cleaning the blackboard with a duster. He turned as he heard me walk into the room and immediately turned his back to me and continued slowly cleaning the board.

He stood perhaps six feet six inches, was built like a rugby player and had bright red hair.

Fuming now, I stood waiting for him to turn around, but he didn't.

"I am Gary Hicks' mother," I said in my best Mrs Bucket voice. "I want to talk to you, so put that duster down and face me, you ignorant man."

Mr Rodgers continued to slowly finish cleaning the board then turned around and, with a supercilious smile on his face, put his hands on his hips, cocked his head to one side and said nothing.

"My son is an eleven-year-old child who has been persecuted by you since he came into this class. When it first started, I was defending **you** and telling him it was something he must be doing. But today you have gone too far. I now realise that you are bullying him and demoralising him. You pulled that plug out of that computer on purpose and then shamed him in front of the class by calling him a liar."

Mr Rodgers interjected, "Your son has an attitude problem, Mrs Hicks, and you should be sorting that out and not standing here accusing me of something he's invented."

My Mrs Bucket voice dropped immediately, and my anger raged as my voice lifted a few decibels.

"It's you that has the attitude problem. Gary is a youngster and a bright lad who wouldn't know what attitude is right now. He's come from another country and is trying to fit in and make friends and you're victimising him and getting pleasure from it. People like you shouldn't be teachers if you can't handle a lad that needs a bit of extra support. We'll see what the principal thinks of it, and I'll get you bloody sacked for this and that's a bleedin' promise!" and I turned around to leave the classroom. In a few swift paces, Mr Rodgers covered the room and stepped in front of me.

"Let's talk about this, Mrs Hicks, before you speak to the principal."

I eyeballed him, anger steaming from every pore. "And what have you got t'say that will change my mind!" I growled.

"I'm sorry, you're right. Gary rubs me up the wrong way. I have often asked myself why. It might be his accent or his voice, I don't know. When I did that today I immediately knew I'd gone too far. I'd like to come over to your house and apologise to Gary if that's all right?" he muttered as he looked down at his feet.

"No, it is not all right, Mr Rodgers. I wouldn't have the likes of you crossing my doorstep. But what **you will do** ..." I stopped to make the point that I was telling him and not asking him "... is call Gary out in front of the class first thing tomorrow morning, and you will apologise to him in front of the other kids and tell them all that he isn't a liar. And then you will award him those twenty house points. I'm telling you now that if Gary doesn't get that apology, if he doesn't come home and tell me that it happened just the way I'm saying now, then tomorrow night I'm straight to the principal's office and if you're not sacked by him, I'll go to the Education Department, and they will sack you or I'll take it to court. Do you understand me!" I shouted as I pushed my finger into his chest which was as close as I dared get as he could probably see that I really wanted to smack him in the face.

This six-foot six-inch huge man bent his head and, with a meek nod, answered, "Yes."

"And while I'm at it, I will believe my son from now on and if you continue to bully him like you have in the past then the deal is off. I see the principal. Understood?" I yelled again with another stab at his chest, desperately holding myself back from a full physical assault.

"Yes," he said again. His face now resembled the colour of

his hair. I turned on my heels and marched back to my house where Gary and Sharon-Louise were waiting.

"Mum, yer shouldn't 'ave told 'im off; 'eel make me life hell from now on," Gary cried.

"Did ye smack 'im one, Mum? Did ye, Mum? Go on tell us?" Sharon-Louise bounced on her feet like a boxer and punched the air as if it was the face of Mr Rodgers.

"I have told him he will apologise to you in the morning, Gary, in front of the class, and give you those twenty house points. If he doesn't do that, you come home and tell me and I'll have him sacked. He won't bully you again, Gary, 'cos now he knows that I know. Bullies are cowards when they're faced with the truth of their actions, Gary, and that man is a bully. Plus, he's frightened of me now and he knows he'll lose his job if he continues. I'll knock his bleedin' carrot top off his shoulders and he knows it," I shouted in exasperation, then we all burst into laughter, including Gary.

"A don't know 'ow ye didn't smack 'im one in the jaw, Mum. I would 'ave," shouted Sharon-Louise as she shadow boxed around the room demonstrating how she would do it.

The following morning Gary was called to the front of the class and Mr Rodgers said: "I'd like to apologise to you all and especially Gary here when I called him a liar yesterday. He wasn't lying and I'm going to award him the twenty house points."

Gary related this story repeatedly to us and went on to say that Mr Rodgers was as nice as pie to him all day from then on. I checked with Gary at least once each week to make sure Mr Rodgers was as nice as pie for the rest of the school year, and he then gave Gary a glowing report.

Working at the mills was a bonus as they made wallboards for building materials, and I could purchase them with a staff discount. The four exposed feet at the base of the house I boarded up with wallboards from the mills which improved the look of the house immensely. I was learning to use a saw and swing a hammer like any other handyman. I hired scaffolding and bought paint and transformed the look of my home over the next few months. I painted the outside walls cream and my brother-in-law Mark painted the iron roof black for me, he and my sister were adamant I shouldn't paint the roof myself. But I was prepared to do it! The window surrounds and front door I painted olive green. When the daylight stopped me from working outside, I sewed drapes and prettied up the inside. With every pay cheque I received, I spent money on my home. A concrete drive was laid from the road up the side of the house with a path off it to the front door and, at the same time I had the concreters build a proper set of concrete steps. I bought leylandii trees to line the outskirts of my land to form a hedge. Weekly I dug out gardens and planted flower beds. The house began to resemble an English cottage.

Dave saw the kids every Sunday but rang me every Friday night to tell me what time he would pick them up. I knew the real reason for his call was to make sure I was staying at home over the weekends. He was still attempting to control my life. Apart from his phone call, which upset me every time, our lives fell into a pleasant pattern. The kids had their friends around at the house most nights and weekends, and my home was always full of happy laughter.

I never questioned the kids about what their dad was up to. Firstly, I really didn't want to know and secondly, I didn't want the kids feeling they were telling tales. But Sharon-Louise would tell me that her father always questioned them both about my movements.

"Tell him very little, kids; you know what he's like," was all I'd say.

Dave seemed to have a full social life with his new friends and often went off for the weekend playing golf and later, armed with a new shotgun, rabbit shooting. If he was going away, he would only tell the kids the Friday he was leaving, which didn't always please them as they had often refused outings with friends because they were supposed to be seeing their dad. Plus, Sharon-Louise looked forward to her day at work and earning some money and so when he cancelled their day together on the last minute I would change my plans to run her to work and pick her up. Gary now looked forward to his game of golf with his dad and was always disappointed on these occasions. I had a social life that suited me – because I worked such long hours, I was happy enough going out perhaps every other month.

The only stain on my own happiness was that controlling phone call from Dave each Friday. As Sharon-Louise and Gary were aware these calls upset me, they often tried to answer the phone first and not pass it over to me when he asked, saying I was in bed or in the bath. But if he wasn't allowed to speak to me before he went out drinking, he would ring when he arrived home when he was drunk. That phone call would be threatening and so we all agreed it was best for him to speak to me the first time he called.

And each night I would still stare at my moon and say 'We're all happy, Moon. We love living in New Zealand.'

Chapter Nineteen

The warrior defeated

1986-1988

Raewyn became a good friend; she was single and was a workaholic like me. She wanted us to have a night out for my 40th birthday with a group of girls we knew from work.

"I'll walk right into trouble if Dave finds out Raewyn – I can't."

"This is to celebrate your birthday!! Everyone is entitled to have a celebration for their 40th birthday," she insisted.

"Go on, Mum," the kids encouraged. "Get a life! We won't tell Dad. He's out all the time;, why shouldn't you go out?"

They convinced me, and I had my first night out with the girls after being alone for more than three years. The evening was wonderful, and I was asked out for a date by a rather tall good-looking man named Simon. I refused, saying that I was still married.

"But your friend tells me that you are separated and have been for more than three years," he said.

"Yes, that's right, but let me think about it. Ring me on Wednesday," I answered and gave him my phone number.

Sharon-Louise and Gary gave me their advice.

"Go for it, Mum. Gosh! He only wants to take you out for a meal. Say yes when he rings back."

"Whatever you do, don't tell your father," I warned them. I

knew I didn't really have to say that to them; they knew what to say to Dave to avoid trouble.

Saturday was the night of my date, and I was behaving like a teenager as I flustered about waiting for Simon to pick me up. Sharon-Louise had advised on my wardrobe as she lay across my bed watching me dress.

"No, not that, Mum! Ye look like a schoolteacher. No, not that, its neckline is too low! Not that; the skirt is too short." And on I went through my clothes until Sharon-Louise was happy with my choice. Simon walked into our lounge to say hello to the kids.

"Ooh, Mum, 'es handsome," Sharon-Louise whispered when she saw him. I introduced him to the kids and we left to have a lovely meal in the city and discovered that we had a lot in common. He was also a very witty, funny conversationalist, so the evening was full of laughter.

On arriving home, I invited him in for a coffee and to meet my children, to perhaps get to know them better. We were all very comfortable with each other as we laughed and chatted for another hour.

Then, the door opened and in walked Dave – drunk! A vicious leer crumpled his face as he stood looking at Simon with evil eyes. Simon stood to introduce himself, but, as he held out his hand, Dave swung his fist, and the fighting began. Simon tried to avoid fighting and blocked the punches; he kept reminding Dave that he was upsetting his children, but Dave wasn't listening – he was going to kill him. Simon ducked and darted to avoid Dave, who then threw furniture out of his way to get at him. The children shouted, "Dad, stop it. Dad, don't!" but Dave heard no one. Simon managed to get out of the door and Dave threw himself on top of him on the front lawn. They rolled about punching and wrestling. I picked up the phone and rang the police. Within minutes, they were there. They took

Dave's car keys from him and then put him in the police car.

"Thank you for taking me out. I did enjoy my time with you," I told Simon, "but, as you can see, I couldn't possibly have a relationship while Dave still lives close enough to watch me. I'm really sorry about tonight. I can't do it again as it's too dangerous."

"If ever you feel like legally standing up to him, Pauline, please ring me and I'll help you. It's a long process but I would be willing to support you through it. It's wrong that he doesn't live with you and yet feels he can control you."

As I sat comforting my kids after this trauma, I swore to myself that I would never put them through that sort of upset again. A social life was something I couldn't afford. I would wait until the kids left home.

As Dave's car was left on the road outside, he turned up in a taxi on Sunday morning. He didn't knock or come in, just drove his car away. "He'll be going home to get his golf clubs," I told the kids. Thirty minutes later he arrived to take the children to the golf club. We all stood in the lounge wanting him to leave the house as soon as possible to avoid an argument erupting over the previous night.

He stepped into the lounge and marched straight up to me, spat his words into my face as he poked my shoulder. "That was all your bloody fault last night. Ye talk about me being selfish … but you knew what I'd do if I saw you with anybody and you went right ahead and did it. *You* put the kids through that by thinking only of yourself – behaving like a whore in front of your own kids. Ye should be ashamed of yerself."

All the while his face was two inches from mine. I tried backing away but he stepped forward each time. I had nothing to say. What he said was right – I was already engulfed in masses of guilt because I did know how he would react, and he piled the guilt on me even more.

"Let's go, Dad!" Sharon-Louise and Gary said, trying to move him out the door, which he then opened. And there on the top step was his suitcase. He picked it up and slid it onto the lounge room floor, saying, "Find some wardrobe space for my things. I'm moving back in to make sure that doesn't happen again!" Then he left with the children.

I stood looking at the suitcase … defeated.

After some hours sitting crying, I rang Babs and told her the full story. She told me not to let him back in! "Leave his clothes in the case. Put it outside again!"

But nobody knew him like I did. My life would be hell again if I tried to keep him out. My strength to fight had dissipated and I slipped into a depression. When they all arrived home, Dave went straight into my bedroom to hang his clothes in my wardrobe. Sharon-Louise and Gary didn't comment about him moving back in. They also knew he would do it whether I liked it or not and it was easier to go along with him. They both just hugged me.

Once the kids had gone to bed, I laid out my boundaries. "I have created this house as far as it is without your help and the children have seen that. If you come back, I don't want the kids or me subjected to any more of your drunken behaviour. We've been happy here without you and had no fighting, arguments, or drunken violence. You need to gain our respect. Finish this house with me, stay in more and stop spending all your earnings on drink and gambling. Start paying money toward the family needs. You've never paid toward keeping your children and if you want to come back, it's time you faced up to it. They're my conditions and the first time you step outside these boundaries I want you to go. I already have a non-molestation order out on you and we are legally separated, I'm going to keep that going. If you step out of line again on any one of these, I'll call the police and have you locked up again. They are my boundaries."

He agreed, and for the next three years we worked together as a couple. He paid me a regular amount for housekeeping for the first time since we were married. He did work to gain our respect and I felt that we were now a complete family. BUT because of our history, I never felt safe. I still had the sleeping lion in the house that I worked around. I behaved as any wife would behave, still smiling around the children so they wouldn't feel any anxiety and chatting with the wives of his friends giving the impression life was normal in our house – but I wasn't truly happy. I was still pretending and living in fear.

Dave even bought me another puppy, another German shepherd. We called him Bruno. He tugged at my heart strings and was my substitute child and brought baby talk back into the house. Billie had been my dog back in England and had died, aged fifteen, the year before we left. I did miss having a dog around and Bruno quickly became my constant companion when I was home.

Forest Products, the company I worked for, had sold the business and I was given a large redundancy package. I decided to create my own business in interior design. Almost as soon as Dave heard how much I was given, he began complaining about his job. Then he came home one night and announced he'd had a row with his boss and had walked out. He was now forty-six and I knew he would find it hard to find work again as a panel beater.

We were both not working now and at home all day. I focused on looking for premises for my new business, but during the day, Dave began visiting the clubs that had pokie machines and spent his holiday pay on gambling and alcohol. I reminded him that he was slipping back into his old ways and the arguments began to build. If I started a business and he was at home, I knew he would be back to gambling, drinking and not looking for a job. I needed to keep him working to avoid this and began looking for a panel beating business.

"I don't want a bloody business. Ye can forget about that," he shouted when I read him an advert for a workshop for sale in the local industrial park.

"You're forgetting that I am buying the business, Dave, not you. It's my money buying the business, not yours. If I buy it, you can work for me if you like, or go and find a job elsewhere, but I am adamant that you find a job, so either work for me or start applying for jobs."

Given that the car repair business had moved there only months earlier and the owner lost his regular customers, I was buying only the workshop. Dave had no idea of how to start what would now be a new business venture. I began by employing one panel beater, a car painter and a labourer, plus Dave who said he'd work for me.

At the same time as buying this workshop, I started a businesswomen's network group to create a source of incoming work. I called it WISE, an acronym for Women In Self Employment. I opened it to any business or trade but accepted only one of each. The idea was we promised to use each other's services and I had approximately forty in the group. Most of these women had businesses with small fleets of cars. From the moment I started the network group, work flowed into the workshop. Word quickly circulated of the efficacy of this women's network group, and I began taking calls from women who wanted to join, but if I already had someone in the group who was in the same business, I would place her name in reserve in case we lost the original one.

Nobody wanted to leave WISE because of how successful it was for all its members. My reserve listings began to grow until I had enough to start a second group and, once again, I was the only female with a panel beating company in this group. So, I now had approximately eighty businesses that brought their work to me. I ended up with three of these networking groups and I began to employ more tradesmen. At the same time, I promoted my business in the local newspapers and around the new local housing estates. All of this fed the work through to my workshop. Within the first year, my workshop was known as 'the' place to take your car for repairs, making the business hugely successful.

Being a woman in a man's world did have its advantages. I brought a different energy to a trade that didn't have a good reputation as far as communication was concerned. Communication started with my staff. When interviewing, I needed them to see the vision I had for the business and they must show they were prepared to work with me to achieve it. I also created a profit-sharing scheme, which kept them enthusiastic and focused on their standard of work and their results. They recognised me as the owner but I relied on them all to keep the high standard of work that would bring the customers back and spread the word about the business. My job was to bring the work in and run the office. We were a team.

I quickly grew to know my workers and classed them as friends. These men and their families became my extended family and my customers became my friends. Dave began arriving to work later each day and behaving as though he was the owner. Once he arrived, he worked alongside the men so I taught him how to prioritise the work and move it through the workshop, and I gave him the title of Workshop Manager. And I never corrected him in front of others when he talked of being the owner of the business. I was still in charge of everything and I kept the work flowing in and managed the office.

So many wonderful stories came from my panel beating workshop - many of them were showing me that Mum was still directing me and working in the spirit world for me and others that I could help.

Chapter Twenty

Panel beaters and Angels

1989-1999

To be a woman in a man's world you had to be a strong leader to gain respect. I had to 'walk the walk' and 'talk the talk' to gain the trust and respect of my all-male staff. They knew my word was my bond. Being a leader doesn't *change* who you are, it *shows* who you are. I led with empathy.

My business was called PRIMA. I chose the right tradesmen (family men) to work for me, those who shared my vision, and between us we built the biggest and best collision repair business in Auckland, New Zealand. I owned this business for seventeen years. These men and their families became my extended families.

Silent Smiley Saul

I first met Saul when I was advertising for a panel beater about two years after I opened. This huge, muscled, Samoan version of the Hulk walked into my office with his wife. He must have been at least 6 foot 9 inches and his wife would have been no more than 5 foot. He stood the other side of my desk and leaned over it with a worried look on his face, gripping the side of my desk and saying:

"I Saul. I come for de panel beating job."

I asked the appropriate questions of his experience but Saul struggled, desperately fighting to find his answers in his head, until he'd blurt out – "I de best!"

This huge man battled against his fear of speaking and, after probably only two minutes, I decided I couldn't put him through an interview any longer as it was painful for both of us. When I heard his only response of "I de best" my gut instinct told me he possibly could be.

"Do you have time for a trial now?" I asked.

He nodded.

I looked over at his wife and she nodded, smiling as she sat in a reception chair.

I introduced Saul to my supervisor, Vaughan, who would oversee a trial job with him. Within the first hour Vaughan could tell if the man knew what he was doing or not. But after an hour and half, I walked into the workshop to see Saul stripped to the waist and stuck into the job as Vaughan walked toward me saying:

"This man is dynamite – he had that bumper off and the new one attached perfectly in less than thirty minutess, and he's now gone onto doing the rest of the repair. He's a keeper."

I nodded. "His wife is waiting for him so call the trial off now and bring him back to the office."

Vaughan and Saul stood before me, Saul with his shirt in his hand crushed into a ball, sweat showing on his muscled chest and visibly shaking with obvious fear in his eyes.

"The job is yours, Saul" I said as Vaughan turned to him and shook his hand saying: "Welcome aboard, mate."

The worry on Saul's face was replaced by the biggest smile showing perfect beautiful white teeth. He looked firstly toward his wife, who beamed her pride in him, and then he said: "Thanks, boss, thanks."

His wife stepped forward, and said, "Saul is illiterate so if you have papers he needs to sign I will do that for him."

So that's why she's with him!

Over the next months I heard stories about Saul's previous employer – he took advantage of Saul and would sometimes not pay him in money but with a bag of food. He never had a rate of pay and would just be handed a couple of hundred dollars at the end of the week, if he was lucky. Because Saul couldn't read and write, he didn't have the confidence to look for another job, and because of his lack of education, he even felt grateful that he was employed at all and so had stayed with this man for seven years. His wife had seen the ad and encouraged him to come along for an interview.

When I heard these stories of how he had been treated, my blood boiled. Saul was not only a good panel beater, he was a loyal, dedicated worker who silently went about his work – he was a humble, beautiful man, inside and out.

The rest of my staff took to Saul immediately and I could see they even protected him in many ways.

His first Christmas with me had arrived and we would close down for two weeks over that time. Every year I gave my employees a Christmas food hamper, in it everything they would need for food on Christmas day, including a turkey. I had placed them on the tables around the smoko room.

I called them all in at lunch time on closing day and one by one gave them three envelopes, their week's pay, holiday pay, and a bonus payment and I indicated their hamper. Shaking each man's hand, I told each one how much I appreciated their support throughout the year.

Saul's turn came. He stood before me looking worried. I told him how much I valued his service and handed him the first two envelopes, this week's pay and his two weeks' holiday pay. He couldn't read or write but he could count his money. He firstly opened the envelope for his week's pay to date and, without counting it, he pushed it into his overall pocket. Then he looked at the envelope for his holiday pay and opened it to see the bank notes but didn't take them fully out of the envelope. His head was bent over this pay packet for perhaps thirty seconds then he looked up and handed the envelope back, the money still inside.

"No, boss," he said, looking me in the eyes, "me and de kids we go camping. I not coming into work … I tell them already."

"No, Saul, the workshop is closed for your two weeks' holiday. Nobody is coming into work. This is your holiday pay while we're closed."

He stared at me, trying to make some sense of this in his head. Another thirty seconds went by. "You pay me for not being here?"

"Yes, Saul … because we close the workshop for two weeks, which means you can't work, we pay you for that time. So, this is your money, it's your holiday pay." He then took the notes out of the envelope and looked down at the wad of money in his huge hands, still trying to process this as I said:

"And here's your bonus for the months you've been with me."

His eyes showed shock as he looked at me and then back down at his hands. Taking the notes out of the envelope, he left them sitting in his huge hands and began shaking his head slowly – then eventually he looked up from his hands to me. "My money as well?"

"Yes, Saul. You've earned that extra money. That's your bonus, and here's your hamper of food to take home."

This was all too much for Saul to process and I could see his desperate attempt to cope with his emotions and not knowing what to say. The smoko room was deathly quiet as we all stood smiling at Saul, waiting for his reaction but aware of his internal struggle with what to say.

Saul said nothing – he simply stood looking at his huge hands as he formed fists around his money. Then his hands began to tremble and eventually he dropped his chin to his chest, rounded his shoulders over – still holding the bank notes in his huge fists – and began to cry.

"Oh, Saul!" I said as I tried to circumnavigate his huge chest to hug him. I began crying myself.

"No one ever do dis for me, boss!" he stuttered as he cried. The rest of the work force began coughing and clearing their throats. Then Vaughan stepped forward, grabbed Saul's arm, pulled him in and gave him a blokey hug and gently punched his shoulder.

"You're a good man, Saul," said the others, automatically drawn into this raw emotion. With tears in their eyes, they surrounded Saul to give him the blokey hug too, and with each one Saul said, "I loves youse guys."

As I look back on that day now, I always remember it being one of the best Christmas presents I've ever had – these big tough men, panel beaters, car painters, tow truck drivers – choking back tears – all having a group hug in my workshop as they witnessed and were drawn into the genuine humility of this beautiful man.

Silent Smiley Saul

Saul is not a small man
Yet he seldom makes a sound
Sometimes I have to check
To make sure that he's still around

His olive skin and smiley face
Will suddenly appear
Thumbs up he'll flash a smile that says
"I happy, boss, I here"

I've seen Saul, single handed,
lift a car out of his way,
His physical strength astounds me
As he goes about his day

And yet this man is gentle
A tender strength shows in his eyes
Saul's presence in my workshop
Is like a breath of summer skies

Years of wisdom lie buried in young Saul's soul
We can only suspect learned from strife
Teaching us all by example – that
Each day we should celebrate
LIFE

An Angel called Breeze

From the following story, it is clear that Mum had once again been busy in the spirit world, sending in my direction those that needed my help.

In the middle of the working week, a quiet time in a panel beating workshop, I sat staring out of the office window, looking at the sky. It was a beautiful, cloudless, autumn day, warm but without the humidity that had plagued us all summer. The phones were quiet for once and the lads in the workshop were all busy and not needing my attention.

Arthur sang as he worked. Hearing him sing gave me comfort as it showed there was contentment in the workshop. Arthur was a great singer, fancied himself as another Elvis. I think he did a few gigs at night but panel beating was his day job and paid the rent. As I dreamily transported myself to Vegas, imagining I was listening to the real Elvis, an old white Toyota Hi Ace van pulled into my vision. An overweight, thirtyish, mousey-blonde-haired woman stepped out. Her jeans and badly worn sneakers had seen better days and her rusty old bomb of a van had more hits than Elvis Presley and wouldn't have looked out of place in a wrecker's yard.

She politely introduced herself as Carol and asked for a quote on the most urgent of all the repairs that needed doing on her van.

She wants this fixed! It'll cost thousands. I hope she's got insurance, churned around in my head as my dreams of Elvis and Vegas rapidly disappeared.

I called Dave to give a quote, ignoring the looks he sent in my direction when he saw the state of the van. I could see what he was thinking. 'Writing a quote is a waste of my time; this van needs to be towed to the scrap yard.'

He calculated the quote and handed it to me. I glanced at the total as I handed her the large quotation and she gave it a cursory glance and said quietly, "Someone's goin' to pay it for me." Then, with conviction, she said, "Can you fax it to this number. I'll be in touch."

I believed her.

The following week she rang.

"This is Carol," she said. "I'd like to bring my van in next Monday please."

Dave was in my office when I replaced the phone. "You'd better check on the person that's payin' for that lot," he snorted. "Pigs might fly before someone pays for that heap of junk."

"She told me we would receive a banker's cheque on completion of the work," I told him.

"And you believe that?" he quipped. "If that person is real, he's got more money than sense," and he stomped out of my

262

office. "Yer'd better ask for the banker's cheque up front for that one," floated in from the workshop as the door closed.

Please don't let me down, Carol, I prayed.

Monday morning arrived; it was bright and sunny. Everything hummed busily along, customers arriving, phones ringing, everyone wanting to be attended to first.

Just the usual, I thought as I prepared for the onslaught that a wet weekend brought to panel beaters – plenty of crashes; no major damages, thank God, as we didn't like the 'nasties'. It upset all of us when people were hurt.

"Not my fault," everyone said. "The other driver was an idiot!"

I sympathised with all of them, thinking, *Yeah right. Still, it keeps the till ticking over.*

Into this chaos drove Carol in her beat up old van, looking excited that it was going to get the attention she thought it deserved. She was obviously very fond of her 'piece of junk'.

"Can you drop me home and fill up my gas bottles on the way?" she asked apologetically. "I've left my daughter at home and I can't fill the bottles this week while the van's in here."

As I was the only person in the office, I would normally ask people to give me notice if they needed a ride home after bringing their cars in so I could arrange for them to bring it in when it was more convenient. But Monday morning was the busiest time for me as the work came in for the week. I had to tell Dave and the boys I was leaving the office for a while to run her home as she'd left her baby on her own.

"Another sob story!" said Dave as he walked into the workshop, but I didn't have to hear his comments – it was written all over his face, though I thought I heard him say, "Pauline will do ye shoppin' too while she's at it!"

I had been in the habit of doing the shopping for a dear old soul who regularly would put a few dents in her car while parking.

"Just fix it for me, luv," she'd say, "before me son sees it. He'll want to take me car away; he's just lookin' for an excuse; thinks I'm too old to drive he does."

Any normal human being would do the same! She was a good customer and sang our praises around her groups of friends who would ring saying, "Are you the panel beaters that do our shopping?" I did have many pensioner customers and would often stop to get some shopping in for them when driving them home.

And so I had to sit Carol down to wait, as I booked all the week's work into the shop before I could leave the office and run her home. Her waiting for me set my nervous reaction off as I worried about work and her baby.

We left the workshop and pulled into the gas station to fill her bottles, and I now felt irritable, having to wait ten minutes for the gas bottles to be filled. Thoughts of all the work I had left behind filled my mind as I began her journey home. I needed to resign myself to at least an hour's absence as Carol started talking:

"Thanks for this. I must keep the house warm for my daughter. She's been sent to this world to teach people love and compassion."

I glanced at her, surprised. *What a strange statement.* A contented dreamy look was on her face.

"Do you know, the toughest, hardest, bikey bloke only has to be around her for one minute at the most and you can see the love starting to show out of them," she mused, as she smiled at me. Her hands were in her lap, and she looked calm and peaceful.

"Is that right?" I replied as I continued to drive, wondering just who I had in my car. She now had my full attention and thoughts of the work I should be doing began to fade as she continued:

"Yes, it's lovely. It's awesome to watch; she's been like that since she was born." She had so much love in her voice.

"And how old is she now?" I asked, expecting to hear she was a few months old.

"Fifteen," she replied simply.

"Months?"

"Years."

This was spoken with a quiet, satisfied pride as Carol went on to explain: "She was born with so many different neurological problems and the doctors gave her no hope, so they didn't give me a lot of help. In desperation, I read everything to do with her disability and talked to anyone I thought could help and, eventually, I heard about this programme in America that had been set up for children with brain problems. I got in touch with them and was told it would cost US $14,500 for me to buy it, so I started fundraising. I've got some really good friends and they helped me. We did cake stalls, car boot sales, everything. You name it, we did it. My partner, her dad, couldn't take the pace so he shot through when she was seven months old. Haven't seen him since," Carol added. "Better off without him; he wasn't much use to either of us.

"We were able to get the programme when my daughter was two and half years old; she was blind and couldn't feel anything. She couldn't tell the difference between hot and cold. It took just three months and she could see for the first time and could feel temperatures. It's amazing; it's a magical programme. The doctors expected her to be dead by now but she can talk a bit and knows everything that's going on around her and she loves people."

She shone with pride as she told me all of this and I was mesmerised by the story unfolding around me. I forced my attention back to driving although I really wanted to pull over and just stop and listen. However, Carol needed to get home as soon as possible, so on I drove.

"She goes to a special school," Carol continued. "At first they were sceptical but when they saw her progress they became very interested and asked me to use it on the other kids with neurological problems. It's helping them too!"

"Do they pay you for that?" I asked

"No!" she exclaimed as though the idea was ridiculous. "I'm there with my daughter anyway and it gives me so much happiness to see the improvements in these kids." She sounded very sincere and it was obvious the thought of payment for her help was unwelcome. "These kids are enjoying their lives more now," she continued. Then she went silent for a while as she thought about these other children and was perhaps considering, for the first time, that she could receive payment; but then she added, "Someone told a charity group about my van and they are kindly paying for the repairs. I think that's payment enough, don't you? People are really good at heart, aren't they?"

Carol was so innocent and humble and I felt she couldn't see what an amazing person she was.

As I drove on, I asked "How on earth did you find my workshop? It's so far away from where you live?" This had been puzzling me since she'd turned up – it had me thinking there must be more to her story.

"I went to the local panel beater and when I told him that the van wasn't insured and someone else was going to pay, he scribbled a stupid amount on a dirty piece of paper and said he didn't have time to do any more than that. So I went further away and they said they were fully booked for weeks and sent me on to another place around the corner from you. When I went there, he said he didn't do that sort of work and told me to come to see you. You were the only one that treated me seriously," she said. "The others just gave me the run around."

Still, she didn't seem upset, just accepting.

"I think you were meant to come to me then, don't you?" I said as I caught her eye and we exchanged a 'knowing' look and smile that said we both understood that the spirit world had connected us and we each knew what we were talking about.

We drove on in a companionable silence into a very affluent area.

"Left here," she said as we turned into a cul de sac. "Straight up the hill to the top; I'm at the end of the road."

Her house perched snugly at the top of the hill, an old wooden cottage with an unkempt garden nestled amongst all these snazzy upmarket houses. I don't think the house had seen any paint or care since it had been built many years ago. At the back of the untidy garden, covered by a tattered piece of blue plastic (attached on one side to a tree and on the other nailed roughly to the house), sat an old settee. This faced the view, which was just incredible. You could see forever across a harbour where islands dotted here and there. Small yachts dodged amongst the larger cruise ships and launches that were going about their business. Even in the rain, this would look spectacular.

"Wow, what a fantastic view!" I remarked. *I could never afford to live here in a hundred years.*

"Yes! My daughter lies on that settee and watches the boats and the water," Carol responded, smiling. "Sunshine and rain, she loves it!"

"Do you own this house?" I just had to ask.

"No," she chuckled. "It's a council house. I've lived here for fifteen years. The council rented it to me right after my daughter was born. We love living here. Just as I moved in, the other houses in the street were purchased and either bulldozed or renovated. It's a lovely posh road now."

As we each took a gas bottle from the back seat of my car,

Carol asked, "Would you like to meet my daughter?"

"I'd love to," I answered and followed her over the broken concrete path and through a front door discoloured by peeling paint. We placed the gas bottles beside an old gas heater in the lounge then Carol said proudly:

"She's through here." She opened a door and we entered another room, calling out, "Hello, Beautiful. I'm home and I've brought someone to meet you."

All I could see was the wooden headboard of a single bed, and bricks that propped up two of the legs, raising the end of the bed facing the window better revealing the fantastic view. Carol walked toward the side of the bed and leaned down out of view to give her daughter a hug and a kiss. As she stood, she turned to me and said simply,

"This is my daughter, Breeze. I gave her that name because she's a breeze to look after," and she stepped to one side with a smile.

I walked toward the bed and looked into the face of radiance. Breeze smiled at me – her whole face and her penetrating gaze reached into my very soul. This angelic child radiated pure love. The warmth of love I felt made me gasp as my inner being began to tremble. I felt a wooden chair being pushed against my legs and I sat immediately. I held the child's hand in mine but didn't say a word. There didn't seem to be any need for words. I looked into her eyes and connected on a deeper level than I had ever done with another living soul. We were both wrapped in a cocoon of warmth as we enjoyed each other and this all-encompassing deep, deep feeling of love.

My throat contracted and I began to cry, not with sympathy but with pure pleasure. Never had I experienced such love. Tears ran freely down my cheeks and I became aware of Carol looking at me and turned my head to see her standing with her head on one side smiling, and I realised that this circle of love included her.

"Lucky, aren't I?" she murmured.

Slowly nodding my head, I said "You are," as I smiled through my tears into her eyes. "You really are."

I left the house sometime later and drove back to the workshop in a dream state, the experience and depth of emotion still warming my whole being. As I approached the workshop, I began to question whether I had dreamt the whole thing.

It was smoko time when I returned and I sat with the men and told them about this little family. They listened in awe. The van hadn't been looked at while I was away and so we went outside and opened the van's back doors and, for the first time we could see why it was so important for Carol to keep this vehicle. It was fitted with a lift for wheelchairs, and Carol had roughly painted the inside with bright colours, plus mobiles hung from the roof and pinned to the sides. It was decorated with all sorts of memorabilia that obviously meant a lot to Carol and Breeze.

Eager to give the van their finest attention, the men worked extra hours on it without even wanting overtime pay. During the time the van was in the workshop, the atmosphere at work was magical. Everyone felt privileged because they had the opportunity to help this little family. Everyone felt good about doing something for someone less fortunate than themselves. Everyone felt special because she had chosen our workshop. And for all his moaning, Dave even went out and bought sheepskins for the seats.

The repairs didn't stop at the main structural damage that needed urgent attention; the panels on the entire base of the van were replaced. My painter was excellent at painting cartoon characters and, on the inside of the back doors so that Breeze could see them, he painted Donald Duck and Mickey Mouse. I found a seat in a wrecker's yard that replaced the ragged driver's seat and this was then covered by one of the sheepskin; the second sheepskin was for Breeze's wheel chair.

Carol arrived to collect her van with the President of a Lions Club and a photographer from the local newspaper. I was handed a banker's cheque outside the front of the workshop as my men who'd done the work stood around the van smiling. I accepted the cheque as it did cover part of the cost of the work. It's important to let people share in giving and the Lions Club was the reason she had found my workshop.

The extra work we'd done was our gift to help Breeze and Carol. We all wished Breeze could have been with them as the men would have loved to meet her, but Carol promised she would bring her to say hello the next time she was in our vicinity (which she did some time later).

Thinking about the whole event after Carol had collected her van, I knew Mum was behind this particular repair as she'd sent her my way. I also realised that I had encountered angels. Angels don't wear the best clothes or drive the best cars. They are disguised more often than not. They are ordinary human beings with the right attitude to life. They accept what comes their way and turn it into something magical that everyone can benefit from.

We had been touched by angels, and the feeling of love permeated throughout everyone involved.

Chapter Twenty-one

Me and my friend Trish

The vehicles I'd gathered for the business were seven courtesy cars, two private vehicles, a tow truck and a delivery van, all registered in my name.

I did lead a double life, working hard in the business, but spending time with my friend Trish was something I looked forward to – it took my mind off my problems.

My usual routine at the end of the working week was to lock the workshop and jump into the courtesy car that had enough petrol in it to last me the weekend. I drove home and picked up Trish, who was my friend as well as my next-door neighbour. The moment she was in the car we started chatting about the events of our week. Trish owned Dog & Cat kennels and she always had a funny story to tell.

On this particular Friday night we drove onto our local shopping complex, a single-storey complex that had a movie theatre and a pub in it. I parked the car and we walked into O'Shaughnessy's Pub and had pie and chips and a glass of wine. Then we left and walked over to the movie theatre and watched a really lovely, weepy movie. When it was finished, we went into a coffee bar and had coffee and cake. We then made our way back to the pub at around midnight and we both stopped and looked in horror – the car spaces outside the pub were empty: my car wasn't there.

"Trish! Someone has stolen my car!" I exclaimed.

"Oh!! Ring the police," she insisted.

I retrieved my mobile phone from my bag and rang the police to report my car stolen. Here's how the conversation went.

"Is that the police?"

"Yes – stolen vehicle help line," said a tired voice.

"My car has been stolen!"

"Where are you ringing from?"

"Outside O'Shaughnessy's Pub in Highland Park."

"When did you last see the car?

"At 5.30 when I left it there."

"And you've just come out and found it gone?"

"Yes, that's right."

"Name?"

"Pauline Hicks."

Address?"

I gave it to him

"Make and registration of car?"

"Oh … I can't remember … I think it was blue … or was it grey? Excuse me one moment please while I check with my friend. Trish, can you remember which car we were in?"

"No, I can't, Pauline."

"I think … I think it was blue."

"Mitsubishi – IG7649," he said in his very bored voice.

"No, the Mitsi's green … it was blue – I think it was the Jeep."

"Toyota – SD1762."

"No. It was blue I think – yes blue, definitely the Jeep."

"Subaru AH1895."

"I've been telling you it was the Jeep – I don't think you're taking me seriously, are you, young man? I said it was the Jeep."

"Look, missus, you've got heaps of cars in your name, and I was just trying to help kindle your alcohol-sodden brain. You've been drinking solidly for six hours and are drunk and completely squiffy, so go and get a taxi and ring again tomorrow when you're sober." He cut me off!!

"Trish, he's just told me I'm drunk and cut me off!!"

"How dare he!! We'll have him reported. I'll ring my Robbie – he's a policeman and he can have him hauled over the coals for that." She retrieved her mobile phone from her bag.

"Robbie, we're in Highland Park and Pauline has had her car stolen and she rang the helpline and they accused her of being drunk and cut her off. I want you to find out who's manning that desk tonight and have him severely reprimanded, if not fired. Yes … thank you … we'll stand by the entrance." Then she turned to me. "Robbie's going to look into it – he's coming to pick us up."

And we turned to walk toward the entrance of the complex chattering away about our plight. "What is the world coming to when the police talk to you in such a way. I think it's disgusting – no wonder there's so much violence in the world – how can you respect the police force when they are so rude and employ degenerates?" and we both suddenly stopped and hung onto each other in horror because there, sitting right where I'd left it before, outside the movies and not the pub door, was my Jeep.

"Ooh!! Oh, God, no!" We clung to each other now hoping that it was a mirage and would disappear as we looked away, and back and stared in shock. Then we both started laughing – not just laughing, laughing hysterically – a belly laugh that was out of control. Trish had her legs crossed as it had affected her bladder. She was red in the face and holding onto the wall, hysterical - whaling like a banshee!

I had to lean over the bonnet of a car because I couldn't stand up straight, my knees kept giving out. The screams of laughter escalated when we each looked at the other, its infectiousness setting off a group of youths in the car park who began laughing with us.

"What are you laughing at Missus?" they kept shouting – but we couldn't tell them – we were choking with this laughter and their remarks made us even worse. Then Trish pointed and managed to splutter, "Robbie!"

I turned to see the police car pull up. Robbie got out and stood there, his face not moving a muscle on – he was in full police uniform, including his hat, and stood with his hands on his hips, so angry.

"Mother," he hissed, "I've never seen you in such a state – you ought to be ashamed of yourself. And you, Pauline – let's gets you both home before any one sees you." He tried to turn Trish to hook under her arm, but Trish wanted to tell him that we had found the car; her words didn't make any sense because of her laughter. And his reaction made this situation even funnier to us. Trish looked as though she was fighting with a policeman as she pushed his hand away and shouted, "No!! No!" and beat him on the chest. The whole scene looked hilarious and made me howl, laughing and screeching as I watched Trish fighting with a police officer.

Robbie eventually grabbed Trish under the arm and then did the same to me. He tried to walk us both over to the car but we couldn't walk straight because we needed to laugh and bend over all at the same time. So we were dragged with one arm up in the air still squealing with laughter. He pushed our heads down to get us into the back seat of his police car as the youths started shouting to defend us

"Are eh, Officer – you can't arrest them for having a laugh in a car park – they're just a couple of old women, for God's sake!"

This made us even worse! "OOOOOOOOOhhhhhhh!" we screamed as we rolled about the back seat –

Robbie took us home and on the way we managed to get our laughter under control, but we couldn't convince Robbie that we hadn't had too much to drink. When we told him we hadn't lost the car. All he said was, "Well you weren't fit to drive it."

We were dumped on the street outside our houses, and we waved to Robbie, thanked him and wished him Goodnight

"Now get straight into bed and sleep it off," he shouted as he drove away.

We stood there waving and playing the part, "Goodnight, Officer."

We had our laughter under control by now and I looked at Trish and said, "That was the best night out I've had for years."

"Me too! I hope we lose the car again next week," she said as we chuckled and hailed each other goodnight and entered our homes. We were lucky her son was the policeman, or we could have been locked up that night.

Trish and I shared the same sense of humour and we had many strange and funny experiences together.

I'd been in hospital for a day to have laser surgery to remove the first of my cataracts and I had to wear a pad over my eye for a week. On arriving home, I opened my mail and there it was!! A personal invitation to Paula Ryan's fashion sale. *Oh!! When is it? Tomorrow!* I knew Trish would have been invited as well so I rang her.

"Trish, did you get an invitation to Paula Ryan's fashion sale tomorrow?"

"Yes I did, Are you going?"

"Too right I am – pick me up in the morning at eight. It should only take an hour to get there –it starts at nine."

"Oh, Pauline, I can't do the driving: Charlie ate my glasses yesterday and my new ones won't be ready until Friday – I can't drive – you know me, I'm as blind as a bat without them."

"Can you still use your reading glasses?"

"Yes."

"Then you get your map book out now and, with your

reading glasses, work out how we get there and I'll drive – I'll see you at eight in the morning."

Next morning Trish got into the car so excited.

"Well, how do we get there?" I asked.

"Go down to the main highway and turn right and I'll tell you when to turn left into Bagdad Road – it's almost straight from there."

Off we went. I turned right onto the highway then Trish shouted, "It's the next one, Pauline. Turn left there."

I turned into the street but we soon realised it was a dead end.

"I must have told you to turn left too soon. Sorry."

"That's okay. I'll do a 3-point turn and get back to the main road."

Bump bump bump. "What was that?!"

Trish opened her door and looked down. "We're on a roundabout in the middle of the road."

"Oh my God, was anyone on it?"

"No, I can't see any dead people, only dead plants."

"Trish, please try harder and watch the road for me. You must remember I can't see either!"

"I'm sorry – yes –I will try, but I honestly can't see a thing." Off we went again and, after more wrong turns and dead ends, we eventually found the Industrial site where the sale was being held – but it was now near 10am.

"This is it, Trish. Look, can you see that huge sign saying Paula Ryan's sale here today?"

"No," she cried.

"Okay, just link my arm and I'll follow the signs."

The arrow pointed to a narrow alleyway between two huge concrete industrial buildings.

"Down here, Trish," and we walked to the end, but there I saw another huge sign pointing down a different alleyway.

"We must be nearly there," I said as Trish allowed me to walk and turn her this way and that. Then, as we turned the next corner, the big signs had disappeared. But, up ahead was a small a frame sign that I couldn't read yet – we approached it and I bent down to make out the words: PAULA RYAN'S SALE HERE TODAY and an arrow pointed to a roller door that was pulled down, leaving about eighteen inches off the ground.

"Oh, Trish this must be it – can hear the noise in there?"

I bent down, trying to peer under the door. "Yes, there are women's feet running around – they must have closed the door because they're full up."

"Oh, Pauline!! Knock on the door and ask them to let us in!"

"Trish!! Can you see those feet under there and listen to the noise!! That's women in a buying frenzy, they're not going to stop and open the door for us," and we both stood with our faces only two feet away from the closed door for a while in silence. I then bent down to measure the opening from the ground to the bottom of the door wondering if our bodies would fit under it.

"Trish, do you think you could shimmy under this door?"

"I was just thinking the same," she said. So we lay down on our bellies and began to crawl in commando fashion under the door.

"I'm stuck. My shirt is caught on something," Trish cried out

"Just a minute I'm nearly there and I'll get you free."

I crawled through, trying to avoid feet until my own legs were on the inside of the door. Turning to Trish, I shimmied around on my stomach and unhooked her shirt. "Now push yerself through, Trish."

"I am, but it's hurting my boobs!"

"Flatten them and push!"

"I'm trying, but it hurts." She became frustrated.

"Look, give me your hands and I'll pull while you push. Come on – push!"

"Ha ha!" She began chuckling as she held my hands.

"Now is not the time for laughter, Trish … push!"

"You're reminding me of when I gave birth to Robbie – you were a bossy boots then just like this," and she started to shake with laughter.

"Stop laughing, Trish, and concentrate – push while I pull. That's it! That's it! Now swing your legs around and you're in."

"I can't get up!" she shouted as she lay like a beached whale on the concrete floor.

"Yes you can. I'll help you. Bend at your waist and stick your bum up in the air. Go on, push ye bum up, now lean back on your heels – go on!"

"I can't!"

"Yes you can, that's right! Now straighten your body up – put one foot on the ground by your other knee – that's it – come on, I'll lift you – there!! We're in – we look a bit dirty but we can get changed into our first outfit when we've bought them."

And we turned to see where we were! We'd arrived on the cashier's side of the counters, the feet we had seen were the cashiers – and they were all now staring at us in disbelief! The customers were all on the other side of the counter and pushing and shoving each other to look over at these strange women that had crawled under a door to get into the sale. Then this snooty woman in a high-pitched voice said, "What *do* you think you're doing?"

I opened my bag with determination and grabbed the paper promoting the sale. "We have a personal invitation from Paula Ryan," I said as I wafted the paper before her. "We have as much right to be here as everyone else," as we held onto each other, determined we would not be thrown out by them.

"Then why didn't you use the entrance like everyone else?" she said as she pointed to the open roller door beside the door we'd just shimmied under. It was fully lifted into the air and the

278

opening was big enough for the Queen Mary to sail through –
and we hadn't seen it – we'd missed seeing that huge hole in the
wall.

But we didn't miss the sale!

Chapter Twenty-two

Mental and spiritual worlds collide

2000

Over the next years of running the panel beaters and the networking groups, the insurance companies began setting standards and would only use shops that had the latest machinery. The workshop needed a chassis machine and a bake oven. I didn't want to get a loan. I felt it best at this time to put the money into the business and so announced to my family I was selling the house and releasing some cash. All three of them didn't want this. I was once again the villain in the house.

Building the business was a priority and, though I soldiered on, they all moaned and complained constantly.

"Give me just two years," I told them. "We'll then buy a really flash house that you'll be proud of, I promise you." But they weren't supportive, and each grew irritable in the house and the atmosphere was awful. All of this began to get me down. Over the days and evenings, my nerves became fraught as I worked around them.

The house I found to move into was fifty years old and was a wooden, weatherboard structure. It was a single-storey with three bedrooms and an L-shape lounge, dining and kitchen. The land sloped down from the road making the back end of the house a double storey. The area under this part of the house had been contained with the brick footings but had not been developed inside; it showed the wooden underfloor of the house and it was plumbed for a laundry. I felt we could make this area into a room for Gary, who was now at university.

The house was old and tired, and my family didn't like it one bit. They all complained about its condition. They had now been used to living in lots of space where everything was new, and this house was not what they'd been used to.

"Just wait until I get my ideas going on it. You'll love it when it's finished," I tried to encourage. But I couldn't convince them.

Dave didn't want the house. His negativity about everything I was planning was hard to live and work with. He was drinking heavily at this time and telling me it was because he had to get out of the house, which was his excuse. Any work on the house that needed to be done, I organised. The installation of the chassis machine and bake oven was my responsibility which was fine with me, except Dave didn't want a part of either the house or the workshop, and his negativity threw obstacles in my way with everything I did. Anything around the house, I faced kids' negative responses. I was used to having to work under these circumstance so I simply soldiered on.

Bruno, my beautiful German Shepherd dog, was still my constant companion and kept me company each evening. He also went to work with me most days. Under the house was an old laundry tub in which I placed Bruno's sack of biscuits. As I arrived home each day Bruno would fuss around me until I went downstairs to feed him.

On this particular day, I opened the door under the house and walked toward the sack of biscuits that sat in the laundry tub. Bruno jumped up and tried to grab the sack and seemed to be blocking my way to it.

"That's naughty!" I shouted at him. "You know you don't do that. The sack had been rolled down from the top because there was only a small amount of biscuits left in it. I unrolled the sack inside the tub and put my arm in to get his biscuits *but* ...there was a rat in there. It ran up my arm to escape, its claws catching on the arm of my short-sleeved, knitted sweater. I screamed and threw myself against the wall to get the rat off me but it then went under my chin, drilling its feet against my skin as it tried to release itself. I was uncontrollable, my screams curdling. Bruno jumped up at me, trying to grab the rat, and knocked me against the wall. Dave was in the shower and Sharon-Louise was in the kitchen. They both came racing down the outdoor stairs to find me, still hurling myself against the wall of the house, but they couldn't see anything. The rat had released itself by this time and had run under the floorboards. Dave and Sharon-Louise stood staring at me, thinking I'd gone completely crazy.

"A rat! A rat!" I kept shouting over and over.

I knew the shower was running so I pushed past them and, in a distressed state, scaled the stairs two at a time, ripping my clothes off as I ran. I stood in the shower crying and scrubbing my skin for thirty minutes. Once I'd calmed down a little, I came out of the shower with my skin red raw. I put my housecoat on and sat on a chair with my back against the wall. I picked up a poker from the hearth and held Bruno's collar for safety.

Gary was at Uni, Dave and Sharon-Louise went out while I sat in the chair all evening without the television or radio on, listening for any noise for fear the rat would come into the house. My mother would say rats are such a bad omen.

The arguments between Dave and I began to escalate and now we had the double problem of not being able to escape from each other during the day. We worked tensely and in silence. Once we left work, Dave would go straight to his club. He would come home sometime later to eat, but worse for drinking on an empty stomach. The children always seemed to have problems of one sort or another and it was a constant battle to keep everyone's spirits up – by smiling, being supportive, doing whatever I could to please them all – but nobody was trying to support me. I was pretending so well again they probably didn't feel I needed support.

As time went on, the renovations were completed, but my family still didn't like this house. I felt it was because the tension inside it was unbearable. Dave was constantly drunk. Even the kids were now telling me to leave him.

I confided with Babs. "I feel you should start making your plans to get out of this marriage, Pauline. Start tidying your affairs so you will have something in the bank before he claims it all. Collect your precious and historical memorabilia and store what you want here in my house. Come up here for a few months as we plan your next moves."

I gathered together my precious possessions and memories and went to stay with my sister and her husband in Takau Bay in the north of New Zealand's North Island. I needed to talk everything through with my sister in peaceful surroundings to work through what I should do. I employed a woman to work in the office and would be on the end of the phone for any queries. Babs and I sat talking through the whole debacle but we hadn't come to any resolution yet. She did however advise that I was not to just walk out and leave him everything. It was complex and needed lots of planning.

On this particular morning, I left the farm to visit the shops in Kerikeri after Babs and Mark had left for work. At around ten in the morning, I heard the local fire engine screaming along the road, coming in the direction of the farm. Then my mobile phone rang – it was Babs.

"Come and pick me up quickly, Pauline. The house is on fire."

In a state of panic, we drove to the farm and arrived to witness the fire service damping down the smouldering ashes.

There was a significant amount of damage downstairs, and the roof area where I had lived was wiped out completely, along with the precious possessions of my entire life to date. My old electric blanket had caught fire and had caused the blaze.

Neighbours and their children in this caring country community arrived to help and Mark put the children to work sifting through the ash, saying, "There's a diamond in that ash and diamonds can't burn. There's a reward for the one who finds it."

He referred to my diamond solitaire ring. The children didn't hand me a diamond, but they brought me something far more valuable; my confirmation book that I'd received as a child. Inside it, I had placed the last letter I had received from my mother before she died. The heat had been fierce, iron girders had been twisted out of recognition, but these two flimsy pieces of paper had survived that ferocious inferno. With this find Mum was reminding me that she was still watching out for me. She was pointing out the important things of life and they are not material. My personal possessions were now reduced to my car, hand bag and the clothes I now stood in. My history had been wiped out.

My shock and grief over my losses were healed over the next weeks as I talked it out of me with my Babs' help.

"That beautiful diamond solitaire," I muttered one day as I reflected back on my ring.

"Pauline!!" she said in her bossy way, "the loss of your memorabilia has been more painful than the loss of that diamond. Anyway, I predict that you will receive another diamond one day and it will have far more sentimental value attached to it than the one you have lost. Am I ever wrong?" she chuckled.

My sister was never wrong, she claimed! Although she was my older sister and the bossy one, she had a big fat heart.

I felt guilt as it was my electric blanket that had started the fire but there was major work to do now and Mark began the rebuild. There was little I could do for them at this point, and I left Babs and Mark and returned to Auckland with some ideas of how I would move forward.

Selling my house and placing it on the market was the first move, and once sold I would then place the money into a savings account to gain interest. I needed to find a rental house for the interim. I still needed to work through how to leave Dave permanently but with enough money for me to move forward on my own. I began showing them all houses we could rent. And they all disagreed with everyone.

"What sort of house do you want then?" I asked in exasperation after showing them yet another house I thought we could live in.

"We want one like the last one we lived in. You shouldn't have sold it," Dave moaned.

"There's no point in going down that track again. We can't go back to it and if nobody's happy where we are then we've got to find something that suits us all so let's rent until we find the right one. Please be a little more open-minded about this," I pleaded.

They moaned and complained about everything at home and this again made my life miserable and full of angst. They seemed to gang up on me. Then both the children decided to get a flat with their respective friends and when this was announced I looked at Dave and decided, *this is it!* If the children were not living at home and he was earning a wage in the workshop, this could be the time we could go our separate ways.

The weekend came when the children moved into their flats. Dave was his usual belligerent self until I announced, "Once we sell the house, you can do what you like. I'm not living with you anymore." This now felt the right time.

I moved out and left Dave there in the house until it was sold. I found a flat over a garage on a small remote farm and moved into that. Every day, I was at the workshop and carried out my tasks, but my general health began to suffer. I was living like a zombie. This sort of tension wasn't good for anyone and the years of keeping the peace had now taken its toll. Over the years to date that I had the workshop, my business brain had functioned well, and the business had improved daily. After some time, Dave became more aware of how the workshop ran and, as his confidence in that area grew, he began giving the impression to others that the business was his. When his friends came in, he talked as though I had nothing to do with it.

"I've done this, and I've done that," he would say, and I had allowed this to happen. I didn't object as they brought work in, and I played the part of 'working for Dave' really well. The problem was that Dave began to believe it and now that I had moved out of the house, he decided to sack me!

When I ignored him, my life at work became even worse. We battled through every day. Each evening I would go back to my little space over the garage, exhausted, and I started to become afraid. Every noise was someone trying to break in. I couldn't sleep because I didn't feel safe. My nerves had been destroyed.

Dave was still living alone until the settlement date. I found a small rental unit in the area, ready for when the house sale was completed and I could move some of the furniture in. Dave discovered I had rented a unit before settlement and, on that day, he shouted in the workshop in front of the staff:

"What the fuck are you playing at?! You've rented that bloody box and never asked me if it suited me."

"It's not for you to live in. I've told you, it's my unit. I don't want to live with you. I'm living there alone! You've got to find your own rental unit now." Only because the staff could hear us the argument didn't escalate. I was safer in the workshop.

I ordered the removal truck for settlement date and went back to the house that day to supervise the packing. When the truck arrived at my rented unit, Dave was waiting. Once the truck was unloaded, he threatened that he would live there, and he wanted no arguments from me.

I was again walking through a nightmare; I couldn't think my way around his actions anymore. It was all too much and I couldn't work out how to live on my own without him thinking it was his right to live there as well.

I didn't move into the unit but left it for Dave to live in after telling him he'd have to pay the rent if he wanted it. I then went back to the room over the garage in the country and slipped into a deep depression. There was nothing I could do about it.

When Dave saw me in work he was used to seeing a confident businesswoman and my behaviour wasn't something he could manage. He kept shouting at me that I had an attitude problem. But I was so very ill.

One evening I returned home to my tiny room over the garage and the woman that owned the main house knocked on the door.

"Did you hear anything last night?" she enquired.

"Why?" I asked.

"A young girl was raped at the side of this garage by her uncle. The police are coming back shortly to ask you some questions."

I began to shake with fear. The police arrived and I couldn't tell them anything – I'd heard nothing. When they left, I barricaded myself into the flat. As the night wore on my mind was in a turmoil and I became extremely frightened. My head pounded with the tension. At 11p.m., I packed my case and drove to the rented unit and Dave.

"I'm frightened. I'll stay here tonight and sleep in the spare room until I find a place to live," I said. Dave let me in.

I sat staring into space for hours. Dave kept telling me to pull myself together but cut back on the aggression. I moved around work and home in a dream state, a zombie. The time between waking and sleeping was too long. I wanted to sleep around the clock. Every noise was something coming to harm me. Dave went out each night as usual and I was thankful for that because I needed peace and quiet. No tension. I slept in the spare room and wanted to hide myself away.

I visited the doctor who prescribed anti-depressant medication, which sometimes worked for a few days, but then I would drift back to this extremely painful mental state that seemed even worse when my body rejected the last trial of medication. Rather than getting better, I became more and more mentally ill each week. My life became a nightmare.

The business suffered because I had no energy to put into it. I had now hit an all-time low!

After being verbally abused by Dave one morning, I finished work at lunchtime, went home to the rented unit and turned all the various bottles of antidepressants I had trialled into a bowl. I collected a bottle of gin and a glass and placed them all on the dining room table and sat looking at them, feeling, *this mental pain will stop soon when I'm dead*. As I filled the tumbler full of gin, I heard the back door opening and then shutting.

"Who is it?" I shouted as footsteps came down the hallway and the dining room door opened. Gary stood there in his school uniform. He was his chubby eleven-year-old self.

"Oh, Gary you're the very person I needed," I stated, as he dropped his school bag and came over and kissed and hugged me, holding his cool face against mine. I held onto him, and the feeling of love flowed between us which eased my head and comforted me. We stayed hugging each other for a few minutes, he then pulled away from me, picked up his backpack and went into the kitchen. As I sat there, I thought, *I want another cuddle; that was just what I needed*. I followed him down the hall and into the kitchen. But the house was empty; the back door still had the chain on it. As I stared at this, I realised that Gary was now twenty years old, and I had just seen him as an eleven-year-old child. There was nobody in the house but me. At first the shock I felt at what had just transpired had me trying to think it through. I most definitely felt his cool skin on my face and I did feel his arms around my neck! Did I create Gary at that age to stop me from committing suicide? Or was he sent from the spirit world? Whatever the answer was, I knew I couldn't do this to my kids and inflict that sort of emotional pain on them. I flushed the tablets down the loo and poured the gin down the sink with a new determination. *Somehow, I must get well!*

After a visit to the doctor where I explained this strange happening and how close I was to suicide, he sent me to see a psychiatrist, who gave me another round of medication. For the first few weeks of this new medication, I began to improve. The money for the sale of the house was placed in the bank and I felt well enough now to move out of this rented unit with Dave and look to purchase another house for me to live in. Somehow, again, he found out I had purchased a house. At work, I was sitting with the men during their tea break when the door flung open and banged against the wall, his anger at boiling point. He took two swift strides toward me and bellowed as he hovered over me.

"What the fuck do you think you're doing?! You've bought another house with *my* money and didn't tell me."

The men hurriedly stood and went back into the workshop.

I stood up to be at the same height as him as I backed toward the door. "I've bought that house with *my* half of the money from the house sale. It's for me! I keep telling you I'm going to live on my own. You can stay in the rental unit." I said all of this in fear as, for the first time, he was showing his evil side of the way he treats me in front of the men.

"When are you going to get the message?" he bellowed further as he punched my shoulder. "I am not the one that will be paying rent, you will! I'm warning you now, you don't use my money for buyin' anythin' else. I'm goin' to the bank now to have that money moved over into my name. I've got other plans for that money. Do you hear me!" he screamed into my face as I backed away, preparing myself to exit the nearest door. But he picked me up by my shirt front and threw me against an old fridge that had a large handle sticking out from it. My back hit the handle and the base of my spine hit the floor. Immense physical pain tore through me.

He grabbed my bag, tipped it up and picked up the new house keys which still had a label on them from the estate agent. Once again he was claiming what was mine and, as he'd had years of getting away with this, he believed it was his right.

How much can I take before my mind is obliterated? I thought. I was ready to walk away from this life completely. I began having thoughts of moving back to England and not fighting for anything I had worked for. Now that the children weren't at home, I could transfer everything into his name leaving him with it all.

I rang my son and daughter and, for the first time since they were now adults, I looked for support from them both. I tried to tell them how their father had just physically abused me and he was moving the house money into his own account. Both said they didn't want to know. I'd made such a good job of protecting them from the abuse I received when they lived at home that they didn't want to hear me complaining about their father.

That night I had a very vivid dream where I discussed my life with Mum. She asked me to go and help my brother Harry. She mentioned England but added that, at this stage it would not help me to heal, and so, with Mum's help, I made the decision to visit my brother who lived in America and had just gone through his second divorce.

After ringing Harry and hearing how depressed he was, I felt we could help each other if I went there for a couple of months. I made my plans and found a lady to take my place in the workshop office until I returned. Little did I know it would be a lot longer than two months before I would return to work.

Sanity
- a poem by the author

Demons start to use me, ripping through my heart and soul,
Fire and knives abused me - I was dragged across hot coal
My spirit wraps me in its arms, escaping, starts to soar
And lifts me to another sphere, adrift without an oar
I see things in my private world that no one else can see,
Ecstatic as I'm floating there, my spirit, my world, and me,
I hear what no one else can hear, whispers in my ears,
Tender warm and loving words, prompting joyful tears
Time stands still, life is sweet, Love is all I feel,
Worldly woes, stress and pain, all seem so unreal!

WAKE UP!! Shouting, stirs my brain, drags me back to 'life'
Spirit now releases hold, reality, and strife
Shocked and maimed, I moan and crawl,
and lose the will to fight,
Fear and pain, stress and shame, grip my senses tight.
Sanity must not include my pleasure-seeking ride,
I'm 'sane' now, no confidence, invisible, I hide.
I look at you, and I can see, *you're* happy I'm 'down here'
But *I* was really happy while I floated in my sphere
I'll try to keep myself 'down here' to please the ones I love,
But crazy really suited me, it fitted like a glove
If I promise not to write it down, or talk to those you know,
Would you mind if I went crazy, perhaps once a month or so?
Because now that I've experienced it, it's obvious to me,
I'm 'normal' when I'm crazy
But I'm 'mad' in Sanity

Chapter Twenty-three

From the frying pan into the fire

2001

My life of stress over all those years had taken its toll and I was so tired and still depressed as I boarded the plane in Auckland heading for Chicago, Illinois, America.

On my arrival, my younger brother Harry and his four-year-old daughter Shirley were waiting for me, and they stood hand in hand. This sight made my heart ache as I saw my brother looking thin, grey and haunted. He was forty-six but looked older, his handsome face now drawn and hollow. His shoulders drooped as if the cares of the world sat upon them. By contrast, Shirley was bright, colourful, pretty, alive and shining. I suffocated the sobs that welled up in my throat as I approached them.

Harry made excuses about his truck being repossessed as we approached a beaten old Chevrolet that looked as tired as he did. "As long as it gets us to your home, I don't care what we ride in," I said, trying to cover the embarrassment I knew he felt.

Shirley and I sat in the back seat on the drive to Harry's apartment. Shirley was only six months old last time I had seen her. She now chatted away, not at all self-conscious.

I'm going to enjoy my time with this little treasure, I told myself.

Entering O'Hare near Chicago, Harry began apologising –

this time for the neighbourhood. It did look quite rough.

"This was the first apartment I could find in my price range. I'm still paying alimony to Cynthia, my first wife, and now the alimony payments to Alma. It doesn't leave me much to live on," he explained.

"I understand that, Harry; you don't have to make excuses to me. It doesn't matter where you live; I'm here to be with you, wherever that might be." I hoped I was making him feel more relaxed about taking me into this depressing part of the city.

We turned into the driveway of the apartment complex. The drive was probably one hundred metres long and led to the central area of the complex with pathways fanning off it leading to the various apartment blocks. On the left, the main office and laundry facilities were flanked by a fenced in swimming pool. On the right of the office were rows of mailboxes that ran along the edge of a car park surrounded by a grassed area, approximately twelve metres deep. The apartments on that side looked on to the grassed area and mailboxes.

Harry turned to the right and drove around to the back of these buildings to where the front doors were. He lived in a first-floor apartment which had a metal staircase leading to it.

The door to Harry's apartment opened onto a short hall with two bedroom doors on the right and a bathroom door on the left. Then the end of the hall opened on the left into a living room about five meters by three meters. As we stepped into this area, directly facing us, was an aluminium sliding window, which opened onto a small deck that overlooked the grassed area and the mailboxes. On the left of this room, a breakfast bar separated the kitchen and dining room from a living area lined with mismatched pieces of furniture. It was all spotlessly clean as I expected from Harry but it needed a woman's touch. *I'll have to put some new life into this place*, I thought.

"I'll show you your bedroom," Harry said, leading me to the

room nearest the front door.

A mattress lay on the floor covered in fresh linen, and against a wall was a chest of drawers. The wardrobe was built into the wall. A Venetian blind covered the window which overlooked a car park and the main highway.

"I've put my mattress in here for you and I'll sleep on the base in my room," he said.

"That's fine Harry; it will be good for my back. I'm happy enough. But will you be okay sleeping on the bed base?" I said.

"Yes, I'm fine. I slept on it last night and it was quite comfy."

Shirley helped me unpack my suitcases while Harry went off to make a hot drink. I looked around the clutter-free room without memorabilia of my life and felt I could live here without stress as I built my mental health again.

Sitting around Harry's dining table with a hot drink, we began to catch up on the happenings of the last four years. I watched Harry's hand shaking as he'd placed a mug of tea before me. My brother was indeed a broken man.

Alma, his second wife and the mother of their child, dropped by some time later to collect Shirley and we had a brief chat and promised to catch up some more when I'd settled in and was over my jet lag. She was a tall attractive woman in her thirties, with long auburn hair.

"Shirley can come and stay for the weekend when you've had a few days to rest," she announced as she hugged me and then took Shirley and left.

Alone now, we decided to walk across the main highway for a quick bite to eat at the shopping mall and then come back and chat some more. Harry wanted to go to a liquor store to get some beers when we had finished our meal. It was now dusk, and night was settling in.

"What do you drink, Paul?" he asked.

"I don't, Harry. I gave it away some years back — it always

made me ill, plus I decided not to have it in the house around Dave as it only encouraged him to drink more."

"I like to have a few beers to settle me down. You don't mind, do you?"

"Go for it," I said, but something stirred in my gut. I was escaping a husband that drank far too much and this ignited my concerns.

Walking back across the road, Harry already seemed different. He strode out, talking and laughing. And there was a confidence about him that hadn't been there a short time before.

Well! I must have made him feel better by being here, I thought and linked my arm in his and felt happy I was here.

As we approached the central area of the apartments, we came across a large group of youths. Their cars were all parked haphazardly behind the mailboxes with the doors open. Loud music blared into the night. Some moved and danced to it, others lay on the grass or sat in their open cars; they were all smoking and drinking alcohol.

Harry's arm tightened around me, and I heard the urgency in his voice. "Don't even look at them, Paul, or they'll knife you. If they say anything, just ignore them. Don't respond to anything. Come on," and he quickly moved me around the youths, down the path leading to the back of the apartments. He hurried me up the metal stairs and through the front door. Once inside, he deadlocked the door and drew two bolts across it, top and bottom. He then walked straight to the ranch slider window which overlooked the mailboxes and drew the blinds before switching on the light.

"I don't want them to see which apartment we came into," he said.

"Aren't you overreacting, Harry? They're just a group of kids doing their own thing, aren't they?"

"No, I'm not overreacting," he said seriously, his voice

raising. "You're naïve. You haven't lived amongst these people; they'd kill you without blinking an eye. Life is cheap to these people, so while your here don't go out without me, and don't let them see which apartment you live in, and make sure you don't speak to them because if they hear your voice, they'll think your wealthy and break in. Just do what I tell you while you're here. They're not kids, they're evil little shits!"

This upset and confused me: I didn't like him speaking to me like that.

A few minutes went by while he stood with his back to me, facing the wall in the kitchen as he calmed down. Then he turned toward me, walked over to where I sat and stood with his legs apart and his head on one side. He smiled.

"I'm sorry. I'm just worried you might get hurt if you don't play their game and you don't even know what their game is," he said. "Come on, give us a hug," and he stretched his arms out to me. I stood and hugged him. I didn't want my first evening with my brother spoiled by anything, and so decided to put it out of my mind, and we sat down to chat.

The journey had made me extremely tired and, after a couple of hours, I bid him goodnight and went to my room.

The noises of the area went on throughout the night. The *hoons* had their car radios blasting out. They yahooed and ran about the complex, screaming, shouting, throwing bottles and cans, smashing car windows. The police and fire station were close by and the alarm, which sounded like an air raid siren, screamed constantly, along with the thundering of heavy traffic on the highway. This meant that morning was a blessing, but I felt exhausted.

As I lay in my bed in a daze, the phone rang, and I leaned over and picked it up. It was my mother crying.

"What's wrong, Mum?" I said.

"You've got to move him into another place very soon," she

said.

"I will, Mum, don't worry. I can see he doesn't fit in around here."

"Bye, luv. I'll keep you both safe, you'll be alright."

"I know, Mum, Bye. I love you," I said.

"I love you too, Pauline. I'm lookin' after ye both," she said, and I put the phone down.

Sitting on the edge of the mattress, my hand groped on the carpet for where I thought I'd just put the phone down, but there was no phone! I'd just received a message.

Mum had been dead for some years now – I had just heard from her spiritually by clairaudience. This had happened before.

As this area was not going to help Harry's mental health to recover, or mine, I agreed with her that he needed to move quickly.

At 7.30 am as I moved into the kitchen to make a cuppa, Harry opened his bedroom door. He came into the kitchen looking much the worse for the beer that was supposed to 'settle him down'.

"Mornin'," he said and walked over to switch on the kettle, not catching my eyes.

"How do you feel?" I asked in a typical, sarcastic, sisterly response.

"I think I had a bit too much last night," he said, smiling and shaking his head. "My stomach's killing me."

"I'm not surprised, Harry," I said. "That wasn't any fun for me listening to your anger. If you want me to stay around for a couple of months, you'll have to stop drinking, or I'll have to go back on the next plane home. You are clinically depressed, Harry, and the medication you're taking shouldn't be mixed with alcohol. I want to help you to recover but of course I can't do that unless you work with me on it," I pleaded with him.

"A couple of beers once a week? Is that such a bloody

crime?" he shouted.

"Yes, it is," I shouted back, full of sisterly concern. "Yes, it is a bloody crime, so you should give it away. You are suffering from depression right now and beer is the worst thing you can have. Drinking it is upsetting your stomach and making you ill." We had both reverted to our teenage years, bickering at each other. We had been raised to speak our thoughts and not mince our words. The Irish in us had been ignited and we verbally battled it out.

He started shaking his head as though what I was saying was rubbish, but then said he'd try not to have any beer for the rest of the time I was with him.

I went off to the bathroom and stepped into the shower with thoughts of going home, but the warm shower mellowed me. Also I couldn't let Mum down as I'd promised to help Harry move. The temperature outside was in the nineties, and with the swimming pool opposite and Harry out at work all day I could perhaps get some rest and not waste my plane fare. Going home would have been a sign of defeat.

With all this in mind, by the time I had dressed in fresh clothes, I came out of the bedroom with some determination to start this holiday again.

"Well, should we go somewhere for the day?" I asked.

"My stomach's killing me, Paul," he said. "Do you mind much if we stay in this weekend? I need to be near the bathroom. We'll go out next weekend with Shirley."

"Okay," I said. "Have you got any books I could read?"

"Help yourself," he said and pointed to the wall unit where a small display of books sat. I sifted through some interesting reading material, and I found a couple of books on numerology.

"Are you into this?" I said, holding the books out for him to see.

"Right into it," he said. "Read them. I'd like your opinion on them."

The sun was shining, and it was such a beautiful day it seemed a shame to be indoors, so I stepped out onto the deck with the books. A large tree planted in the grassed area in front of the left side of the deck provided shade from the sun and privacy from the traffic of the central area, so I settled myself behind the tree on a deck chair and began to read.

The subject caught my attention, and I spent the day reading, except for short cold drink breaks, and some lunch, while Harry lay on the couch taking his medication.

At 4 pm, I became restless and asked if we could go to the supermarket to stock up on food for the week. He changed his clothes and drove me across the main highway to the nearest store.

"I didn't realise it was so close, I could have walked. I"ll shop here through the week while you're at work," I said.

"Make sure you go in the mornings while the hoons are sleeping it off," he said.

I nodded. "I'll take that advice."

Back at the apartment I prepared a meal. During this time, I'd decided there was no point in holding grudges. Alcohol was a major factor in my unhappy marriage and that was colouring my opinions. *I can't stop my brother from drinking. This is his life, and I am in his home. I have to make the most of the circumstances I have found myself in and try to tolerate the small amount of beer he drinks.* We ate our meal and discussed numerology.

Harry was a mine of information and had absorbed all the information in the numerology books and more. Showing me readings he'd done on various members of the family, I saw how accurate they were. He had fed calculations into a programme on his computer and could produce readings in a few minutes.

"Why don't you do it as a sideline?" I said. "You could earn extra money that way," and I started to get excited about the prospect of him starting a small business from home to enable him to boost his income. While I was staying with him, I could take the phone calls and he could do the readings at night after work.

"Pop them in the post and hey presto! You've made yourself another fifty bucks!" I said excitedly.

Harry was intrigued with this idea, so I spent the rest of the week reading up on numerology and practising it while he was out at work. It kept my mind occupied and stopped me from getting depressed. We discussed my progress at night, and I worded an ad to place in the local paper on Saturday when we planned to visit Chicago with Shirley.

Harry worked in a sports factory and was a supervisor on the production line. He had been a paralegal and I felt this job was a waste of his brain, but he claimed he made so much more money and didn't have to think. His working hours were 6am until 2 pm then he would collect Shirley from school and bring her home where she stayed for her evening meal and waited for her mother to collect her.

Harry was an hour's drive from the factory, which meant he rose at 4.30 am and, because of this, was in bed at 8.30 at night.

I quickly fell into his routine and pottered about the apartment, collecting materials from the supermarket each morning to smarten the place up. I reorganised the kitchen cupboards, placed pot plants about, put colourful posters on the walls and generally enjoyed myself. All this was greatly appreciated by Harry, who now looked forward to coming home each day where I had a meal prepared for all three of us. I aimed to improve our general health while I was there.

In the early evening, we would spend time with Shirley until her mother collected her, then Harry and I would chat until his bedtime. 8.30 pm was far too early for me to retire, so I read or sat on the deck behind 'my tree', and watched the hoons from my hidden position. Staying inside on these lovely warm evenings was suffocating, and I would take my Walkman outside and listen to my music, partially drowning out the noises of the night with earphones. Harry slept with a noisy air conditioner going all night to block out the noises. He offered it to me when I said I couldn't sleep because of the hoons' noise and the highway but I refused his offer – it was more important for him to sleep because he was working. "I can cat nap during the day," I said.

Swimming on the occasional morning before the hoons took over the pool, reading and generally relaxing during the day, after a few days I started believing my plan would work. The only thing I couldn't get used to was the noise of the night. The hoons, heavy traffic on the highway and the sirens every night meant getting a full night's sleep was impossible.

Shirley stayed from Friday evening until Sunday afternoon, and I made plans of what we would do that weekend. When Friday evening arrived, Alma turned up at the usual time.

"What are you doing here?" I asked, smiling. "Shirley's staying, isn't she?"

"Yes," said Alma. "I've called in to have a word with Harry."

They walked into the kitchen, and their voices grew louder as they argued over money. Harry claimed he shouldn't have to pay her a full alimony if he fed Shirley every night.

Shirley shouldn't have been subjected to this, so I took her out onto the deck, shut the door and began to play a loud singing game to drown their escalating, loud voices.

Eventually Alma stormed out and Harry, now agitated, paced the apartment. Shirley and I finished our game and I bathed her, read her a bedtime story, and put her to sleep on the mattress we would have to share. I returned to the living room where Harry was drinking a beer.

"Oh, Harry! You promised! You've fallen at the first hurdle.

This is going to bring you stomach pain and make you ill."

He didn't respond so I took a book and went outside and sat reading. An hour went by before he stepped onto the deck, his eyes smiling, and he had a stupid grin on his face. Holding his drink and a cigarette in one hand, he stood before me, legs apart and his head tipped to one side. In a little boy voice, he said, "Is my big sister going to talk to me then?"

I gave him a disdainful look but said nothing.

Pulling a dining chair out, he sat down. "I'm not going to be angry, Paul." Then he continued to chat, trying to instigate a conversation with me, but I wouldn't. I tried to show I would have no discussion; that I just wanted to read my book. Now it was me being stubborn. I waited for the right opportunity to say I was going to bed. Then he stood up to stare at the hoons.

"I'm going to bed now," I said, "and I suggest you do too."

"Don't you worry about me sis," he said as he reached out and took hold of my hand. "You just go and take care of my little beauty in there, but just before you go, Paul, I want you to know that you're the best thing that's happened to me for a long time. You comin' out here to be with me will put me back on my feet. I love you, Paul; I want ye to know that." He said all of this with genuine brotherly love in his eyes. I felt ashamed of myself for my thoughts, and felt like crying. Instead, I gave him a hug. He stepped into the living room so I took the opportunity to do the same and closed the door and blinds.

Harry was in the kitchen. "I'm going to bed now," I said, and went to my room. Pushing Shirley over toward the wall, I slipped beneath the covers, and lay chastising myself for wanting him to change his routines for me when he too had just gone through a difficult divorce. I lay awake until I heard him enter his bedroom. The noises of the night became louder. It was Friday night and the hoons were in fine fettle. At three in the morning the police came and moved them away, then it was silent at last except for the highway traffic, and the emergency calls to the police and fire department. I drifted into a sleep full of nightmares.

Next morning, I was up and showered before Harry and Shirley awoke. Shirley was first in the kitchen and was so excited to be with us and said she looked forward to going somewhere special.

Her bubbly enthusiasm gave me strength, but Harry came out of his bedroom looking like death and lay down on the couch. Shirley asked him where we were going today but I could see Harry was ill and in no fit state to drive.

I had to think how to get Shirley out for the day and not disappoint her.

"Come on, Shirley," I said. "Let's go buy you a swimming costume and we'll go swimming. What do you say?" I said, smiling.

"Yes!" she cried excitedly. "I want a pretty one with lots and lots of colours."

"Then that's what you'll have," I said, and we walked across the main highway to the supermarket. She picked out the prettiest, most colourful costume in the store, and skipped all the way home, so excited and eager to show her father when we returned.

Shirley and I spent the day by the pool and Harry remained in pain as he lay on the couch.

When that small amount of alcohol upset his stomach so much, he never bothered about it for the next week because he'd be in pain, but as the effects wore off and Friday night loomed, I knew he yearned to have a beer again. And I did have to admit, he only needed one or two to make him feel ill.

We took Shirley to church on Sunday, and I could see Harry took religion seriously. We hadn't been raised religious but we had all attended the Church of England schools and church, and being in church cleansed him, he told me. Hearing this, I encouraged his attendance, hoping the church would help him heal his soul.

The following week I kept my routine around the apartment, but felt I would go stir crazy if I didn't get out somewhere on the weekend coming up, and I told Harry this.

"I'll sort something for next weekend," he said.

Alma rang me on Friday afternoon and asked if I would like to go out with her for the day on Saturday. "I'd love to!" I exclaimed, delighted, and grateful that at last I would get out and see something of Illinois.

"That's great," Harry said when I told him. "I'll catch up on some letter writing while you're out."

"What time do you think Alma will collect us tomorrow, Harry?" I asked. "She didn't tell me."

"Oh, Alma's always late for everything, so I wouldn't be up at the crack of dawn," he said.

"Okay," I said. "'night then."

"'Night, sis."

The night as usual was disturbed by the hoons, the sirens and the traffic, but I did sleep a little more than I had over the last days.

I was as excited as Shirley the next morning with thoughts of getting out at last! I was up and showered and had my bag packed by nine o'clock. By eleven o'clock Shirley and I had grown agitated.

"What's Alma's number, Harry? I'll ring and ask what time she is coming."

"I'm running late," she explained. "I'm sorry about this, but we'll have our lunch then come over and pick you up. Have you packed your costumes?"

"Yes, we have," I said and winked at Shirley.

"I'll be there about one," she said.

305

I felt disappointed that it was only going to be half a day, but I thought, *that's better than not going at all*, so Shirley and I filled in the time until after lunch then sat on the deck to wait for Alma.

Three o'clock arrived. "Do you think everything's okay, Harry? She said she'd be here by one."

"I've told you what she's like, Pauline – she can't be anywhere on time."

"Still," I said, "I think I'd better ring."

"I'm sorry," she said. "I've been giving the house a spring clean and re-arranging Shirley's room for you to sleep here."

"Sleep there?" I said, turning and looking at Harry, who now looked embarrassed but stared straight at the television pretending he couldn't hear me.

"I don't know anything about sleeping there. I thought we were just going out for the day."

"Oh lord! I've put my foot in it," said Alma. "Harry wants you to stay the night here – he wants to have a beer."

"Does he?" I exclaimed, looking at Harry, "and he didn't have the guts to tell me, eh!"

"We'll be there in about an hour," she said.

I put the phone down and glared at him. "You organised this to get me out of the house so you can have a drink?" I snapped. "Why didn't you discuss this with me?"

"You don't want me to drink in front of you, so I asked Alma to take you around there. Don't make a song and dance about it."

"I'm feeling very uncomfortable being here upsetting your routine, Harry. I'm going to organise my trip home." And we then sat in silence until Alma arrived.

Alma turned up at five o'clock and found Shirley and I both dispirited after waiting a whole day, thinking we were going out. Alma had a man and a young boy in the car.

"Who are they?" I asked as we descended the stairs.

"That's Steve, my boyfriend, and his son, Kurt. I've got to drop Kurt off at his mother's; he's been staying the night with us." I hadn't given it a thought that Alma might have a boyfriend.

"Steve's got a drinking problem," said Alma. "He's been doing really well until last night when he fell off the wagon. That's one of the reasons we're late; I've been waiting for him to become compos mentis." She dropped this news on me as we approached the car.

Steve struggled out of the passenger seat and held his flabby, clammy hand toward me which I gingerly shook and let go of quickly. *What a feeble excuse for a man*, I thought. Standing there with no shoes on, his skinny, bandy legs hung like loose threads of cotton from his baggy pink shorts; he had a pigeon chest under a lilac vest; his arms (which looked very much like his legs) dangled either side of his body in the stance of an orangutan. Long curly dreadlocks hung unkempt and matted around a deathly grey pallor and, somewhere near the back of his head, I saw these dull, piggy, yellow eyes. He couldn't have been more than thirty-five, and Alma smiled as if she was proud of him. *Love is blind*, I thought.

Then Steve's son jumped out of the back seat. "Kurt's the name; pleased t'make yer acquaintance," he said with some authority, although he was only ten. He stuck out his hand which I reluctantly touched. *Grubby little thing; it's probably just been up his nose*, I thought. Then he turned and spat on the ground. I took an instant dislike to them both.

The greater the distance between Shirley and this obnoxious child the better, so when we were asked to get in the back seat, I sat between them. Alma started to drive.

"I'm sorry, Pauline … I've got to make one more stop at my mom's to deliver her shopping to her and I'm late. She's already been on the phone. When I sort her out, we'll go to the indoor swimming pool."

We drove to Alma's mother's. "Did Harry tell you Mom's an alcoholic?" she said as we got out of the car.

"No," I exhaled. *What's next?* I thought.

Alma's mother's apartment was depressive, the air filled with cigarette smoke, the blinds all shut blocking out the daylight. The electric lights were burning, and noisy air conditioners blasted out in every room, yet I could still smell the alcohol.

Alma's mother tottered around the corner of the kitchen holding onto the wall. She had blue hair, cut short around a painted doll, flabby face, and saliva oozed from one corner of her mouth, which was smeared with bright red lipstick. Her eyes seemed to looked in different directions and were a dull yellow. She wore a man's grey cardigan over a loose-fitting floral dress and her feet protruded from the bottom of this ensemble in bright pink, fluffy slippers, which pointed east and west. The whole creation was topped off with a cigarette holder, waved in the air in her other hand.

"This is Harry's sister, Mom, visiting from New Zealand," Alma shouted, then looked at me and said, "You have to shout; she's a bit deaf."

"Hello!" I shouted and held out my hand.

"Oh, hello darlin', how are you? It's lovely to meet you." All this was said in a soprano voice, as she tried to focus on my hand, then aimed herself in my direction. As she moved her hand from the wall towards my outstretched hand, I caught it with my right hand while my other hand went into the crook of her arm and saved her from falling.

"Sit here," I shouted as I steered her towards a dining chair.

"Thank you, darlin'," she said, still in her soprano voice. "I've not been too well lately so I've had a little brandy and it's gone straight to my legs." She tried to laugh but didn't quite make it and it turned into a cough that spluttered and scraped around in her throat to clear the phlegm.

Alma put the shopping away and began to clear the glasses, cups, and dirty ashtrays from around the house. During this time, her mother attempted to tell me something about her illness, or I think it was about her illness, but I couldn't understand her drunken vocabulary. I "ooh'd" and "aah'd" in what I thought were the right places, shook my head, nodded, and tutted and it seemed to satisfy her.

Approximately twenty minutes later, Alma approached her mother. "We've got to go now, Mom," she shouted.

Her mother looked confused. "But y'jus' got here, darlin'?" she sang.

"No, Mom, we've been here all afternoon," said Alma, looking at me and winking.

"Oh, have y'darlin'?" said her mother and knitted her brow. "It's me illness, y'see; a' lose track o' the time." She tried to laugh and again started coughing.

No wonder she's confused, I thought, though I disagreed with the way Alma treated her but I wasn't going to argue; I needed to get out of this suffocating place.

Back in the car, Steve reminded her how late it was and he had promised to have Kurt back by 5.30 pm.

"We'll go straight there now," said Alma.

My god, I thought, *this is some day out.*

Driving across the city back to O'Hare, where Kurt lived with his mother, I wondered why Alma hadn't dropped him off when she collected me. Kurt got out of the car spitting abuse at his father because he'd promised he'd take him swimming. Kurt and Steve walked up to the front door and knocked, but nobody answered. They waited and knocked again, but nobody was home.

"What should I do, Alma?" Steve shouted in a pathetic whimper.

"Hasn't he got a key?" Alma shouted back.

"I can't leave him alone. I don't know how long his mother might be out," he whined while he lifted his top threads of cotton up in the air then dropped them again to hit his thighs.

"Let's find a phone booth and ring his grandma; she might know where his mother is," shouted Alma.

The little brat ran back to the car with an evil grin on his face and jumped in, while Steve moved towards us, balancing on his bandy, stringy legs which threatened to break at any moment.

Alma drove into a supermarket car park for Steve to use a pay phone and I recognised it as the supermarket I walked to each day. The thought of escaping came into my mind. We all got out of the car and Steve rang Kurt's grandma.

"She doesn't know where she is, and she can't have him 'cos she's goin' out herself," he shouted as he put the phone down. Alma stood staring for a while then looked at me. "He'll have to come home with us then," she said. "Would you mind if he slept on a cot in your room with you and Shirley?"

The thought of spending the night with this lot was more than I could possibly comprehend. I leaned in the car and grabbed my bag. "I'm going back to the apartment," I announced and started to hurry away.

"You can't!" Alma screamed. "Harry will be angry with me. Please, Pauline; we'll put him in our room then."

I wasn't going to be talked around. "I'm sorry, Alma. I can't take any more today. I'll take my chances with Harry," and I aimed myself toward the exit of the car park.

"Pauline, don't please," she pleaded. "It's dangerous to walk alone around here, especially at this time of day. Let me drive you then. Please get in the car."

If I got in that car, she might take me straight to her place and I couldn't trust her.

"I'll be alright, Alma; I need the exercise. Now please stop making a scene and take that lot home." I indicated toward my beautiful Shirley, the brat and cotton threads. Shirley looked confused and upset, but I knew I couldn't take her with me because I was about to crack up. My mind was going crazy and all I wanted was to be back in New Zealand. *How can I get back there as quickly as possible?*

"I'll see you on Monday, sweetheart," I shouted to Shirley and blew her a kiss.

I jogged across the main highway, dodging the traffic, and entered the driveway. Picking up speed now, I sprinted toward the central area where I came across the hoons. Some of them jostled me, trying to block my path. My fears of what they might do to me filled my mind. I dodged and ducked, trying to keep on moving toward the pathway that ran behind the apartments. As soon as I was clear, I aimed for the metal staircase, frantically trying to avoid them, but the hoons followed, laughing and shouting abuse. I was moving through a nightmare, my fear choking me. I scaled the stairs two at a time, crying on the outside but screaming inside.

"Harry, open the door, Harry!" I cried.

The hoons reached the bottom of the stairs. "Get away from me!" I screamed. "My husband's a policeman."

They mimicked me, "My husband's a policeman! My husband's a policeman!" as they threatened to climb the stairs.

I hammered on the door, trying to be heard over the loud music coming from the apartment. Thumping with both fists I now screamed, "Harry, it's me, Pauline. Let me in quickly."

The hoons mimicked me again.

Harry eventually opened the door, and stood there looking confused. "What are you doing back here?" he uttered.

"I'm not staying the night with them. You just carry on as if I wasn't here," I said and pushed past him into my bedroom and shut the door.

He opened it again, saying, "Come on into the lounge and talk about it, Pauline. Come on. I'm sorry I sent you away with her." He obviously wanted to make peace. "I knew she'd let me down. I've told you what she's like, now ye might believe me."

I hit his hand that was on the door handle and heaved at the door to shut it again. He stayed quiet for a while then began speaking through the closed door. "Open the door and let's talk about it all, Pauline."

My head was in a state of flux and confusion, bursting. I threw the door open and saw Dave ... in Harry's face. "Don't speak to me, don't come near me, and leave me alone!"

These words rasped through my throat with such vengeance I sounded evil. "Do you *un-der-stand!*" My blood pumped around my face and head and I felt at any moment I was going to explode. In the state I was in, I didn't recognise my brother but was instead fighting Dave and speaking out after all those years of abuse. Harry raised his hands in submission, then I could see the shock in his eyes as he looked at me. He stood rigid, not twitching a muscle, just shaking his head. I slammed the door shut and stood with my hand on the handle for a few minutes.

I heard nothing from the other side of the door but knew he was still there. When I opened the door again to look at him, I saw my brother again. We looked at each other in shock. "I'm organising to go home tomorrow so you'll be free of me – this place is making me ill," and I shut the door.

As I sat on the mattress, it was hard to comprehend my behaviour. *Did I dream all that?* Never before had I mentally sank to such a state. "My God!"

Hugging my knees, my back supported by the corner of the room, I sat cold and confused for some time. Motionless. Stunned. Then slowly my insides began to quiver, and my body began to feel warmer as the blood started to pump normally and the muscles around my neck and face began to relax. After some time, I settled down and I was able to cry.

The music was turned off shortly after my outburst and, soon after that, I heard his bedroom door shut.

Heaping clothes on top of me to create some warmth, I lay down and slept – through the noise of the hoons – through the noise of the sirens – through the noises of the night. I slept for the first time since I had arrived in America. I slept right through the night.

Waking with a migraine, I went to the kitchen and made a cup of tea and took some medication, but I wasn't in the mood for a confrontation, so I went back to bed.

Harry got up and after a short while knocked on my door. I sat up but chose not to answer and he opened the door. "Are you alright?" he asked.

"No!" I replied and said no more.

"Come on out and talk about it," he said.

"No!" I repeated.

Standing with his hand on the door, he said, "I'll go make some tea. Come on, we need to talk," and he walked away.

I sat for a while longer, but began to feel like a stubborn child, so I decided to join him at the dining table.

"I really am sorry about last night, Paul," he said.

"Are you?" I didn't care whether he was or he wasn't. "So, you remember it this time, eh! You made plans to get rid of me without even consulting me. That says such a lot about you. I will never be put in that situation again by anyone," I said. "I didn't like what I turned into, I saw Dave's face in yours. I'm going mad, Harry. I want you to take me to the airport to change my ticket. I'm going on the first available flight." This was said without emotion, flat. I felt nothing.

"Please don't go, Paul. I promise I won't drink again while you're here. You've got nothing to be afraid of. I want to show you I can do it. Please, Paul, last chance eh? You are ill, I can see that now. Please stay and let me look after you?" His voice wasn't pleading or condescending; it sounded as though he had given some thought to it and had planned his speech. I could see he wanted to help me.

"I've got a migraine, Harry, and I'm not prepared to give you an answer now. I'm going back to bed, and I'll let you know what I think when my head is better."

Waking only for a drink or the bathroom, I slept all day. Harry woke me twice to ask if I wanted anything to eat but I declined. I still felt sick, and continued to sleep without waking through the following night.

Monday morning arrived and Harry had gone to work. At 10 am, I moved from the mattress to the dining table, still in my night clothes and still feeling numb. I stared through the window at the tree and at the residents as they went about the complex. It took a great deal of self-persuasion to have a shower, after which I sat in the recliner chair, and placed my Walkman over my ears. The day dragged on. Pushing myself to prepare a meal for Harry and Shirley was a major task and I was not able to be jolly or chatty with Shirley when she arrived because I desperately needed quiet. I couldn't even bear the sound of my voice.

Alma arrived to collect Shirley, and Harry chastised with her over the way she'd behaved toward me on Saturday.

If I don't get some peace I'm going to crack, I thought and moved onto the deck and closed the ranch slider to muffle their raised voices.

Shirley left with her mother and Harry started to talk to me about staying.

"I came here because I was already ill, Harry. I've been taking medication for depression and I was close to a breakdown when I was in New Zealand. My overreaction to your drinking is probably because of the life I've led with Dave. This is your

314

home and you're entitled to behave in it any way you wish. It's not right that I come here and demand you stop drinking. But I'm frightened of this place and staying here is making me even more ill. I've given it lots of thought, Harry, and the only solution is for me to go home." I said all this showing there was no discussion.

"Okay. I'll take you to the airport on Saturday," he said.

"Thank you," I replied as I stood and gave him a hug, then went to my room and slept again.

When Tuesday morning arrived, I felt a little better, the thought of going home beginning to sink in. Saturday couldn't come fast enough.

Before I had left New Zealand, friends had asked if I would be interested in minding their house during August and September when they were going overseas. They lived at the top of the North Island in New Zealand, and their house was a cosy cottage, beautifully decorated, and with immaculate gardens. The windows all looked over a peaceful valley. I had told them I'd let them know when I came back from America.

That's what I need, I kept telling myself, ... *to be away from people and have total peace for a couple of months.*

Although Harry offered to help me I could see how stressed he was and I knew how ill I was and felt sure us being together was only making both of us worse. I knew I had to go home. Would Mum understand?

As the week moved toward Friday, I began to feel stronger. Harry announced on Thursday evening there was overtime going for the weekend and he would be working Saturday and Sunday.

"You promised you'd take me to the airport," I said, feeling frantic that my plans to go home would be cancelled again.

"No, it's okay, I will still, I'll be finishing at two on Saturday. I'll come straight home and collect you and Shirley, and we'll go into Chicago then."

"Please don't let me down, Harry," I said as I touched his arm, feeling desperate.

In the apartment below Harry lived a young couple in their late twenties or early thirties, with two little girls aged four and six. Although Harry had told me not to talk to anyone, I often spoke to her and the children and sometimes allowed Shirley to play with them in our apartment, because they seemed to be the most 'normal' of all the residents. They were both on 'social' and, on the odd occasion, she would call to borrow sugar, milk, or some necessity until her 'social' cheque came through.

Often at night when I was on the deck, I could hear these neighbours talking beneath me as they sat outside. He had shaved his head completely bald, which to me seemed a bit odd, but his wife seemed quite normal.

My Friday went according to its routine, and Harry went to bed at 8.30 pm because he was working the next day.

Shirley was also in bed, and I turned off the lights and took my evening cuppa out onto the deck and sat behind the tree watching the hoons. Cigarette smoke drifted up from the deck below. The hoons were worse than ever that night, racing each other up the driveway in their cars and slamming on the brakes trying to do a 360 degree turn in front of the mailboxes, flattening a few of them. Another group fought each other with smashed beer bottles, and others staggered around the grassed area, obviously drunk. Suddenly, explosions erupted around me, three or four explosions near my ears. I had heard enough since I'd been here to know this was a gun being fired. I dropped to my knees and frantically crawled along the deck to get back inside the door. My heart pounded madly, fearing the next bullet would hit me. While moving, I shouted through the deck slats to my neighbour beneath me, "Was that gunfire?"

"You can keep a gun in this country to protect yourself," he answered loudly. Two more shots. Now lying with my body inside the door, I leaned over the deck and shouted through the slats to Baldy, "Will somebody call the police?"

"I would say so, Ma'am," he calmly answered.

There were two more shots! I pulled the ranch slider shut, closed the blinds, and crawled into the dining area to reach the phone. I dialled the emergency number and told them the hoons were shooting at us.

"I'm really frightened," I said. "I've got a little girl in the apartment – she's only four. Please hurry!"

After telling them where we lived, I placed the phone back on the table and crawled over to the couch. Frightened and panicky but trying to move quickly, I grabbed the cushions from the couch and threw them one by one down the room toward my bedroom door. I crawled after them, opened the door and threw them into my room. The walls were wooden, and I was afraid if they started shooting towards the apartment from the back entrance, the bullets would come through the walls. By crawling on the floor, I felt I was a smaller target. Manoeuvring Shirley away from the wall and toward the edge of the mattress, I placed the thick cushions against the outside wall and got in between the cushions and Shirley and put my arms around her to protect her. I lay there terrified for approximately ten minutes when I heard the police car sirens entering the complex.

The Police did their job and moved the hoons away. The silence was golden, but I was afraid now that they might find out who called the police and so didn't sleep all night, and lay listening to every move outside, fearing they would return.

Harry rose at 4.30 am and I went out to tell him about the shooting. He immediately shouted instructions at me not to go out of the apartment or near the windows then stormed toward the front door. Before he slammed it shut, he looked over at me and said, "I wish I could get out of this hell hole." And I was

317

reminded of the promise I'd made to my mother. But right now, I was exhausted, and Shirley would be up soon and would want to play.

How am I going to get through the day? I thought. I tried to keep Shirley busy, but I moved on automatic.

From the window, I saw the couple from downstairs and I stepped onto the deck. "Wasn't that awful last night?" I shouted down to them. They just looked at me and said nothing.

They must be so used to that sort of thing, I thought. "We're not used to guns in New Zealand," I ventured. "It really frightened me."

"Bring Shirley onto the deck tonight – I'm setting off fireworks for the kids in the neighbourhood," said Baldy.

It was the fourth of July celebrations.

Harry rang from work at 2 o'clock and said he was working until six. I told him not to worry about my ticket I'd get a taxi on Monday and sort it out then.

When he arrived home, we talked about the shooting, and I told him about Baldy putting a fireworks display on for the children.

After our meal we sat on the deck watching Baldy and his wife acting as though they were circus masters. They strutted in front of the neighbourhood children, who sat in a circle around the grassed area, shouting instructions to them all about what they should and shouldn't do and throwing their arms around to emphasise their words.

They really loved an audience. Baldy set the fireworks off while he drank his beer and took long strides around the front of the audience, shoulders back, chest puffed out, having a wonderful time. Harry went to bed but Shirley and I watched the fireworks until 9.30 pm.

Desperate to get some sleep that night, I took a couple of sleeping pills. The hoons were kept at bay because of the firework display so I felt safe enough to knock myself out.

Placing the cushions from the couch around the outside wall again, I pushed Shirley over to the edge of the mattress. It had given me a sense of security the previous night, so I repeated the procedure. As I snuggled between the cushions and Shirley, I put my arm around her and prepared myself for sleep.

The fourth of July parties were in full swing around the area. *The fire station sirens will be running hot tonight,* I thought. Explosions from firecrackers, loud whistling noises from fire rockets, constantly, people shouting, screaming, laughing, glass smashing, cars revving, cans being kicked, people arguing – but my sleeping tablets had begun to work. *Gunshot noises again,* but I knew the authorities would be on alert so I ignored them. The noises of the night began to fade, and I slept.

My sleep was interrupted occasionally by other loud explosions, people screaming and glass breaking, but my sleeping pills put me straight back to sleep.

The front door slammed shut and I heard footsteps running down the metal stairs. Harry's car was parked under my window. I heard it start up and drive away and I looked at my watch 4.55 am. I dozed off again.

Waking with a dreadful thirst, I looked at my watch and it was 6.35 am. Slowly climbing over Shirley and being careful not to disturb her, I tucked the covers around her back, wrapped my dressing gown around me and went to the kitchen. After switching on the kettle, I opened the drapes and looked down on the grassed area. *Shock horror!* It was completely covered in household bric-a-brac and pieces of furniture.

What's all that? I thought as I opened the ranch slider door and stepped out onto the deck, peering into what looked like a bomb site. In the centre, sitting hunched with her arms around her knees, her chin perched on them, was the girl from downstairs, dressed only in a T-shirt and her knickers. Peering closer to make sure I was seeing clearly, I shouted, "Are you alright?"

Her head moved up slowly until she met my gaze.

"Are you alright?" I said again. "What's happened? Do you need any help?"

Crying and shaking her head, she gestured with her hands towards me and towards her apartment.

"Do you need help?" I asked again and she just repeated the gestures.

Flustered, I stepped back into the lounge, shut the slider, and picked up the front door key from the computer table. I placed it in my dressing gown pocket, and ran out and down the metal stairs, around the pathway and to the front of her ranch slider when she shouted, "Stop! Look!"

She pointed again towards her apartment, and I turned to my right: the ranch slider had been ripped from its runner and smashed into pieces on the deck, leaving her home wide open. Baldy sat crouched on a stool on the patio, pointing a gun right at me. I froze. I stood directly in front of him, blocking his view of his wife. His elbows were on his knees and both hands were holding the gun with his head directly behind it as he squinted to focus. The gun slowly swayed left then right.

"I've rung the police; they'll be here soon," his wife whispered loud enough for me to hear.

I stood like a rock again, but this time a rock with no anger. Not knowing what I felt, and unable to take my eyes off the gun, I became aware of saliva oozing from the side of my mouth because I couldn't swallow. I wanted to go to the bathroom, but I couldn't move as I stared down the barrel of the gun.

Baldy was no more than three feet from me and looked drugged. A pulse throbbed on his bald head, and my gaze kept coming back to it. Somewhere in the distance I heard a police siren growing louder as it came closer. Then car engines stopped behind me, suddenly, with a screech of brakes. Then car doors opened.

"Get down, Ma'am," said a strong female voice. "Get down, Ma'am."

But I stood frozen, transfixed by the sight of the gun, not knowing who she was talking to.

Police had parked on the other side of the mailboxes, and now crouched behind their open doors with their windows rolled down, pointing their guns in my direction. My back was to the police, with Baldy facing me. I realised we were in a straight line, with me in the middle. Guns pointed to my back and one pointed at my face. In shock, I just stood there.

"Get down, Ma'am!" the female voice shouted louder. I still couldn't move. Time stood still and, in the silence, it seemed like hours passed.

Then action!! A rustling noise behind me of people running. A hand clamped on my neck and another in the middle of my back, which pushed me to the ground. Uniforms ran past me in Baldy's direction. A loud gunshot! I threw my hands over my head as I lay face down on the grass.

This is a nightmare! I thought, but never moved. Then, some minutes later, hands were under my arms, and I was hauled to my feet.

"You alright, Ma'am?" the policewoman asked, looking into my eyes. I nodded, still stunned, and looked toward Baldy, who lay face down on the deck, his legs wide apart, his wrists handcuffed behind him. A policeman had his foot planted between his shoulders.

"Did you make the call, Ma'am?" I heard the policewoman ask and slowly turned to see her talking to Baldy's wife, who now stood amongst the debris.

"Get your clothes. You'll have to come down to the station to fill in the charge form. Will you help her, Ma'am?"

The policewoman looked at me. I nodded and put my hand out to Baldy's wife, who came toward me and threw her arms around me. "I've had a whole night of sheer hell. My kids are scared to death." She started to cry, and I put my arms around her to soothe her.

"There, there. Let's get you dressed," I heard myself saying, but I knew I was running on automatic, not thinking about what I was doing, or saying, because I didn't feel it was happening to me. It was a dream I was going to wake from any minute, so I had no emotions.

We walked over the broken glass and into the lounge area, where every article of furniture she had was in pieces either on the grass or smashed to splinters on the carpet. The fridge freezer did not escape, it was on its side with the doors ripped off.

"He's pissed all over my clothes," she cried.

"There, there. We'll find something," I mouthed while I walked through this nightmare and into her bedroom, the same room by the front door that Shirley and I occupied in Harry's apartment directly above.

"I was screaming for you last night," she said. "Couldn't you hear me?"

"No dear," I said. "I'd taken a sleeping pill."

"He had the gun to my head and kept telling me he was going to kill me, then he'd shoot up to the ceiling instead. He thought it was funny," she cried.

"There, there," I said again as I looked around the devastation in the room and her words began to filter into my numb brain.

"He shot up to the ceiling," I repeated to myself, and my eyes slowly moved upward to look at the ceiling. There were four bullet holes. *Four bullets*, I thought, and something began to stir. *In the ceiling! That would be our floor!*

Realisation set in, and I turned and bolted, screaming, "Shirley, Shirley!" Her name came out of my mouth, but my brain screamed *No!! No!!* My legs moved like wings getting me over the debris, around the building and sailing toward the metal staircase. A policewoman followed me. "Shirley!! Shirley!" I screamed. *No! No!* my brain repeated.

As I ran up the metal stairs, my slippers got caught and I kicked them off. The key went into the lock, and I flung open the door and ran into the hall. I burst into the bedroom, fear choking me. The policewoman was behind me as I pulled back the covers and grabbed Shirley under her arms and lifted her up off the mattress and out of her sleep. She started to cry.

"Are you alive, sweetheart?" I stuttered, hugging her, inspecting her, then hugging her again. The policewoman pulled the mattress back off the floor, and the tips of the bullets were obvious in the carpet.

I stared in horror as a bellow rose in the pit of my stomach. It began to rumble, started its climb as it grew. Inch by inch, it moved up my body and shook my frame like a volcano about to erupt. My head flung back as it forced its way through my throat, determined to be born. Violently, it spewed forth upward to the heavens, demanding "God Help Us! Help Us! Help Us!" and I collapsed onto the mattress with Shirley in my arms, crying like I'd never cried in my entire life before. Bellowing loud, then wailing moans and sobs forced out of me into the atmosphere as though the power of them would stop the insanity I felt I was being forced to endure. I had lost control.

Shirley cried with me, and we held onto each other.

The policewoman led me into the living room, she sat me on the couch and fetched me a glass of water. My arms stayed locked around Shirley, afraid to let her go.

"I'll be back shortly, Ma'am," said the policewoman. She left. Suddenly, I stopped crying, not wanting to, but I was upsetting

Shirley.

"It's alright, sweetheart," – gasp – "I'm alright now," – gasp
– "Silly Aunt Pauline, I got a fright." I kept kissing and hugging
her, my speech stunted as I gasped for air.

"It's alright, Aunt Pauline," she said as she wiped the tears
from my cheeks. "I'll look after you. I love you."

I started crying again.

"Oh, Shirley. I love you too, sweetheart."

With my crying under control, we sat kissing and hugging
each other.

The policewoman came back with the two children from the
bottom apartment. All were wearing T-shirts and knickers. They
each held one of my slippers in their hands.

"Could you look after these two, Ma'am, while their mother
comes down to the station?"

"Yes," I said.

I didn't want to, and I felt truly sorry for them, but I was in
no fit state to look after children. The door closed and we all
looked at each other, the two little ones standing holding hands,
their pretty little faces puffed from crying, their eyes wide with
the fear of what they had witnessed through the night.

I've got to pull myself together, I thought. *These children need me.* I
stood up. "Come on," I said. "Shall we have some waffles for
breakfast?"

"Yes!!" cried Shirley in her usual bubbly manner and ran to
the kitchen. The little ones just nodded.

Somehow, I got through the day without falling to pieces.
Jumbled thoughts raced through my mind, planning how to
move forward, and what I should have done in the situations I
had found myself in. They all pushed to the front of my mind,
shouting to be heard and during this gabble of information came
the realisation that the previous night's happening was Baldy
shooting at the hoons, and I had been talking to him while he

was shooting the gun. *He could have turned the gun up at me*, and I shuddered at the thought.

I kept a writing pad and pen on the kitchen bench throughout the day and wrote down thoughts that entered my head of how to get Harry out of this apartment ... and places Harry had spoken of and vicinities near his workplace. Almost on instinct I was writing various ideas of how to move and I had no idea these names had been filed into my memory.

Baldy's wife made the most of her free trip into town and went visiting her relatives and friends to spread the word about Baldy being jailed.

On arriving to collect the children at 2.30 pm, she wanted to relate all the sordid happenings of the night to me, in all their gory details, and I didn't want to hear. My mind didn't have room for anything else. All I wanted her to do was take her children and go. That morning I had felt sorry for her, but she'd had time to collect her thoughts, and was now enjoying the importance this gave her. Neighbours had been watching for her; they followed her to my apartment to hear the story, and so she had an audience again, and wallowed in it. *These people aren't my people!*

Somehow, I moved them out of the door, closed it behind them and sank to the floor with my back against it.

"Are you sad again, Aunt Pauline?" I heard.

Shirley stood looking down at me as I crouched behind the door.

"They're noisy people, aren't they, and they made me tired," I said.

She sat down beside me. "They made me tired too." She reached out and held my hand.

I needed to do something to help release some of the feelings battling away inside me, but Shirley's presence kept bringing me back to reality and responsibility and I had to keep suffocating the release of emotions.

An hour later, Harry walked in, his eyes wild.

"What's been happening!" he demanded.

"Sit down," I said. "I'll tell you." And I tried to relate the story without emotion.

His first reaction was anger and then he dropped his head into his hands and started to cry. "We're gonna die in this place. We're gonna die!"

I tried to console him

"We're not going to die in this place, Harry. I've been speaking to Mum and she's keeping us safe. We're just going to move you out." I tried to explain to Harry this strange relationship I had with our dead Mum.

Shirley was put to bed as early as I could as I wanted some time to speak to Harry. She was staying for a few extra days because it was school holidays.

I explained what I had planned for the next few days and that I had written things down while trying to make sense of the turmoil that had gone on in my brain all day.

"You're not going to work tomorrow, Harry. We're going to look for another apartment," I said.

"I can't move out of here … I've been wondering how to tell you. I've signed a six-month lease. It's got another three months to go," he said, looking at me defeated. "They'll make me pay for those months and I haven't got it."

"That's okay," I said. "I've thought of that and worked out how much it will cost. I'll pay it with my Visa card."

"You have to put a bond and a month's deposit on a new apartment. I don't know where I'll get that from."

"It's okay. I'll cover that as well. We're going to find an apartment you can move into next weekend, then I'm going home. Please forgive me, Harry, but if I stay here any longer, I will lose my mind completely."

"I'm really sorry, Pauline, that all this has happened here when you needed a place to recover. I wanted to help you get well again," he said. "You're right … this place can't help you to recover, I can see that, and I do understand. But we've still got to pray that we live till next week."

"We will live through this, Harry. I know it sounds strange to you but Mum spoke to me, telling me we'll be safe. She's on our case." His tearful eyes lifted to mine and we both held out our arms as we gave each other a hug that we both needed so much.

After dinner, I followed my routine of evening preparations while Harry quietly sat with his own thoughts. "I'm going to bed," I said as I began to calm down myself.

Next morning, he appeared in the kitchen looking ill again. "My stomach's killing me, Pauline. I don't think I can go anywhere."

Walking up to him, I calmly said "You will get a shower and drive us to look at apartments. I'm not leaving until I know this child can visit you and be safe. We are finding an apartment today, so move it." His big sister had spoken!

He listened, and fifteen minutes later he appeared at the bathroom door looking a little improved.

We drove around all day. I had circled an area on the map close to his work place because that would save him two hours each day. While he was showering, I telephoned a few apartment blocks in that area. I had a list of places and prices to start and was surprised to discover that most of them were around the same price he was already paying. He had obviously been distressed when he walked out of his marriage that he'd not been thinking straight when he found this place.

We eventually found an apartment near to the factory where he worked. It was perfect – he could walk to work if he wanted to get fit *and* save money on petrol. There was a Catholic church next door (this for his support when I was gone), families with children (for Shirley), and it also had beautiful park-like grounds. The manageress promised me the place was quiet at night and assured me they never saw the police unless they needed them.

"We have our own night patrol for security," she said.

"That'll do me!" I said as I looked at Harry. "What do you think?"

Harry half-smiled and nodded, his appreciation showing in his eyes. I paid the appropriate monies while Harry signed the forms.

"The apartment will be ready in another two weeks," she informed us.

"I'll pack everything up for you, Harry; you'll just need help on the day you move. There's not much here."

"Just stay until I'm in the new apartment, Paul, please!" he pleaded.

"I"m frightened for my sanity, Harry.; I'm going to Chicago on Saturday with you if you'll take me or I'll get a taxi and go without you. I'm going to be asking for the first available flight. I've desperately got to go, Harry. I've sorted you out – you don't need me anymore – the rest is down to you. I love you, Harry, but this country is too dangerous for me," and I hugged him.

Daily, I carried boxes from the supermarket and packed his few possessions. By Friday, I had everything ready to move, leaving a few necessities around the kitchen for the following week. On Saturday, he dropped me at the office of United Airlines, the airline I had flown with. He stayed in the car waiting for me.

Within the airline office, a tall, dark-skinned young man in a white shirt with a huge smile stood behind the desk.

"I need to get the first available flight back to New Zealand. This is my return ticket, but I must go back now," I said as I handed the ticket over. He tapped his computer and said that there was a seat on the 5.30 pm the following day.

"Can you get me on it please."

He tapped his computer some more then announced, "That's it, Ma'am, the seat is yours, but you will have to pay a penalty for bringing your flight forward."

My throat contracted in fear, and my head swirled as I heard these words. "How much?" I asked. A very real fear rose that I wouldn't have enough money to get me home. I began to shake. This could stop me.

He tapped the keys again and said, "$900, Ma'am!"

"No!" I screamed desperately. "You can't. I haven't got that much left on my card … please." Tears began to flow. "I've got to get that flight." My throat began to close over, choking me, but I pushed the words through the constriction. "Please help me get out of this country. I can give you the money when I get to New Zealand!! *Please* … I won't let you down. You've got to get me out of here, *please*. People have been shooting at me; I can't stay here any longer. *Please, please* help me."

Somehow, I was moving through the air with his large protective hands around me, and I was placed on a chair in the back office. A cup of black coffee was placed in my hand.

"Calm down, Ma'am, calm down. It's okay. I'll see to it," he said, and I looked into his caring face, *but* could I trust him?

My cheeks were wet with tears, and he wiped them with a tissue. "Will you be okay while I sort it out, Ma'am?"

I nodded and clung to my coffee mug. He came back in a few minutes.

"There you are, Ma'am, compliments of United Airlines. We are so sorry you've had such a tough time in our beautiful country," and he handed me the tickets. "Safe journey, Ma'am."

At first, I felt stunned as I looked unbelieving at the tickets, then, jumping from the chair, I threw my arms around him and planted wet kisses on his lovely dark cheeks. He released me with a beaming smile.

"You've got no idea how much this means to me," I said. "Thank you from the bottom of my heart."

"You're most welcome, Ma'am," he said in a very caring voice. That response, delivered with feeling, made me want to continue hugging him, it was so genuine.

I walked out of the office with the tickets tight in my hand and smiled for the first time in ages. My head held high, I strode out like Harry did when I first arrived.

I had encountered another angel; I had found another apartment for Harry and so hadn't let him or Mum down, and I was going home.

Chapter Twenty-four

The dark night of the soul

2002

I flew from O'Hare to Los Angeles airport, which was in bedlam. My plane had been heavily over-booked, and accommodation, tickets and compensation was being offered to passengers who would wait for a flight the following day. People were agitated and angry, or greedy and pushing. Two very flustered attendants at the desk tried to deal with all this chaos and their patience was being tried.

After thirty minutes of watching this insanity, I began to feel I would lose my seat and be left behind because I did not join in with it. Doubt set in, and I pushed my way through the crowd, my fear and anger building as I went. I pushed and shouted like the rest until I got the attention of the attendant at the desk and, at that point, burst into tears while I screamed that they were not to put me off the plane. I exaggerated my circumstances and threatened legal action if they gave my seat to anyone else. I was a mad woman!!

The attendant assured me that my seat was safe; that they had enough people who were taking up the offer of compensation and free accommodation for the night and that I would get on the plane. Feeling I couldn't trust her, I worked myself into a state as I did not trust anybody anymore. I stood with my hand luggage at the front of the queue to the gate for three hours. I wouldn't sit down, fearing the chaos would result in my seat being double-booked.

When it was announced we would be boarding the plane, I showed my boarding pass and, now panicking, I ran down the air bridge to the plane door. I would be first in my seat and would not get out of it for anyone! However, I tripped over the lip of the open door to the plane and hit my temple against the metal surround and fell to the floor. The flight attendant stepped forward to help me back to my feet.

"Let me get you a cold compress for your head," she said. I felt no pain.

"I'm fine – just show me my seat please," I responded as I blustered down the aisle. She stowed my hand luggage above me as I buckled up my seatbelt feeling so determined that this was my seat and nobody would put me out of it! The flight attendant came back with a wet cold compress and placed it on my temple.

"I don't need this!" I said. "I'm fine!" as I tried to push her hand away

"You have a small swelling beginning. We'll keep an eye on you during the flight, don't worry." I touched my temple with the flat of my hand and felt the top of the swelling, then traced my fingers down my head as it fell back to where my head 'was/should be', but I immediately misinterpreted what I was feeling – the top of the swelling was my normal head and, as my fingers slid back to my head, this was a hole!

How did I get a hole in my head? More confusion began. I sat for some time trying to work out what had happened to me. The plane took off and levelled out and as I looked up, walking down the aisle toward me was Mary, a friend who had died three years ago. Shocked and surprised, I felt I should keep this to myself – it needed some explanation. I struggled to make sense of everything. Mary walked past me without recognition, and the flight attendant was right behind her with another cold compress. As she handed it to me I felt I had worked it all out – Baldy from the bottom apartment had shot me – that was how I got the hole in my head! I was dead! – all these people on the plane have died! We are all spiritual beings. I decided I was about to discover what happens to our souls right after we die. With a look of 'dawning' on my face, I looked at the flight attendant and said, "I've worked it out! You are an angel, aren't you?"

She just smiled.

I decided she was afraid I might tell the others that 'we are all dead' which could start a great panic up here in the sky, so I gently took her hand and said, "I won't tell anyone. Our secret is safe," and I sat back staring at the other passengers, trying to work out how each of them had died. This occupied me throughout the flight.

Half-awake and half asleep, I heard my mother speaking into my ear and reassuring me that I had done the right thing for Harry. On the day of suffering the aftereffects of the gun incident, she had moved me along, pointing out the various places where Harry would feel safe and having me write them down. She told me to relax now, that she'd be healing me.

After hearing Mum, I remembered dozing for some time and when I woke I was being asked to get off the plane, which I did. I wandered along with everyone else and showed my passport etc., thinking it was some secret code that St Peter needed to let us into heaven! I was asked by the person checking my passport if I was going on to Christ Church.

"I don't know," I answered. "I could be, but nobody has told me yet. Is that heaven?"

He merely smiled, and I followed the crowd and picked up my suitcase and then heard my name being called. I turned to see a man who had my name on a card.

I walked up to him. "That's me," I said.

"These are your keys, luv," he answered as he handed me my

house keys. I recognized them. "Your husband will be in touch tomorrow. Your home is in Howick, right luv?" the driver said.

"Yes," I responded. I drifted along without feeling! I was spiritual, and spirits do not have feelings. I sat quietly in the back of the car and was dropped at the door of my home. I let myself in with my keys and climbed straight into bed.

The next morning, I awoke in my bed … in Christ's Church. Or had I? Perhaps I was in New Zealand? I vaguely remembered this room! I began to feel very confused. I wasn't sure where I was! *If I am dreaming about being in a bed in Christ's Church, then will I wake soon and find out where I am?* I hugged the pillow while my mind battled the confusion. Fear enveloped me; I was afraid to move. I couldn't work out if I was awake or asleep! Dead or alive!

Remembering the plane journey but 'knowing' I was dead on the plane, I pondered that *if I'm alive now, then the plane journey was a dream. But if I only dreamt about the plane, am I still dreaming; will I wake in my home in Auckland or back in Harry's home in USA?* The phone rang. I looked at it for a short time knowing I couldn't pick it up as my stomach squirmed and my nervousness rattled my entire being. The phone switched over to the message service and I heard Dave's voice.

"I'll be in touch in a few days. I've got a girlfriend and I'm staying with her."

From that point on, I didn't give Dave and his new situation with a girlfriend another thought.

I felt my head. The hole was still there, which confirmed that I'd been shot, but now I was 'feeling', and I didn't *feel* anything when I was first dead. My mind screamed, trying to sort out my confusion. My stomach knotted in spasms and my chest hurt with the tension. I knew I had no way of sorting it out and my head was in a chaotic tangle of confusion, panic, and pain. My emotional pendulum was oscillating wildly. A state of mental and physical imbalance tipped my mind and body upside down and inside out. This felt as though I was in a tumble drier! I had no way of controlling any emotions, thoughts, or feelings.

Suddenly I felt weightless. My spirit was a balloon escaping, and about to rise into the atmosphere, buffeted by these out-of-control emotions. In fear, I gripped the edge of the mattress, bore down, trying to feel anchored, trying to force myself into the bed with every ounce of energy I could muster. Like this, I tried to stop these feelings from enveloping me and lifting me out of my body. The effort eventually burned up my energy. I started screaming, "No! Don't do this! Don't do this!" Then I couldn't hold on any longer. I had to let go and allow these feelings to run amuck inside me. They were eating away at my soul, and I decided I was in hell, and this was part of being dead.

Vomiting, emptying my bladder, my bowel, all without my control. These feelings I identified as the demons in hell! They had taken control of me and had a will of their own. They were not part of me, but *they* had moved into my body demanding to be expressed and I was being used by them. I didn't know what *they* would do with me next; they controlled me, and they possessed me. They ripped through my inside, slicing me with blades, causing pain that was so excruciating I eventually passed out.

"Please, God, I'm sorry. Please save me," I prayed when I woke, but the daylight continued in this way, followed by a black night of more suffering, to another day where it all continued without any ease, straight on into the night again. I moved from one painful incident to another without knowing if it was sleep and nightmares or I was awake and feeling the demons inside rip me to pieces with their knives.

Exhausted, I would close my eyes but these feelings, which I now began to call 'the happenings', would torture my soul. I began to witness waking moments which were short reprieves from 'the happenings', allowing me to recoup slightly before the next 'attack'. In desperation, I forced myself to stay awake to escape 'the happenings', but exhaustion took over again, and 'the happenings' violently abused my being. I never experienced refreshing sleep, just violent happenings. Then these happenings became my reality. This reality was interspersed with video nightmares when I fell into brief exhausted sleep. I couldn't distinguish between waking and sleeping, being dead or alive, a reality or a dream state. Everything and everyone around me was there to harm me.

Hell was worse than I had imagined when I was alive. I vividly experienced yellow-eyed evil entities with grotesque faces, rotten teeth, and putrid breath, drooling saliva and biting at my body; each one violating me … constantly. I couldn't escape from them!

Huge thundering ocean waves would pick me up and throw me against a brick wall, attempting to drown me. Not once but daily and without warning, each very real to me. I fought to breathe, and felt and suffered the pain of my body hitting jagged rock surfaces.

In one single incident, when my arms began to burn and the pain was excruciating, I looked at them as they burst into flame. I felt the pain of this fire consuming me. Screaming in agony, I ran to the bathroom and, as I ran, I watched my skin burning and peeling back, my flesh melting and dripping to the floor. I slipped on my own fat, hit the floor, and passed into unconsciousness. When I woke, I was lying on the bathroom floor. I looked at my arms – they had no visible marks of being burnt but the after pain of my perceived burned flesh lasted for many weeks.

Daily, I suffered earthquakes that ripped open great chasms that I was falling into. Bombs dropped all around me. Lightning struck me. All very real, and the pain was excruciating. "Please

God, let me go! Please let me go! I can't suffer any more!"

My cries were those of a tortured soul. I didn't know if this was permanent or for a period sufficient to pay for the bad I had done in my life!

On a good day I would have perhaps a couple of hours to recoup from what was happening to me and, within those hours, I would sometimes quickly walk to the local supermarket and collect the things I needed. I would hold my head down and not make eye contact with anyone. I would fumble with my wallet to find my money and rush out of the shop, my heart frantically beating in my chest.

"Don't speak to me. Don't speak to me," ran through my head and I would run through the streets back to my home.

Moving into another stage of the illness, I would wake knowing I was alive and not in hell. This knowing would last for an hour or two and it was slightly reassuring, allowing me to feel I could perhaps survive this mental illness.

In my short remissions throughout the day, I would send an email to my children telling them a story about a life I wasn't living. It was all invented but necessary, I felt, to keep my contact going and not have them worry about me.

Will I ever be well? I thought daily, and eventually began to think that I would never recover from this constant mental pain, my living hell. Where was my mother? I felt I was going through the toughest period in my life and I needed her reassurance that I'd get through it, but she wasn't whispering in my ear. *Does this mean I am in hell and she can't reach me here?* The weeks began to painfully pass by.

During a brief remission I sat before my doctor, but there were no words adequate to explain exactly what was happening to me. To the sane mind, this was incomprehensible. He prescribed sleeping pills along with anti-depressant tablets. The medication made me sleep more, which only gave the 'happenings' more time to abuse my body. I suffered constant violent nightmares!

I *treated* myself to a local psychiatrist, which was costly but necessary for me to try to understand this illness. At this time, I became aware that Dave had cancelled my medical insurance, but also that the insurance I once had didn't cover mental illness even if it was still valid. In the four short sessions I had with the psychiatrist, I felt he at least understood plus what he explained about my illness gave me some insight into how I could work with it myself. The medication he prescribed began to reduce the 'happenings'. I knew I was seriously mentally ill. He suggested I go into hospital, but I was convinced if I did I would never be freed.

"I can do it myself," I told the psychiatrist. I began to talk to myself, promising me I was going to conquer this illness; I was not going to give in to it.

Physically, I had pain in my head like something I'd never experienced before. It was as though my brain was expanding and straining against my skull. The muscles in my chest were pushing against my rib cage and every nerve in my body was vibrating as though I was suffering an electric shock. And my thoughts raced through my mind out of control. No single thought was completed before another fought to have me listen to that. With the psychiatrist's understanding and help, I tried various antidepressants. All seemed to help for a couple of days and then I would have an adverse reaction, or the happenings would begin to increase. I would double my medication without instruction when I'd had nights without peace. After possibly the fourth attempt at a new drug, I sank to an all-time low. I just couldn't take any more pain.

This sort of life was not worth living. I dressed and walked down to the beach. The tide was coming in and the beach was free of people. I walked as far as I could into the water and began to dig a hole in the wet sand big enough for me to sit in. When I felt my body was almost completely covered by sand, I lay back and waited for the tide to come in and drown me. After only a few seconds, hands appeared under my arm pits and dragged me out – and saved my life, but I wasn't thankful. I thought a person had saved me but, on looking around, I didn't see anyone. *Am I dreaming or did I actually try to drown myself?* I didn't know! I couldn't distinguish reality from dreams.

"NO!" I shouted as I stood up. "Let me drown, Mum, please let me drown?" It must have been my mother that had dragged me away from the water and now I felt frustrated and ran home crying and shouting, "Mum! Why are you allowing me to live in this pain?"

Hiding in my home, and not answering the phone or opening the door to those knocking, became a stress all its own. The lady I had employed for the office would leave messages with questions about her work and I would ring back when the workshop was closed and leave the answers to her queries on the message service, when my head was clear.

Apart from the first message Dave had left to tell me he had moved in with his girlfriend, I'd heard nothing from him, and that suited me. It also needed to be filed somewhere in my head for the future when I was well and could possibly make a clean break from him while he had another partner. My friend who lived in the North of New Zealand left me a message to say she was leaving for her 3-month trip to Europe. I rang her as soon as I was able to speak coherently.

"Can I still look after your house?" I asked. She was grateful for the offer, and so was I. I rang the workshop and spoke to Dave, telling him I was still ill, and that I was going away again to recover.

"Leave the keys to the house in the shed as me and my girlfriend are moving into it. And another thing – I've stopped your money. You don't work here so I'm not paying you anymore. I've told the office lady to stop paying your medical insurance."

I checked my online banking and he had stopped my money the week I went to America. Once again Dave was claiming what was mine.

I had a small amount of money in my savings that I could live on for a while, but I knew that sometime soon I would have to go to the authorities and ask for welfare.

I drove the four-hour journey to my friend's house in the North of New Zealand and then settled myself in just as they were leaving. The house sat on the side of a hill, the front of it looking like a single story dwelling but, on entering, you realised it was two-storey, the base of the house having been built into the hill and had stairs to the base where the bedrooms and bathroom were. These rooms had their back wall built into the land so there were no windows on that side - only windows on one wall with a view from all bedrooms that looked down the valley toward a small stream at the bottom. It was a beautiful view, serene and quiet, and exactly what I needed at this time. I told the psychiatrist I was going, and he asked me to keep in touch via email or phone once each week. Which I did.

With discussion with the psychiatrist, we'd worked out a plan to help me recover. I would write down every painful happening and then I would burn the paper at the bottom of the garden to signify the end of that happening. When the 'happenings' tried to take control, I would obstruct them by taking myself off for a walk. I began pounding the pavements and walkways of the area until I was tired and then would go home and write.

The happenings are trying to move into me but I'm not going to let them. If I relax, a 'happening' will take over and I'm not allowing that.

This stance I took was me delaying the 'happenings' which was a small victory. Day by day, I obstructed the 'happenings', but never for very long; but they now knew they had met a resistant force and couldn't choose any old time that suited them. They were still stronger than me, but now I was fighting back with every ounce of courage and determination I could muster.

My resistance began to reduce the violent carnage into 'unusual happenings'. My mind had moved to another level. At this stage, I was able to step out of my body at will. When my nerves were beginning to twang and I knew the next attack was imminent, I could avoid the emotional pain by sucking my spirit out of my body and rising above it. I would look down at myself from above and my mind would go onto a 'high'. I could spend hours 'sitting up there', chattering in an animated way to animals or birds or myself, genuinely laughing at myself over incidents in my life; staying 'up there', refusing to come back down because I was frightened of the next attack. Eventually the 'happenings' would take over and drag me back into the next pit of pain that was waiting for me.

Some days there was no pain and no emotion. I would rise from my bed in a zombie state. Showering was too much effort, and I would sit in a chair in my night dress looking down the valley with nothing going through my head. Apart from a heavy weight on my chest, I felt nothing; I just sat like a statue, staring into space. Hours upon hours was spent staring like this. As the day turned to night, I was aware of the dark and then went back to bed and on those nights I slept. These times gave me some respite from the pain.

My children knew that I was only listening to the answerphone service. They would leave messages thinking I was out somewhere. But I had to psyche myself up to talk to anyone. Most days I would watch the phone ring and couldn't lift the receiver. Only if I was in the right head space could I pick up the receiver, but more often I would write down the name and call them back when I could talk coherently. When I did speak to anyone, it had to be for a very short time as my nerves couldn't cope with long telephone calls. They made me anxious and agitated and would set me back after the work I had been doing on myself.

I began to realise I had entered another stage when a feeling of expansion of my awareness kicked in. I began walking down the valley to a place beside the river. On the bank was a picnic bench. When I first started to visit this place, an old golden Labrador would come and sit beside me. At first, I patted and made a fuss of him. Then I would begin writing the happenings of the night as he sat with his head on my lap. I began looking forward to my visits to this spot to see my friend, the golden Labrador. He never let me down and would always turn up soon after I arrived, no matter what time of the day it was. The opposite bank of the river was quite steep, and one day I arrived at my bench and saw my friend, the dog, on the opposite bank, way off in the distance, looking the size of a coin. In my mind, I tuned in to him and said, "Come on, boy, come and see me."

He immediately turned and pricked up his ears as he recognised me and started running down the bank of the river. He swam across the narrow expanse of water and arrived at my side with a grin on his face. I knew he had heard me. From then on, I had mind conversations with him. He sat and stared into my eyes and spoke to me through his mind; he gave me the answers I needed to help me recover. Knowing I could converse with him in 'mind' gave me an amazing feeling of expansion. Birds and animals became my friends and confidants. I would sit in the garden and watch the birds and 'tune' into them. If I held out my hands, they would come and sit on them. This was all so comforting to me. What used to be me in my small world of aloneness was now widened to include the animal world, and the feeling of being alone fighting this illness was now dissipating.

The happenings began to reduce in number and the 'feeling' I was being helped spiritually was a daily blessing. Once I had accepted that I could survive this illness, my mother began contacting me by speaking into my ear through my suffering. She told me she had been with me from the start and had urged me on so many times to survive another day. She told me the fear I had been living in had prevented me from becoming aware of her presence. Fear builds up a vibration that spirits can't penetrate, she told me. But she had never left me.

"You must plan your way out of this mental state, Pauline; that's the only way for you to recover as your personal determination is crucial. I can point the way but you must do the work. I'm right here with you."

Hearing these utterings from my mother was always comforting and supportive. Though she was long gone, she wasn't finished with me yet.

On one occasion, once my mind was well entrenched in the feeling of spiritual help, I went to bed at my usual time and was not afraid to sleep. The electric clock beside the bed had red illuminated digits on the face. In the middle of the night, the buzzing alarm on the clock began blurting out intermittently to wake me. I woke to see the red digits were flashing 2.00 a.m.– 2.00 a.m. on and off with the sound of the alarm buzzing. Rousing from my sleep, I sat up on one elbow and pressed the appropriate buttons but couldn't make the alarm stop. I pushed back the covers, brought my legs out of the bed, and leaned behind the bedside cabinet and took the plug out of the wall.

I was still sitting on the bed and turned to get back under the covers when suddenly the room turned to daylight. Shocked, I sat for a moment thinking, *Oh, I must have slept throughout the day, it must be 2 o'clock in the afternoon.* But something made me stay where I was. This light was startling – it was a brightness I had never experienced and seemed to be 'too' bright. I had the drapes closed but the light in the room was even brighter than the daylight when I was sitting on the bank of the valley in the middle of the day with no roof over my head.

My feelings were calm. This brightness gently hugged my body and gave me a sense of great happiness. I knew that, in the brightness, there were spirits. The brightness was full of them, and the feeling of warmth and the protective spirits all wrapped around me. It was the first time I had felt this sort of happiness.

As I sat staring into this brightness for some minutes, a thought moved into my head that this was not 'normal', and therefore there must be a reason for this brightness.

It's my time to go! I decided. *I am being collected by these spirits that I can't see but know are in the brightness.* Instinctively, I held up my arms, waiting to be taken. Not just waiting, but wanting to be taken. These were the good spirits and I knew my mother was with them; I was reaching out to 'them' filled with a great feeling of love. I *wanted* to be with them. I sat in this position for some time until the brightness faded, and the darkness of the night took over again. My inner being felt very calm and peaceful as I sat in the dark. I lowered my arms and basked in this feeling of love for some time until ordinary feelings of tiredness took over.

Moving back under the covers of the bed, I contentedly closed my eyes and drifted into my first full six hours of restful sleep for some time, without depression and without any happenings. Total restful sleep!

When I woke, I lay in bed feeling an amazing sense of calm. This was wonderful after all those months of waking and catapulting myself out of bed in fear of dozing off into another 'happening'. As I lay there, the memory of the night came to mind. I relived it in my head and told myself what a lovely dream it had been. I still remembered the feeling of happiness and love and the brilliant light with the spirits in it. Turning to the clock to see what time it was I noticed the power was not running through it.

That couldn't have happened for real last night, could it? I thought as I threw back the covers, swung my legs out of bed and leaned over to see the plug out of the wall and lying on the carpet right where I'd left it in the night.

I began my day with my shower, churning over the night's happening while trying to make some sense of it, but I couldn't come up with an explanation that suited me. I went upstairs to the kitchen. The feeling of love and warmth were still with me but, as I began to approach the day, I felt an energy building inside me that was healing. I recognised this was a powerful positive healing energy working through my body that increased in power as the morning progressed until I felt I had more than I needed. Sitting at the dining table I began to write a list of all the people I knew that needed some healing. My list was extensive and after lunch I decided to send some of this healing power to every one of them. I stood in the kitchen and focused on each name and held my arms at a 90° angle from my body and 'sent' this healing power in their direction. I spent approximately twenty minutes on each person on my list. I visualised this power reaching each person and healing each one. Throughout the rest of the day, my time was spent continuing this process. That night I went to bed and slept another peaceful sleep, and the following day was spent again sending this healing power out to my list of people which had now grown from the day before and for the next few days my time was spent directing this healing energy. I ended up listing so many people needing help that I had a busy time filling my days from dawn to dusk, healing!

The bedroom I slept in had recently been redecorated and

had new carpet. The door to the bedroom was difficult to close because it dragged across the carpet which was obviously thicker than the previous one. My friends had pointed this out to me and said they would have the door shaved down at some time when they returned. On one particular night I had been asleep for some time when I heard a wind howling around the house. It whistled so loudly that it woke me just as it came roaring down the hall and the door I had to heave at to shut it, was blown open. I sat up feeling this great rush of cold air hit me in the face and disappear. Getting out of bed, I looked through the drapes to see the air outside was still and calm, not a tree was moving. I investigated the house, but all the windows and doors were shut and there was no evidence of any way this gust of wind had entered the house. As I sat in the kitchen after making a hot drink, I wrote the details of this happening in my journal. It didn't bother me; it was a mystery I would have loved to have solved but I had no explanation for it. I left the kitchen and went down to the bedroom and climbed into bed, with 'amusement' more than anything else. In this time of 'feeling' that the spirit world was protecting me, I concluded they were playing games with me. I settled into my sleep feeling totally protected and happy.

After what I had been through, this period was wonderful. Inside I was still shell shocked, and my emotions still needed to settle properly, but the violence had stopped and for that I was eternally grateful.

My mental health was improving but, on a few occasions, I found myself confronted with 'people' and it would take a few days to recover from the anxiety that this caused. Men were my biggest problem as I was afraid they would hurt me. I shuffled along the streets and tried to avoid a walkway, or road where I might see one. The treatment I had worked out for myself was working and I had to be strong and keep moving forward. I felt

I was being faced with a giant marshmallow that was the antidote to my illness. I knew I would get there eventually and had to keep progressing bite by bite. Confrontation with people would regurgitate more marshmallow. I needed to be vigilant and ensure I didn't see people who would ask me questions and therefore be a setback for me. Dainty bites of marshmallow daily kept me on track.

On a day after another peaceful night, where peace was my experience more than happenings and pain, I had finished my breakfast and picked up my journal and pen and opened the door to go down to the bench beside the river and meet my friend, the golden Labrador. As I looked out at the 'world', it looked 'different'. It was filled with the same intense bright light that had been in my bedroom on the night of the spirit gathering. It was so inviting and full of love. This 'new' feeling of love and happiness became an ocean that rushed over me and I stepped into this ocean feeling an immense power of love and happiness that I had never felt before in my life – not even when I had given birth to my children. The trees were alive and welcoming me. The sun was dazzling, crisp and shining just for me. Everything around me in the world of nature was waiting to welcome me.

I walked down to my bench by the river and this feeling engulfed me. I *had* to take off my shoes and feel the grass under my feet and thank it for being there. I *had* to hug the tree beside the bench and thank it. I *had* to put my hand in the water of the river and thank it for its beauty. My beautiful friend, the golden Labrador, came bounding up to me and placed his head on my lap with a 'knowing' expression on his face. *This beautiful world has turned all of this on just for me.* I began to cry with this amazing feeling of 'love'. It was overpowering.

Staring into my canine friend's eyes, I had my mental exchange of words with him.

347

"Is this what other people have called happiness? I have used that word before when I was extremely happy, but it never did feel like this. Is this what I have missed out on all my life?"

"No," he said. "What you are feeling is 'bliss'. This is just for you."

"Thank you." I cried and hugged my friend for giving me this wonderful feeling.

On this occasion, the feeling of 'bliss' lasted perhaps one more day, but the feelings of happiness and healing kept me going on my path of recovery. I began to walk around the neighbourhood and familiarise myself with it. I could now enter the local store and browse, searching for what I needed rather than frantically grabbing my needs before anyone spoke to me. And my fear of men was over.

Am I waking from a nightmare?
Was that young bride really me?
She had youth and life and passion
Dreams and hopes of living free

Tell me why she wasn't treated,
With care and gentleness?
Why wasn't she protected?
Didn't someone see her stress?

Bit by bit that precious energy
That bubbly happy life,
Was sucked and snatched and stolen
Leaving an empty shell called 'wife'

Like a robot she responded,
Living out a life in fear,
Never knowing what was missing,
Plodding on from year to year

Children raised and safe from harm now,
She looks around in strife,
Though the violence has now stopped
There is no 'feeling' in her life

Is it worth a burst of energy
To peak outside the door
To see if somewhere out there
This world could offer more

Again and again her curiosity
Would fill her daily mind,
With each abusive tantrum,
Whispered callings came behind.

Beneath the cliff that whispers 'freedom'
Friends arms beckon, shouting "DIVE!"
One deep breath, steps out, she did it!
What's that feeling?

She's Alive

Chapter Twenty-five

Time with my sister

2003

While recovering from my mental breakdown, I became aware of the transformation in myself: I had healed so much of my past and could see I was a very different person. I needed to 'level out' and familiarise myself with my 'new' interpretation of me and my life. I realised I would need a period of time to acknowledge I was now stable with a new purpose for moving forward, and I needed time to plan what I would do with my business and my property. I had already recognised that I was about to begin a new life and needed to plan what that would be. I moved in with Babs and Mark to bounce my ideas off them both.

In this new mindset I had, I checked in with my mind and body regularly as I planned various things. I listened to my body these days and, if I felt uncomfortable, I wouldn't do it. Each time I sat thinking about returning to Auckland and starting my new life, it didn't sit comfortably with me, I didn't feel as though the time was right but didn't know why. Then the reason I had to stay in Takau Bay became clear.

Babs announced: "I've got cancer." This was spoken with a false half-grin on her mouth but fear in her eyes. She sat in the corner of the settee, looking small and old.

I felt as though she had just smacked me across the face.

As I stood motionless, anger surged through me. My immediate thoughts were that she had embellished stories all her life. She could entertain like nobody else I knew! A minor incident could be turned into a side-splitting, rip-roaring belly buster when my sister told the story. She had inherited that from my father, the greatest storyteller God had ever put on this earth.

She took after him in stature as well. She was our older sister: two years older than me and five and eight years older than my two brothers. Being the two older girls as children, we shared a bedroom, shared clothes, and shared makeup. Being of Irish descent, we fought like cat and dog, and when she left England to go to live in New Zealand, it was automatic when I needed to find solace and start my life again, I followed her. We raised our children side by side and our combined families had two Mums. We continued to verbally fight. *Isn't that what sisters do?*

She would call me 'fit to burn' and I would call her 'fit to burn', but don't let anyone else call her 'fit to burn' in my hearing or I'd have their guts for garters. I am her sister: only I have the right to call her 'fit to burn', nobody else. But I wanted to shout:

"This statement is not funny, Babs!"

How could I laugh and joke with her about some of the funny incidents in my recent life when I'd just walked into the house, and she had greeted me with such a statement. How dare she! I felt so angry.

It threw me into confusion. I wanted to start a conversation but she hadn't let me hug her. She always hugged me, and I could smell her familiar smell. As children we slept in the same double bed. The smell of her always made me feel safe. At that moment though I felt frightened and hurt and confused and I needed her to hug me and make me feel safe. I wanted her to squeeze me hard in her arms and I wanted to say, "Tell me who it was that did this to you and I'll smash their face in!"

I decided to take my own hug and spill my anger. I dropped my bag and walked over to the settee, sat down beside her, and grabbed her in my arms. I hugged her so hard and smelt her familiar smell but fought with my anger still.

"Who told you this?" I demanded as I pushed her back to arm's length, but not letting go of her.

"The surgeon is going to operate on Monday. He might be able to get it all, but he won't know until he operates." She looked into my eyes with the pain of confession in hers and concern about how I was taking it.

"Too right he'll get it all!" I shouted. "What's his name? What's his reputation? How many times has he done this operation before?" I bombarded her with questions about this man that I obviously needed to know all about before I punched his lights out.

Words came tumbling out of my mouth. "I've told you about those cream cakes you keep eating. This might be a warning to you now, stop eating the rubbish you eat." I vented.

This reaction is the Irish in my family: when we are faced with something we have no control over, anger is our first port of call. But it's only ever a reaction and within a couple of minutes my anger dispersed and I was ready to nurse her through this illness until she was back to perfect health.

Throughout the weekend we reminisced over some of the stories she was famous for telling as we calmed down and accepted this situation. I was ready to do everything in my power to help get her through this ordeal. We laughed and chatted and talked about where we would visit when she got out of hospital. We packed a small bag of nighties and toiletries, and she entered the hospital on Monday morning ready to entertain the staff and patients as she always did. As they wheeled her down to theatre she was telling one of her stories to the orderly who was pushing her trolley and he was convulsed with laughter. I stood at the entrance of the ward watching her, frightened, but smiling while she could see me my face. *She will survive this*, I told myself. Then, looking up, I added, 'Mum, are you watching?'

When I walked into the Intensive Care Unit to see her after her operation I had to sit down abruptly to stop myself from falling. Leaning over her serene face with closed eyes, I grabbed her hand and whispered, "I'm here, you're going to be fine, you have my strength."

She opened her eyes and said, 'thank you' with them and closed them again. Somehow, I managed to get back out of the Intensive Care Unit and collapsed into a chair in the waiting room beside Mark.

She survived the operation and grew stronger by the day and was out of hospital in a week. "You can only get better now," I informed her as I tucked in her covers and administered her drugs and chatted of the places we were going to visit.

"Don't let any visitors come to see me like this. My hair's gone grey, and I don't feel like chatting."

"I'm not listening to that sort of talk," I said. "No visitors until you're stronger is absolutely okay but we can soon put pay to the grey hair problem." So off I went and bought a hair dye. The next morning, I helped her out of bed and into the shower.

"Do you feel strong enough to sit for a while and I'll dye your hair?" I asked with an encouraging smile.

"Okay," she said. "Let's give it a go."

I covered the deck outside her bedroom with newspapers and placed a chair on it and helped her into it. Putting old towels around her shoulders, I began to brush in the dye. She sat looking at the beautiful view of the land she and Mark owned, an emerald green valley with the azure blue water in the distance covered by a sky that always seemed baby blue. "I still love that view," she said dreamily.

"This reminds me of when we were teenagers," I said as I

parted her hair and brushed in the dye to cover the grey.

"You just make sure I don't turn green!" she ordered.

"I've never done that to you!" I exclaimed. "You might not have always had the colour you wanted when I was finished with you but it was never green."

"It was *never* the colour I wanted, and you never put it on properly. You always streak it!"

"No I don't!" I shouted. "You're always moaning about anything I do for you. You're so ungrateful. I enjoy putting your hair dye on, but you always spoil my fun by moaning."

We argued as we always did which brought normality to both of us. We laughed and chatted, fought and bickered until I finished the job and I left her with her head wrapped in cling film as she sat looking out at the view. I went off to the kitchen and made us each a cup of tea.

When I got back with the tray she was leaning uncomfortably over the side of her chair.

"I'll have to lie down. I'm so tired, Pauline!" she muttered.

"You can't lie down with that colour on your hair, it'll get all over the bed sheets," I said "We'll have to wash it off." I stood thinking how to do this.

"Then wash it off" she muttered in frustration

"You'll have to get to the vanity and lean over that," I replied and realised she couldn't bend over and I'd just created a problem. "I know what we'll do!" I said. "I'll run the shower and it will come off quicker in there."

I ran into her bathroom and turned on the shower but, as I did, I knew I wouldn't be able to wash it off her hair without my being in the shower with her. And so, as I went through her room, I took off my clothes and arrived back on her deck in only my knickers.

"Good God! What are you doing with no clothes on!" she exclaimed.

"Come on, get up, I'll have to get in with you," I said as I lifted her out of her chair and moved her firstly to sit on her bed as I took her nightie off. I somehow managed to prop her up in the corner of shower and as I washed the dye out of her hair, it ran in rivulets down our skin, staining us red. We laughed and slithered around each other's naked body. Although she was so very weak, she laughed and cried, and held her stomach where her stitches were.

"Dear God, nobody would believe two women of our age would be in a situation like this," she said. "We look like a couple of red Indians." And she chuckled and gasped for breath as we completed the job. Once the colour was off, I wrapped her hair in a small, clean, dry towel, dried her body and put a clean nightie on her and popped her back in bed. She was exhausted after the ordeal but still chuckling.

"You get a good sleep now," I said as I dried myself, dressed and left the room.

Sometime later, I heard her shouting for me. "Pauline! Get me out of this bed! I'm ready to meet the world."

"That's what I like to hear," I laughed as I entered her room "You're going to look great when I've finished with you."

Picking out her best casual clothes, I dressed her in her finest. We spent a couple of hours blow drying her hair, putting on her make up and painting her nails. We behaved like teenagers. We argued about the colour of the eye shadow and lipstick. We wiped off a few assorted colours before she felt we had chosen the right ones. I then took her photograph.

"Just wait until the family see that, two weeks after your op'. You look fantastic!" I smiled.

And so she did. You would never have known from the photograph that she was so ill, but she never saw the photograph when it was developed. She left a hole in the world that could never be replaced. She died on 2nd April. Her timing with her stories had always been so precise that it wouldn't have surprised me if it had happened on 1st April, and she then sat up and shouted, "April Fools!!" But it was for real when it happened on the 2nd April in the year 2003.

Her ashes were scattered on the land she loved. A pilot took them up in a private plane to swoop low over the land. We gave him the urn, but he said he had to put them in a bag because if you try to scatter them from the urn they fly back into the plane.

Her ashes were scattered from a Pak-n-Save plastic bag. They landed on the backs of the cows and the plastic bag ended up in the stream.

I can hear her now telling the story to all the relatives that had gone before her and watching them all splitting their sides and having belly laughs over the way she'd tell it. She could always laugh at herself.

Letters and cards came pouring in over the next weeks to Mark and me. With one letter addressed just to Mark, he carefully opened the seal and lifted out the single sheet of paper that was folded in half and in the centre of it, wrapped in a piece of toilet tissue, was a diamond. Shocked, we sat looking at it.

"Where did it come from, Mark? What does the letter say? Who is it from?"

"It isn't signed," he said, "but it says:

Dear Mark,

I am deeply saddened by the news of Babs. Even though I have not seen you in many years this news has had an effect on me. For many years I have been withholding a burden in my possession. As a very young child I took something from your house during a clean up after it had been burnt. I took this home and buried it in the yard for some years till I moved away from Kerikeri. During that time, the case was damaged and so it was discarded. This stone has traveled with me for some time now; and so has the guilt. I sense there is great meaning and love behind this stone which I can't contemplate or appreciate. Babs was a wonderful person, and from now on this stone should be kept closer to its meaning. I deeply apologise for my actions as a child and even the continuous withholding of this stone as an adult. Confirmation that this has been received would be very much appreciated.

And it ended with a hotmail email address with no mention of the person's name.

I acknowledged receipt of the diamond and simply said, "Have a clear conscience; the diamond is safely home where it belongs."

But!! It wasn't the diamond from my engagement ring. It wasn't even a real diamond. It was a zircon that had been a gift from my sister Babs. I had kept it in the ring box to await a time to take it to the jewellers and have it mounted in gold and placed on my charm bracelet. That young man had tortured himself with a guilty conscience for all those years since the fire, because of stealing a piece of paste.

He had punished himself.

If I had set that zircon in gold and placed it on my charm bracelet as my plan had been, it would have been obliterated in the fire along with the bracelet itself. It was meant to survive, and I then did have it wrapped in gold and attached to a gold chain bracelet which was a present from Gary and the first piece of jewellery I received after the fire. This 'diamond' now reminds me of my sister and often when I look at it, I hear her words – 'You will receive another diamond, Pauline, and it will have far more sentimental value attached to it than the one you have lost.'

You were right again Babs.

Babs was only fifty-nine. My heart was broken. I didn't know how I would ever get over losing her. She was my best friend and confidant.

After some weeks, Mark asked me to clear her clothes out and go through her possessions. He also wanted me to sort and clear her study.

Her wardrobe and clothes were my first job and for three days I cried constantly as I sorted through them. I was aware of the smell of her favourite perfume on them as I placed them into black plastic bags, taking each bag when full to my car. My plan was to keep the finest for myself and Sharon-Louise and take the rest to a charity shop in Auckland rather than the local one so people in the local village would not be walking around in my sister's clothes and upsetting Mark. My car sat on the gravel drive and the sun beat down over those days heating the plastic bags. Each time I opened the door of the car to add another bag, the powerful smell of my sister surrounded me.

I then spent the next two days clearing her study as Mark made bonfires of years of papers that would not be needed again. As he stood before me surrounded by two walls of books he asked:

"Babs had a habit of hiding money in the books, Paul, and somewhere in here is $2,000 in notes. Do you think you could firstly look for that money as I really need it right now? I thought perhaps you could go along the shelves and put your finger on the top of each book like this," and he put his finger on the top of the spine and tipped a book toward him, "and if it has gaps in the page like that …" he said as he pointed out the gap in the pages he was showing me," then it could be the money I'm looking for."

As he took the book off the shelf and opened it to demonstrate how to remove only books with these gaps, right there was the $2,000 in notes. We looked at it in shock, and then looked at each other and burst into laughter as we both shouted, "Thanks, Babs!" knowing she had waved her magic from the spirit world.

On completion of my work in her study, Mark made morning tea and shouted to me that he was serving it on the deck.

As I stepped onto the deck and looked out to the beautiful view that my sister had so loved, something gently landed on my chest under my chin. My hand went to it and I picked off a perfect yellow tulip – heavy with dew! I sat down and looked at it in my hand! Then looked up into the clear blue sky without a cloud or even a bird in sight and no wind.

"What's that?" asked Mark as he took the flower from my hand. "Where did it come from?"

"I don't know – perhaps a bird dropped it," I uttered slowly.

"It would have to be a pretty big bird to carry that flower – it's heavy with dew!" He kept it in his hand, obviously trying to work out how this had landed on me, then he leaned toward me, looked into my eyes, opened my hand and placed the flower back in it. I held it to my chest and began to quietly cry.

"That's a thank you from Babs, Paul."

"Yes, I think it is," I said as I closed my eyes and heard her voice in my head saying: "Thank you, Pauline. I love you!"

My body told me it was time to return to Auckland and sort my life out. My few possessions were added to my car and, as I opened the door, the smell of my sister filled the interior. As I waved goodbye to Mark I thought, *How am I going to drive all that way to Auckland and stay focused with her powerful smell all around me?*

"Four hours, Pauline, remember – four hours," Mark said as he waved goodbye. This was always a statement my sister would make when I was leaving to go back to Auckland. I had a reputation for speeding and she always worried when I was driving there to see her. I had got into the habit of ringing her to say I'm on my way about one hour before I left so she wouldn't worry about me speeding. I'd had many speeding tickets on that road between Auckland and Takau Bay as it was almost a straight road and quite boring and my mind would wander. If I kept to the speed limit it should take four hours but I'd even done it in two and a half hours driving through the night, which I would never tell Babs as I'd never have heard the end of it.

"Yes, Mark, I'll try," I answered. "Bye now."

I drove along the two kilometre dirt road from their gate that led to the main road, already unfocused and ready for tears again. *Oh I don't know how I'm going to do this*, I thought as her smell drifted all around me – it was as if she was in the car with me. My tears began to fall. I indicated left at the end of the road and right there on the left side of the main road was a young man hitchhiking. He wore a white polo shirt and camel-coloured knee length shorts with a brown belt, thick grey knee-high socks and hiking boots, and, with his light blond hair and fresh open face, he looked European. A small backpack sat beside him and he held out a card that said: 'Auckland'.

That's it! I thought. *If I have someone to chat to all the way home it will keep me focused.* I stopped the car in front of him and jumped out.

"I'm going to Auckland. Please hop in!" I shouted to him. He smiled at me as I picked up his backpack, opened the boot and placed it on top of the plastic bags. When I opened the driver's door again, he was already sitting in the passenger seat and I jumped in smiling, held out my hand and said:

"My name is Pauline. I can take you straight to Auckland. That's where I'm going too."

"Yah!" He said as he shook my hand and nodded his head.

"What's your name?" I asked.

"Yah!" he answered.

Oh no! I thought. *He doesn't speak English so I don't have anyone to chat to.*

He settled into the seat beside me and looked straight ahead.

I began driving, and he eventually felt relaxed in my car, and let his head lean back into the head rest. After a short while it looked as though he had fallen asleep. After many kilometres, I became oblivious to him – forgot about him – as my foot began to press down on the accelerator without my conscious knowledge. Babs filled my thoughts again as he suddenly shot up and leaned forward and looked at the needle on the speedo which was sitting on 120. He looked back at me, fear in his eyes. Immediately, I took my foot off the pedal and slowed down as this was frightening him.

"Sorry," I said, feeling very guilty that he had suffered fear in my car. "I'm very sorry," I said again, but he stayed leaning forward and kept looking alternately at the speedo and then at me, flicking his head back and forth for the next ten minutes until he felt safer and I showed acceptance by sticking to the speed limit. He then tentatively leaned back again with the odd glance at me and the speedo from time to time, then placed his head back into the head rest and closed his eyes. Approximately half an hour later, I forgot he was there again and my foot automatically began depressing the accelerator. Once again he shot up and leaned forward to look at the speedo, then back at me – backwards and forwards his head turned again and again with fear in his eyes until I slowed down to seventy.

"Sorry," I said again, feeling very uncomfortable and ashamed that this young man had placed his life in my hands and I was a threat to him. But I kept wandering off in thoughts of Babs each time he fell asleep. This behaviour between us continued all the way back to Auckland.

As I began driving along the road from Orewa and just before the Auckland Harbour Bridge, I looked out again at the view. This was the time when Babs would say:

"Let's stop and look at that view for a minute. There's the bridge and water welcoming me!" She loved that view.

Suddenly my passenger said, "Yah!" as he looked at me and pointed to the grass outside.

"Here?" I said. "You want to stop here?" *Why?* I thought. There were no buildings or people around and no cars, only great expanses of emerald green grass undulating over and down to the water and bridge in the distance, which was approximately two kilometres away.

"Yah!" He nodded again as he pointed to the open grassed area surrounding a small monument that was perhaps two feet high. I stopped the car and again he looked at me and said "Yah!" as he opened the door and stepped out. I hopped out of the driver's seat, opened the boot with one hand, holding the lid up as I lifted his backpack out and placed it on the grass verge. The black plastic bags seemed to inflate, so I began pushing against them to depress them back into the boot.

Closing the boot lid, I then looked at the grass verge and the backpack was gone, *so he must have picked it up*, I thought and walked around to the passenger door. He wasn't standing on the grass; he wasn't by the car, or even back in the car! I looked around and there wasn't a single person on this part of the road, not even a car!

Visually scanning the area, I wondered where he had gone and why he wanted to leave me here! *There's nothing around these parts*, I thought in confusion. I stood there for a minute or so – I couldn't work this out! I even walked over and around and around the small monument, knowing it was too small to hide him but even thinking he may have been the other side of it perhaps having a wee! *Nothing! Where did he go to?* He was nowhere to be seen.

Confused now, I opened the driver's door and sat back in the driver's seat and turned on the engine. As I looked at the clock on the dash of the car, my mind suddenly said *Eureka!* and I looked up to the heavens and said:

"Thanks, Babs – I did it in four hours."

I laughed and then cried, acknowledging that my sister had sent me an angel from the spirit world to ensure I arrived home safely.

Angels can instantly appear in human form, quite often as a mysterious stranger (generally a young male) when urgent intervention is needed. I knew without doubt that day I had travelled to Auckland with an angel in my car who had been sent by my sister to stop me from speeding.

Chapter Twenty-six

A fresh start and a 14-inch footstool

2005

Today was the first day of the rest of my life and I felt excited as I drove into Auckland and went straight to the workshop. My office lady was so pleased to see me as she wasn't happy working with Dave and was ready to leave.

"I'll take over again on Monday," I promised her.

Dave walked into the office from the workshop and growled, "What are you doin' here? I've told you yer not welcome. I don't want you back. I'm going to give the office job to my girlfriend so yer'd better have another think of what yer'll do 'cos you're not staying here."

I stood quietly looking at him. In the past I would have been afraid of him but now I looked at him without fear and gave him time to spit out his thoughts, then slowly I spelled out my plan.

"This is *my* business, Dave. I bought it with my redundancy pay and built it myself while you received a salary the same as the rest of the staff. You asked to work for me, do you remember? If you wish to stay working here and have your girlfriend run the office, then I suggest you purchase the business from me. I'm putting it on the market and will get a valuation next week. I'm also selling my house that you and she are living in rent free, so perhaps you might want to look for somewhere else to live as well. As Sharon-Louise and Gary are now both living in Australia, it's my plan to go and join them once everything is sold and settled."

He stood looking at me, gobsmacked! "Ye can't do that. I'm your legal husband and entitled to half of everything you own so I'm not agreeing."

"Then my suggestion is you buy me out. I'll get valuations for both the business and the house."

"Ye know I've got no money to buy you out. Yer talkin' rubbish."

"I own both the house and the business, Dave. I built that house with my money while you drank and gambled what you were earning. It was my redundancy pay that purchased the workshop and it was me that saved and did without to get the money for everything that was necessary for the business and so I'm entitled to sell if I wish. You received a salary as an employee because you didn't want a panel beating business. Do you remember this now? I've told you my terms if you want to continue working here and living in my house. Make your decision soon. While I'm at it, I'll be applying for divorce papers."

He stood for a while, eyes like saucers with his jaw dropped, then he opened the office door and left the building. I went into the workshop and caught up with the men who had worked for me all this time. For most of them, it was seventeen years. It had been such a long time since I'd seen them, and they all stopped work to have an early smoko so I could be updated on what had been happening. Dave had been neglecting the workshop and had run the business down. The guys said the problem was that he was ignorant of how to run the business. Apart from upsetting various customers, he had been financially bleeding the business dry. They all knew he had stopped paying my salary, the office lady had told them. I let them know I was going to sell

365

the business and if any one of them felt they would like to buy it, I would give them first refusal. But I was going to write into the condition of sale that they were all to be kept on as staff.

When things move quickly almost all of us say: 'it was meant to be' – and that's exactly how it was. A young man we had known since we started the business had heard the news and called on Monday morning asking how much I would take for the workshop. I received the valuation that day and rang him back and he was happy to pay that price.

The law stated that the finances in most marriages of more than two years needed to be halved 50/50 when they divorced. If the boot was on the other foot in this divorce, and he had owned everything I would be expecting half. My days of fighting were over. I wanted no more stress from him as I knew he'd drag me through a court to get half.

He rang me when the workshop had sold to say he wanted half the money from the sale of the workshop, but he wasn't moving out of the house. I discovered the bank had loaned him money on the business while I'd been away and so the money received from the business was greatly depreciated once the bank paid that loan back to themselves. I informed him of this and agreed to sell him my half of the house, which I would take out of his share of the depleted workshop sale.

Friends told me to give him nothing but I knew he'd fight and I wanted no connection to Dave anymore, therefore the legal paperwork cutting me out of his life was for me, urgent and vital, to ensure I couldn't be guilty by association and responsible for half his debts that would raise their ugly heads into the future.

Money had never been my main desire or drive. At this moment in time, if I ended up with no money and only had the papers to say we were divorced that would be more important to me than anything else.

I lived in a motel as I tidied my affairs and called in on my friend Trish, who I hadn't seen during that time I was ill. She told me her father's unit was going up for sale as she'd placed him in a nursing home, but she would let me rent her dad's unit until I left for Australia.

"It could be a few months, Trish," I said, "but let me go and see it."

The single-storey 3-bedroom 2-bathroom property had a garage attached but was in desperate need of renovation. I immediately became excited about doing up another house as I waited to leave New Zealand. I went back to Trish and offered to buy the unit. I rang the builders I had always used and told them the project needed to be completed in six weeks. They swung into action and renewed the kitchen and bathrooms and put a fireplace and new French doors in my lounge. The decorating was my job. I needed to hang sixty-four rolls of wallpaper and paint the ceilings and woodwork and varnish twenty-seven doors. Plus, landscape the grounds. I was there at 8am at the latest each morning where I beavered away into the night for six weeks until it was finished.

Everyone told me I'd never do it, but you don't say things like that to someone like me who never walks away from a challenge. Of course I did it. I finished on Thursday. The carpet was laid on Friday and my lovely new furniture was delivered Saturday morning. I had heard that furniture was a little more expensive in Australia and so I had bought new furniture and would have it all shipped when I was leaving. I would live in this unit until I was leaving for Australia and would then have a better idea of my financial state and would either rent it out as an investment property or sell it to start afresh in Australia.

Once the renovation was finished, it looked beautiful and it was hard not to feel smug. I decided that I now needed a well-earned rest. How to relax was something I'd never got the hang of, so here was my opportunity to practise before I left the country. Plus, Sharon-Louise and Gary were both coming home for a couple of weeks to go through their storage and whittle it down. I would then pack their things with mine into the shipping container when I left. It was my time to relax and catch up on some reading. *I deserve this rest*, I told myself. *I will never be a workaholic again. Life is for living and I've got a lot of living to catch up on. If I want to sit for a week reading, there is nothing wrong with that. I am going to be the biggest slob from now on.*

The feeling of freedom I now felt was overpowering, mainly because my divorce was imminent. From time to time, I'd close my eyes and whisper to his girlfriend, 'Thank you, thank you!' He was her problem now.

Choosing the books I wanted to catch up on, I placed them on a table beside my lovely new lounge suite. I poured myself a glass of wine and placed that beside them. Looking around, I felt I needed to raise my feet and went into the garage and saw my old, upholstered footstool and brought that into the lounge. I settled myself into the corner of the settee and placed my feet on the stool which was covered in an old floral material that didn't match my lovely new suite. I placed my feet on it and as I looked at it, I decided it must be the next thing on my list. It had to be recovered and I would do that when I arrived in Australia. I leaned over and picked up my glass of wine and raised it in the air:

"Here's to you, House!" I laughed and felt decadent. "And here's to being a slob ... cheers!" and I sipped my wine and looked at the footstool. The material was faded and shabby. It looked awful. *Why did I ever choose that material in the first place?*

I placed my glass on the coffee table and picked up the first of the books I wanted to read. With my feet on the stool, I opened the first page of my book but, as I looked down, all I could see surrounding the page was the awful material of the footstool.

It will only take me an hour to recover that, I thought, so I went out to the garage where I had my working boxes and found an offcut of the material I had used for drapes. Perfect. I picked up my heavy old pliers and a thin chisel to remove the tacks and staples that held the material in place, and took the footstool out onto the concrete patio to do the job.

The footstool had castors on it and kept rolling away from me while I was trying to work on it, so I jammed it between my knees to keep it still, taking on the stance of a sumo wrestler. The tacks and staples had been in the stool for many years, and I had made such a good job of recovering it on a previous occasion that the tacks were buried into the wood frame and were difficult to release. I had to prise them out with the chisel and then grab the head with the pliers and yank them up and out. This was a bigger job than I had first thought. As I yanked on a difficult tack with all my might, it suddenly left the wood, and the pliers hit the left side of my face around my eye. I saw stars, and the pain became excruciating. I dropped the pliers and the stool from between my knees and ran to the kitchen to get a cold compress. As I passed the mirror in the dining room, I looked at my face. My eye was closing over, and a deep red stain was beneath it.

My God! I thought. *I could have put my eye out!* My cheek bone was sore and swollen, my lip was bleeding and became twice its size. I ran the water onto a sponge and placed it on my face and sat coming to terms with the pain for approximately thirty minutes. When it had eased a little, I thought, *I'm not going to let a 14-inch footstool beat me – I'm going to finish that job.*

Back I went to the patio, picked up my chisel and pliers and once again grabbed the footstool between my knees to keep it still. I knew I had to be more careful this time so, as I pulled the tacks out, I tried to pull to the side of my body rather than the

369

middle as I had done before. This, of course, was not a natural movement for the body. After the third or fourth tack had been removed in this way, I heard the area around my hip make a cracking noise, and pain ran through my spine and into my legs. I dropped the pliers and chisel. My knees gave way, releasing the footstool as I dropped to my knees, slamming them on the concrete and knocking my head and arm on the upturned footstool. Each movement added more pain to my body.

The pain in my hip and knees was unbearable and I had to lie flat on the concrete on my chest. *I've dislocated my hip!*

Oh my God! I thought. *I need help. I've got to get inside somehow and ring for help!*

Using my forearms, I crawled forward, inch by painful inch, dragging my body and legs over the rough concrete toward the open French doors. My legs wouldn't bend at my knees or move on their own. The rough concrete ripped the skin on my knees and shins and blood started to spread over my new carpet as I pulled my body across it. When I reached my chair, I couldn't get up off the floor and so, painfully stretching my arms as much as I could before the pain became worse, I pulled cushions down onto the carpet and somehow rolled myself over to place them under my head. I then tried to straighten my bruised, battered, bleeding body out on the carpet.

I thought of all I had just accomplished. I had renovated an entire house in six weeks without a scratch but the recovering of a tiny 14-inch footstool had put me on my back. I couldn't see through my eye – it was closed over, swollen and now yellow and black. The back of my head and shoulders were in pain from hitting the stool. I also had a swollen cheek and jaw, a fat cut lip, a dislocated hip and bloody knees and shins. And I needed to clean the blood off my new carpet. *This is unbelievable!* I lay on the floor for at least another hour trying to work out how to get help. Then I heard:

"Where are you, Mum?"

Thank goodness! The kids have arrived early.

I tried to shout, "I'm in the lounge," but the words came out sounding, "hmmnn inda lowng." I couldn't speak properly through my bloodied mouth and sore swollen jaw. They walked into the room and fear and shock showed in their eyes and on their faces. At first, they froze. There was their mother, lying with bloodied legs and with blood streaked across the new carpet. My face was distorted with lumps and bumps, black swollen eyes, a cut fat lip, a swollen jaw.

Gary was ready to beat somebody up as he dropped to his knees, demanding to know, "Who did this to you, Mum? What happened?" Gary's 'family' anger showed in his voice.

It suddenly became funny. "I beat meself up," I tried to say and began to laugh as they both dropped to the floor. Tears of laughter began to seep from my swollen eyes.

"You beat yourself up, Mum?" Sharon-Louise repeated, trying to clarify my mumbled words, half smiling as she said it. I gave them half a nod and tried to splutter the story of trying to get the nails out of the footstool. Even though my face was excruciatingly painful, I began laughing as I could see how all of this looked to them. We were all three now lying on my blood-stained carpet in my beautiful room, laughing until the tears ran down our faces.

Divorce was simple in New Zealand if both parties agreed. We both turned up at the Department for Courts and signed the divorce application before the Registrar. After ninety days, if we hadn't changed our minds or requested a hearing, it would become final. We followed the rules and while I waited, I put my affairs in order and prayed that his girlfriend wouldn't leave him before it was absolute.

Chapter Twenty-seven

The Ripple Effect

2006

When the spirit world sends me off to do some work I don't get a letter or an email asking or have a conversation spelling it out. A situation is thrown before me that ignites my passion to help someone. Something isn't right and needs to be addressed by me and, since my mental recovery, I now swing into action sooner as I realise I wouldn't have been chosen to do it if I couldn't handle it. But more often than not, I only realise it's a spiritual challenge when it's all over.

We live in this sea of humanity and everything we do, good and bad, has a positive or negative ripple effect. This spiritual challenge ended up being a rather large transformation and one I'm proud of.

My friend Raewyn was mentally and financially struggling and I feared for her mental health. She needed help to untie herself from a heavy financial debt she was suffering because of her sister Rose, who was mentally slow. Seven years previously, their grandmother had died and left her house unit and all she owned to both sisters. Immediately, Rose moved out of the unit she rented in the same block as her grandmother and moved into grandmother's unit; she locked the door and stopped talking to her sister. Raewyn couldn't get into the unit or even speak to

Rose about the situation. If Raewyn rang Rose she would immediately put the phone down. Because Raewyn's name was now on the title of this unit as a 50% owner, she paid all the overheads, including the phone, so that her mother could keep contact with Rose, who didn't work but received a disability pension. Raewyn alone paid for all the council rates and overheads on the property to keep herself from the debtor's court as she knew Rose wouldn't pay for anything. Raewyn was now paying the full costs for her own and her grandmother's property. Grandmother's money was in a tin box in the unit, therefore Rose became the sole beneficiary of that as well. All Raewyn inherited was a debt.

Their mother was ill for some years and never visited her daughters, but only saw them when they came to visit her. She died five years after their grandmother and now their father had recently passed away and left his property and possessions to both his daughters. Once again, Rose locked grandmother's unit and moved into their parents' house. She locked the door to everyone, including Raewyn, and wouldn't even communicate with the lawyers and so their father's estate couldn't be settled.

Raewyn was now paying the overheads on three properties. She was drowning in debt, which was making her ill. The money their father had left them was in the bank but frozen until his estate was settled. But Rose wouldn't listen to anyone and wouldn't open the front door.

I was extremely worried about Raewyn when I called to see her and her genuine tears made me feel her pain. I offered to help but she felt I would never be able to get Rose to open the door. I never start something I can't complete so I knew I would get in to talk to Rose.

I knocked on the door of Rose's 'new' home – her late father's house.

"GO AWAY! YOU WANT TO THROW ME OUT!" she

shouted through the window.

"I don't want to throw you out, Rose. I just want to talk to you," I would shout back, but she would begin screaming until the neighbours thought I was attacking her. They would stand on their drive watching me as I tried to speak to her, making sure I wasn't hurting Rose.

I persisted and arrived at the house daily but she wouldn't let me in. On one particular day, the gardener that had worked for her father arrived to cut the lawns. I managed to speak to him out of sight of her windows and asked him if she paid him on completion of his work.

"Yes, she does pay me, but I don't know for how much longer. She's giving me old dirty notes as though she's dug them up from somewhere."

"Then you've noticed she's a little slow mentally and she's holding up the settlement of her father's estate as she won't talk to anyone. Her sister Raewyn is at her wit's end and I must get in to speak to Rose before Raewyn becomes so ill she ends up in hospital."

"Oh dear! I remember Raewyn. She's a lovely lady. Please tell her I'm so sorry about her father's death and all the trouble she's having right now. I'll knock on the door as usual for payment when I've finished and will step into the hall and keep her chatting until you get in the door, if that helps."

"Yes, please. I'll sit in my car around the corner and if you let me know when you're about to knock on her door, then I'll come around and catch her off guard."

I received the nod from him as he disappeared around the corner. Jumping out of my car, I hugged the fences hoping she couldn't see me. Her door stood open as the gardener chatted in the hall so I was able to walk in and stand beside him.

"Get out of my house! You're Raewyn's friend and you want to throw me out of the house!" she screamed in front of the gardener.

"Rose, I'm your friend as well. I've come to tell you your sister is ill and you've only got each other now that your Mum and Dad and your grandmother have all died. She wants to speak to you." These words stopped her screaming and she looked at me for a minute or so, saying nothing, and obviously turning these words over in her head. 'Her sister was ill' were the words that bothered her so I remained silent as I watched those words navigate her thinking process.

The gardener left and I closed the door so that the neighbours couldn't hear as they were stood deliberately against the fence near her front door, keeping an eye on Rose. For almost a whole day, I explained Raewyn's situation to Rose, approaching the problem from this angle and that angle until eventually I saw Rose grasping the situation. She then asked what she could do to help her sister. I explained that both needed to sit and talk to the lawyer about her father's estate.

"Raewyn wants you to stay in the house, Rose, so the lawyers need to take her name off it and leave it just for you. But she needs to get the keys to your grandmother's house so it can be sold now, and this will help Raewyn so much as she doesn't have to pay all the expenses on it once it's sold."

After almost a whole day of talking, at last she gave me the keys to Grandma's unit.

Raewyn cried with relief when I told her.

"That unit will be filthy, Pauline. She doesn't do housework. Will you get someone to clean it up ready for sale?"

"I'll do it myself. I've got some free time at the moment!" I answered, not knowing what I was letting myself in for. "I'll go around there tomorrow."

I drove to the unit block the next morning, armed with cleaning materials. *Ahhhhh!*

The small unit complex was a U-shape of seven two-bedroom units. From the main road there was a drive leading into the centre of the U-shape which was a carport for all the residents' cars to share.

Grandma's unit was totally surrounded by mounds of rubbish. A tree in her garden outside her front window had grown out of control and lifted the rusty iron car port roof up off its supports – it was now dangling precariously in the air amongst the branches. This same tree had a branch that had grown through the bedroom window, where I could see it was resting on top of rubbish perhaps five feet high in the room. The windows were filthy with old net curtains stuck to them. All the other units looked dirty and unkempt and the grounds were like a jungle. But even this didn't prepare me for what was to come.

I picked my way through the rubbish to the front door and turned the key in the lock of this filthy unit – and pushed – and heaved – I even kicked the door at various places to loosen the lock, until finally I was able to open the door only inches but just enough to peer inside. *Oooooh!!!*

The rubbish inside was piled high up against the front door, stopping it from fully opening.

Have you ever visited a council tip and stood before the mounds of wet rotted rubbish? Well, this unit was filled to at least five feet high just like that, and the smell was gut churning! I stared through the small opening of the door in horror .....then a rat rustled through the rubbish and ran toward me. *AAGGHH!*

I snapped the door shut again! *How do I clean up this amount of rubbish!* I ran back to my car and looked back at this gathering of seven scruffy units that had baby prams outside a few of the doors, showing that babies and small children lived there. Now that I had witnessed the way in which these young families were living I couldn't just walk away. I sat in my car staring at this scene, building my resolve to help these families to right this disgusting and dangerous living environment.

Once I felt settled within myself with an initial plan, I stepped out of my car with determination to do something about this situation. I knocked on each door saying who I was and asked for the owner/landlord's contacts. Luckily, I had chosen a time when those living there were all home. I called them together and began a discussion with them asking how long this place had been in this state and also asked if they were still paying rent. Every one of them was paying on time, they told me, with the exception of one older New Zealand man who owned his unit.

Each of the other families were immigrants and their English was poor but I persisted until I was able to let them see I was here to support them and determined to do something about the way in which they had been forced to live.

That evening I rang each of the contact numbers I had gathered and firmly stated that these units weren't fit for animals to live in. The heavy rusty iron car port roof could collapse at any time on any one of these young families with children and would kill them. I gave them one week to inspect it for themselves and if they weren't prepared to do anything about it I threatened to contact the authorities. I offered my time freely to be the project manager and clear and clean this small community and make it safe, but they must share the costs. I gave them all my telephone number.

Over the next few days, each owner visited to inspect their property. Within days, they all agreed to a shared financial responsibility in the clean-up operation. And so, I formed the body corporate. They never asked who I was or questioned me in any way.

I began doing what I'm good at and happy doing: detailed planning. Action. Firstly, the tree was cut down, the car port demolished and within a week all the rubbish was taken away. This included all the rubbish in grandmother's unit as it took almost five days to bag it. A specialised company had to be given this role and the cost was astronomical. This cost had to be an individual cost of Grandma's unit. The glazier replaced the bedroom window and the new car port was built. I oversaw all this work and, once the rubbish had gone, the unit had to be aired out as the vermin that had infested the property had defecated and urinated on everything, and this had soaked into the floorboards, they needed to dry out. I placed large de-humidity machines in there for a week.

"How did it all get in this state?" I asked the kindly young and appreciative neighbours that called daily with hot tea and biscuits as they filled me in with the details, but old Fred, the New Zealander that owned his own unit, had the history to relate to me:

When Grandma was alive she took pride in her little unit and it set the standard for the rest of the group. Her unit was one foot on the leg of the U-shape and Rose rented on the end of the other. Rose had moved in to this small complex and began collecting rubbish – and stored it in and around the unit she rented. She was an obsessive-compulsive hoarder of rubbish. When Grandma died, Rose couldn't fit another item of rubbish into her unit and so closed the door and moved into Grandma's unit and began to hoard all over again.

Single-handedly, Rose had brought the tone of this tiny neighbourhood down. Rats infested the area – the other owners lost interest in their properties – they rented them out for whatever they could get and didn't do any repairs. Rose had created a negative ripple effect. The owner of Rose's first unit couldn't get a response from her. She never opened the door to him when she moved into her Grandma's unit and the mail he sent her was never acknowledged. Even when he threatened court action, he couldn't get her to the court proceedings and she simply ignored every attempt at contact. And so, eventually, the cost of emptying and cleaning that unit was left to the owner.

The tenants of this small community were all young families with children – Maori, Indian, Chinese, Philippines – and then there was Fred, a man in his late 70s, living alone, with a daily negative opinion on everything I did.

"Huh, women!" He sat outside his front door on a dining chair, arms crossed and commenting on my work constantly, inspecting everything I did and telling me how it should have been done.

The bathroom and kitchen were replaced and when I'd finished decorating the unit, which included polishing the wood floors, I made curtains and blinds for the windows. During this time, I also asked the tenants to inspect the inside of their units and, if some part of it needed repair or replacing, they were to let me know. When they reported a problem, I contacted the owners stating my expectation was that it be done immediately.

I did realise that these property owners were a little afraid of me. I don't know who they thought I was, but they never argued over anything. They did the work inside their own property and paid without complaint for their share of the body corporate work.

Once the inside of Grandmother's unit was finished and the car port rebuilt, I had the exterior of all units painted in fresh new creams and light greens. I now needed to start on Grandma's garden and brought my own motor mower from home to start this job. When Fred saw my motor mower, his eyes lit up. "Ére, give us that," and off he went – not just mowing Grandma's grass but mowing the grass for everyone in the unit block – everyday!! I gifted Fred his new toy as I wouldn't be taking it to Australia with me. I also persuaded and then organised the owners to pay him fortnightly to keep the grass down. They all agreed.

Fred began to smile more. He had a new job and felt useful

again. I also gave him the title of Body Corporate Manager which made his chest swell, and he took the responsibility seriously, not wanting another tenant to ever move in and do what Rose had done.

In my interaction with the owners, I stressed that these young families had paid their rents regularly and yet had been living in squalor for some years. I would be keeping in touch with them from now on and the owners must not put their rents up. They must allow them to pay only what they were now, paying for some time going forward as a compensation for the years of neglect. They all agreed.

I walked away from that unit block totally satisfied with the transformation – but that transformation wasn't just the units: Fred had a new lease of life, a managerial position, and a gardening job he received a salary for – the children could now safely play outside – and the young neighbours got to know each other.

On behalf of the sisters, I sold the unit to the Indian family in the complex as their parents had come to live with them. All the unit owners now had a property that had increased in value. The standard of living for everyone had been lifted. That freshly painted unit block of seven was now one of the best in the area, and Fred had begun to plant rose trees and bushes, making this area look an absolute picture.

The sisters were now friends again and able to windup their father's estate. With the sale of Grandma's unit, Raewyn was able to pay off her debts. Rose still wanted to live in their father's house and with a strong 'exaggerated' word from me about the authorities insisting that Raewyn be allowed into the house at least once each week to ensure this rubbish hoarding never happened again, (a letter I created and said was legal and to be signed by Rose and Raewyn) the house was then placed in Rose's name only. After paying overheads on three houses, Raewyn now only had one – her own – and was at last mortgage free. Raewyn and Rose had been left enough money to live comfortably for the rest of their lives.

This all started because I was concerned about the mental health and financial pain of a friend. I had no idea what I was getting into. And this is usual in the creation of a positive ripple effect. It's always something done for another without any thought for yourself.

It wasn't until I was walking away that I became truly aware of the magnitude of that project, and that then put a smile on my face and gave me happy goosebumps every time I thought of it. I am so grateful to Spirit for sending me.

Some weeks later, I was invited to the units by the young Indian man; he was having a BBQ on a Saturday afternoon. I accepted. When I arrived, all the neighbours had placed tables under the car port and each family had cooked something of their home country cuisine and I was the guest of honour. They all thanked me and presented me with a beautiful emerald green and gold sari. I was weepy, humbled, and extremely grateful.

A person's actions – good or bad – creates positive or negative ripples. Why not try it yourself. Throw a good deed into the sea of humanity and stand back and watch those ripples spread out. Helping one person alone isn't possible – it doesn't stop there. He or she, in turn, consciously or unconsciously will pass on something from that experience to another and the ripple goes on and on. The same thing happens in reverse with a negative action or deed. Think of Rose who set off a negative karma with her hoarding – it affected all those around her. She 'infected' a whole neighbourhood.

Sometimes consciously, and sometimes unconsciously, the Law of Karma is set into action – it cannot be avoided. Now that you know, be aware of your actions and words – and begin every day with a positive action that will ripple out before you and make this world a better place.

Epilogue

Releasing a life of trauma

Thirty-six years of my life had transpired since marrying the wrong person. That was quite a price to pay for choosing the wrong man at the age of twenty-one – I was only a child. Thank goodness my crazy sense of humour never left me as I dealt with all I was subjected to.

The trauma I had experienced within my marriage was repressed as I tried to hide it from the children and was never in a safe or stable place to allow me to deal with it and heal. I was locked into an arena, protecting my children but living with the sleeping lion from whom there was no escape. To manage this situation, I had to brainwash myself.

Within my mind, I had created a storage room and here I placed every violent episode I suffered at his hands. After each traumatic event, it became my 'go to' place. I threw my painful experiences in and slammed the metal door shut. I didn't allow any of it to enter my conscious mind again. I became so adept at this that each time I was abused I could do this automatically and not give it another thought.

During and after my mental breakdown, and throughout my recovery period when the metal door was blasted off its hinges, behind it were a series of veils that had to be lifted 'by me' in trepidation – I had to force myself. One by one, each violent incident was then revealed slowly for me to process, working backwards as I was recovering. I spent some time in shock as these happenings were once again played out in my mind. I kept wondering how on earth I didn't think of these incidents again until I was processing my mental breakdown. There was never any question of their validity as I did then remember these incidents with absolute clarity. The brain will only reveal what a person can cope with and so the repressed memories took many years to uncover until the last veil was lifted in 2019, which was the first violent incident dating back to 1971 when he sold the workshop I purchased and gambled the money. This was almost fifty years after the event.

From reading many psychology books I learned:

My relationship with my husband wasn't 'normal.' Normalising the abnormal causes one's spirit, which would normally leap to correct the situation, to instead sink into ennui, complacency, and eventually into blindness. An important study that gave insight into the loss of the self-protective instinct was carried out in the early 1960s. Animal experiments were used to determine something about the 'flight instinct' in humans. A dog cage was wired on one side of the floor to give the dog an electric shock if he walked on it. Within an hour the dog learned to avoid that side of the floor. They then did the same to the opposite side of the floor. Again, the dog quickly learned to avoid it. Eventually the entire floor was wired to give random shocks. No matter where the dog lay or stood, he would eventually receive electric shocks. The dog acted confused at first, and then panicked. Finally, the dog gave up and lay down, taking the shocks as they came. No longer did he try to escape or outsmart the scientists. Next, the cage door was opened, and the scientists expected the dog to run out, but it didn't flee. Even though it could vacate the cage at will the dog lay there being randomly shocked. From this, scientists speculated that when a human is exposed to violence, they tend to adapt so that when the violence ceases or they are allowed freedom, the healthy instinct to flee is hugely diminished and the person stays put. This is the mindset of a woman that has spent many years in an abusive relationship.

The pain of that mental breakdown was excruciating, but I needed something that severe to shake me out of the brainwashing I had done on myself. I survived it, and have learned so much about life, people and most importantly myself. Although those memories slept in my subconscious, it was necessary to uncover and deal with them and let them go, as only then would I have my second chance at life.

So many lies surrounded my life. So many people had made assumptions of who I was, based on what they knew about Dave. My mother was right: he was a liar and a gambler and even I don't know half of what he did in the shadows and behind my back.

Although I was married to Dave for thirty-six years, I can honestly say I don't know who he is. I never met the real man. Liars are actors. Nothing they say or do is real; they are always hiding their real self for fear of being caught out. He lived a separate life to me under the same roof and I still don't know how he spent most of his days. He lived in his world of addictions – a family life with wife and children wasn't part of his consciousness. I was his cash cow providing the funds for him to live the life he wanted.

And how do I feel about him? Very sad. I have forgiven him.

When I think of him, Socrates' words always come to mind "The unexamined life is not worth living."

Like all of us, Dave had no choice in any attributes he was born with or without. He was given a life and chose not to face his demons and missed his opportunity to learn so much. He allowed his demons to steer his course through life. He hurt many people but, in the main, his children and me. He missed out on creating beautiful memories to keep him contented in his old age. He has nothing to show for the life he led. He is now in poor health, alone, penniless and experiencing Karma. Even if he faced up to the pain and damage he did throughout his life, it's too late for him to start again as his health isn't strong enough. He is a very sad case.

When we should have been a family enjoying adventures together, I substituted my kids absent father with my sense of humour. I tried to implant beautiful memories by laughing and doing silly things with the kids, creating some magic that they will hopefully have stored away in happy memory files of their childhood.

My adult life was a challenging one, and necessary as my 'baptism of fire' for the spirit world. It honed my intuition and made me wise. I was lucky enough to be born to a woman with one foot in this world and one in the spirit world. I was a channel for her work. Subsequently, her support was the reason I survived my many traumas. She guided me through them and never left me even after she died.

Apart from the years I was recovering from my mental breakdown, during my adult life I continued to support those who were leaving this world and crossing over to the next. Those moments helping others also helped me – holding space for those dying is an honour. I believe we are all living to be of service to our fellow man.

I don't regret my past as from it came my children and grandchildren and they bring me so much love. My childhood was magical. My adult life was hard as it tested my resolve to understand spirit and successfully work with it. Not easy but necessary.

My funny, crazy, painful life was a life I would call 'Practical Spirituality'. I lived, and still live, a spiritual life.

The aftermath of that life has left me with a delicate mentality.

My sharply tuned intuition will sometimes raise a red flag and I will retreat into my safe space, carefully assessing a situation for some time before I spring into action to either deal with it or take a different path. Those who know my story will understand and wait for me. With those who don't understand, I've learned to accept that that's not my problem. My life was complex and 'at last' I've faced a truth that I can't fix everybody. Hence, I wrote it all down to firstly, help psychiatrists and psychologists understand the mind of a woman that has suffered domestic violence and a gambler for many years in order for them to help her.

My second purpose for publishing my story is not that it is less important but equivalent to my first reason for publication – it is to highlight my family life living within domestic violence and gambling. Historically, these men have got away with it because the laws have never changed, and domestic violence is in a lesser class of its own even though women are murdered, and children are traumatised for life after what they have witnessed in their homes. If that man was to walk across the road and into another home, and physically abuse and even kill that women in front of her children that man would be given a lengthy jail sentence. (She wasn't his partner!) If he physically abuses his partner, this isn't taken so seriously until it becomes murder.

When the police are informed of domestic violence, this is a threat that could end in murder. What I believe should happen is … the women and children should be left in their home (not placed in a safe home, living in fear that these men will find them) and *these men* should be apprehended and jailed – not left in the family home. There should be a weekly report online, and free for publication naming and shaming these men that have harmed women and children that they should have been protecting. This alone 'could' be a repellent as these macho men need others to think they're Mister Wonderful.

Some measure of education must be imposed on these men within their time of incarceration, and they must reach a certain level of acceptance of how to behave before they are released. (A psychiatrist/psychologist could plan this better than I can.)

The time in jail should match that of any person that was intending to murder. The monies saved on safe houses could be used for a special jail and education of these men.

The women should also have free counselling, teaching them that they don't have to accept this behavior – that they are worth more!

Education and counselling should be mandatory when applying for a marriage license. If they choose not to marry but to live together, social welfare should make the education and counselling mandatory as part of the information needed for any financial support they are claiming. Therefore I ask: please … please consider my proposals – **Change the laws!!**

If that were to happen, I could then close the cover on this book and get on with a peaceful life. **Please help me to do this**.

As I work to bring my proposal to those that need to change these laws, I am in my twilight years living on the Northern Beaches of Sydney, Australia, near my children and grandchildren. Once or twice a month, the ferry boat will take me from Manly to Circular Quay in Sydney and back again. These beautiful old ferry boats remind me, every time, of the ferry boats crossing the Mersey in my youth, and I hope with all my heart they don't replace them with modern ships until I've popped my clogs. Sometimes in the dark of night I create my magic as I listen to my Beatles music; I look across the creamy swell of moonlit water, observing the twinkling lights of the boats and houses on the far banks, and I feel my life has come full circle as I relive my teenage years. I will sigh with contentment thinking once again, *How Lucky Am I?*

I'm in my 70s now and still living my purpose. My mother's pagan spirituality called people such as me Angels of Death. That title frightened me as a child, but I later understood it to mean 'soul comfort and release' and came to see it as a privilege. Now in the 2020s, we have a new name which is accepted in the medical world. We are called

Death Doulas

Lightning Source UK Ltd.
Milton Keynes UK
UKHW010630060223
416537UK00001B/84